Jane Austen on Film and Television

A Critical Study of the Adaptations

by SUE PARRILL

McFarland & Company, Inc., Publishers
Jefferson, North Carolina, and London

Library of Congress Cataloguing-in-Publication Data

Parrill, Sue, 1935–
    Jane Austen on film and television : a critical study of the
adaptations / by Sue Parrill.
        p.   cm.
    Includes bibliographical references and index.
    ISBN 0-7864-1349-2 (softcover : 50# alkaline paper) ∞
    1. Austen, Jane, 1775–1817—Film and video adaptations.
2. English fiction—Film and video adaptations.
3. England—In motion pictures.   4. Women in motion
pictures.   5. Love in motion pictures.   I. Title.
PR4038.F55P37   2002
791.43'6—dc21   2002000752

British Library cataloguing data are available

Manufactured in the United States of America

*McFarland & Company, Inc., Publishers
  Box 611, Jefferson, North Carolina 28640
  www.mcfarlandpub.com*

To Bill for his love and loyalty

Contents

Preface

The researching and writing of this book has occurred over about three years. In previous writing projects I have found that I tired of my subject long before I completed the project. This project was different. Throughout my research, I have thoroughly enjoyed reading and rereading Jane Austen's novels, watching and rewatching the films and television adaptations based on them, and reading the opinions of critics and reviewers writing on the topic. My approach has been to trace the history of the adaptations, to compare the adaptations to the novels, to compare the way the different adaptations treat the novels, and to analyze the adaptations as examples of cinematic art.

I have watched the adaptations or read the screenplays for the adaptations of all except three items on my filmography.* Andrew Wright's article "Jane Austen Adapted" in *Nineteenth Century Fiction* (1975) was of great assistance in my preliminary searches. Since I have concentrated mainly on the criticism dealing with the adaptations, I make no claim that my bibliography covers all of the important literary criticism on Jane Austen and her novels. Neither is it a complete listing of everything written about the adaptations, since I chose not to include many film reviews. I have included everything that I cited and some other items which I thought would be useful to a person researching the adaptations.

I particularly acknowledge the support which Southeastern Louisiana University has given to my project. I received two faculty development grants, which paid for travel to research BBC adaptations in England and for photographs to illustrate the book. Personnel at the Sims Library were also helpful. Laverne Simoneaux discovered a videotape of an early NBC

Screenplays or video versions of the following were unavailable, and probably not extant: Pride and Prejudice, *BBC 1952/1958;* Persuasion, *BBC 1960-1961;* Emma, *CBS Camera Three 1960.*

Emma at the Library of Congress. Rosemary Hanes in the Library of Congress tracked down two screenplays of early NBC *Philco Television Theatre* productions.

Staff at the BBC Written Archives, Caversham Park, Reading, were very helpful in unearthing several screenplays which I requested. I would especially like to thank Michael Websell for his assistance in finding materials and arranging to have screenplays copied and sent to me, and for responding to my e-mail requests for information. I also found the staff at the British Film Institute in London helpful in allowing me access to their files of press releases and newspaper articles.

I am appreciative of the kindness of Andrew Davies and Patricia Rozema. Davies e-mailed me his screenplays of *Northanger Abbey* and *Pride and Prejudice* and responded to my questions concerning the fate of the projected film of *Northanger Abbey*. Rozema sent me a draft of her screenplay for *Mansfield Park*. Through her intercession, Miramax also sent me a tape of the film shortly after the film's release.

In my pursuit of illustrations, the Film Stills Archive of the Museum of Modern Art in New York, Photofest, and the BBC Picture Archives were my primary sources. Mary Corliss at MOMA and Bobbie Mitchell at the BBC were very helpful. I appreciate the assistance of the several British talent agencies and of English Equity which helped me secure permissions of the actors shown in the BBC productions. When I sought permissions from the actors, I was gratified that a few actually volunteered to supply insights and information about the making of the films or their critical reception. Celia Bannerman and Irene Richards were extremely helpful and encouraging. I also thank Linda Troost for her valuable suggestions regarding illustrations.

I further acknowledge the assistance of my office staff. I thank Michael Libersat, who created my web page and who was primarily responsible for creating the book's index. Anna Woodall provided valuble support in copying and collating. Finally, I express my appreciation to my husband, Bill, for his proofreading and editing efforts, and for his film expertise and extensive library of film criticism. I have found it a great advantage to live with a combination English teacher and film expert.

I

Why Jane Austen?

Why adapt Jane Austen's novels for film or television? From the point of view of television and film studios, adaptation of these novels can make sense. They tell good stories—simple love stories which are still appealing, particularly to a female audience. Anyone who goes to the movies can testify that Hollywood movies are sorely in need of stories with interesting characters, strong motivation, and plausible endings. Since most educated people, even in America, have at least heard of Jane Austen, this name recognition is another selling point. It may also be relevant to point out that since Jane Austen's novels are in the public domain, it is not necessary to pay the author for their use. It is relatively inexpensive to film an Austen adaptation. It requires no expensive special effects, no exotic locations, and only a small cast. It can get more expensive if the studio wants to populate the roles with stars—such as Hugh Grant or Gwyneth Paltrow (who commands a bigger salary now than she did when she was cast in the Miramax *Emma* [1996]). Douglas McGrath, scriptwriter and director of Miramax's *Emma*, summed up the advantages of filming Austen:

> I thought Jane Austen would be a good collaborator [...] because she writes, you know, superb dialogue, she creates memorable characters, she has an extremely clever skill for plotting—and she's dead, which means, you know, there's none of that tiresome arguing over who gets the bigger bun at coffee time. [Purdum 11]

Hollywood film studios have always been interested in producing a few medium to low budget films which have some intellectual cachet and which may win prestigious awards. In 1979 Morris Beja estimated that 20 to 30 percent of American films released each year are adapted from novels and that 75 percent of the top Academy Awards have gone to adaptations. Further, of the twenty top money-earning films of all time, reported in *Variety* in 1977, fourteen were based on novels (Beja 78). The tendency for films to be based on novels continues into the twenty-first century. Since 1977, over half of the films nominated by the Academy of Motion Pictures for "Best Picture of the Year" have been based on novels. Of the recent Austen-based theatrical releases, *Sense and Sensibility* received the most recognition in Hollywood. Emma Thompson won the award for best screenplay, and the film was nominated in six other categories. In England, the film won the BAFTA awards for best picture, best actress (Thompson), best supporting actress (Kate Winslet) and was nominated in nine other categories. *Clueless*, however, was the biggest surprise, earning 56.63 million dollars in the USA and 3.433 million pounds in Great Britain, after costing only 20 million dollars to make (IMDb). Its success surprised even the director, Amy Heckerling, who said in an interview, "[...] [W]ho ever thought that a movie about teenage girls called CLUELESS would be taken so seriously" (AFI 5). Heckerling won the National Society of Film Critics Award for the best screenplay in 1995. The film also spawned a successful, if not very good, television series.

Adaptations of classic novels have been staple fare on BBC television since its beginnings and on BBC-2 after it was created in 1964. During the seventies, commercial television stations such as Granada, ITV, and Channel Four also produced literary adaptations or purchased them from independent companies. The BBC's *Vanity Fair* (1967), the first color broadcast of a classic novel, stimulated public interest in such adaptations during the seventies. Such high quality series as the BBC's *The Pallisers* (1974) and *I, Claudius* (1976) and Granada's *Hard Times* (1977) helped to sustain this interest. During the eighties, the BBC seemed to have lost its touch, but Granada presented two masterpieces during this period—*Brideshead Revisited* (1981) and *The Jewel in the Crown* (1981). Giddings and Selby define the turning point for the BBC as the presentation of *Clarissa* on BBC-2 in 1991 (84). This adaptation prepared the way for what they call the "renaissance of the classic serial" (80). During the nineties, the classic serial did appear to be reborn. Stendahl's *Scarlet and Black* (BBC-1) in 1993, *Middlemarch* (BBC-2) in 1994, and *The Buccaneers* (BBC-1) in 1995 were followed in 1995 by *Persuasion* (BBC-2), *Pride and Prejudice* (BBC-1) and *Emma* (ITV). Ironically, the BBC found itself winning in the rating wars with commercial stations—winning with its high-culture product (Giddings, Selby 120–121). And, the BBC also found itself making a profit by selling the adaptations to a world-wide market. *Pride and Prejudice* has earned the BBC 1,620,225 pounds. By November 1995, the

Penguin/BBC edition of the novel *Pride and Prejudice* had sold over 150,000 copies, and the video version had sold 150,000 copies (Giddings, Selby 122).

Even in the United States, where more money is available for the making of both films and television series, the studios have allowed only a few large budget films of classic novels, and then only by auteurs of enormous prestige. Examples include *Barry Lyndon* (Stanley Kubrick, 1975), *The Age of Innocence* (Martin Scorsese, 1993), *The Portrait of a Lady* (Jane Campion, 1996), and *Bram Stoker's Dracula* (Francis Ford Coppola, 1993). Alone among independent filmmakers, Merchant-Ivory Productions, headed by producer Ismail Merchant and director James Ivory, have consistently managed to turn out quality literary adaptations by keeping their budgets within reasonable limits. Among their notable adaptations are *A Room with a View* (1986), *Howard's End* (1992), and *The Golden Bowl* (2000). Even film companies such as Miramax and Mirage occasionally take on a classic novel if the budget is small enough to make the gamble worthwhile. The Miramax *Emma* cost 6 million dollars, and the Mirage *Sense and Sensibility*, 16.5 million. The theatrical releases of these films made respectable grosses—*Emma*, over 22 million dollars and *Sense and Sensibility*, 49.3 million (IMDb). However, American television companies invest mainly in well-known classics, such as Dickens' *A Christmas Carol* (1984), *Frankenstein* (1993), and *Heart of Darkness* (1993). Public television, TNT, and the Arts and Entertainment Network are the chief venues for films made for television and mini-series based on British classic novels. Many of the these, of course, have been made for British television, by British film companies. Increasingly, these adaptations have been jointly financed by American corporations, such as Mobil Oil, TNT, and WGBH-Boston. According to Rebecca Eaton, Mobil Oil Corporation, which sponsors *Masterpiece Theatre* and which co-produced *Persuasion* (1995), has invested millions of dollars in adaptations of classic British novels over the past several years, including *Middlemarch* and *The Jewel in the Crown* (Tristan Davies).

It is surprising that after the filming of *Pride and Prejudice* in 1940—a film which was very successful at the box office—no other film adaptation of an Austen novel was made for theatrical release until 1995. There were live television adaptations in both England and the United States in the 1950s and early 1960s, and in the late 1960s, the 1970s and the 1980s, the BBC made and presented filmed or taped versions of all of the novels. Amazingly, during 1995 and 1996, six adaptations appeared—first *Clueless*, then *Persuasion*, followed by *Pride and Prejudice* , *Sense and Sensibility*, the Miramax *Emma* , and the Meridian/A&E *Emma*. It is not unusual for filmmakers to hop on the bandwagon after a successful adaptation and bring out an adaptation of another novel of the author. However, several of these adaptations were being planned or even being filmed at the same time. Emma Thompson had been working on the screenplay for *Sense and Sensibility* since 1990 (Thompson 208). Sue Birtwistle and Andrew Davies had talked of doing a film version of *Pride and Prejudice* as early as 1986 (Birtwistle, *Pride* v). *Persuasion* and *Pride and Prejudice* were being filmed at the same time, and their production teams even competed at times for the same props and costumes (Giddings, Selby 103). Apparently the Miramax *Emma* was being filmed at the same time as the Meridian/A&E *Emma*. Miramax hoped to cash in on the Austen fad with *Mansfield Park* (1999), but the box office failure of this film put an end to the string. After Miramax purchased Davies' screenplay of *Northanger Abbey*, the studio shelved its projected film of the novel. Davies has expressed doubt that Miramax will ever revive the project (e-mail 1/11/01).

The question might well be, "Why was Austen so right with the mid-nineties?" One of the answers usually given, with a disparaging sneer, is that the public, especially the British public, has a nostalgic longing for the order and beauty of the past. Julian North sums up this appeal succinctly. He calls Austen "a canonical author whose life and work signify English national heritage and all that implies of the past as an idyll of village life in a pre-industrial society, of traditional class and gender hierarchies, sexual propriety and Christian values" (38). Charles Denton, Drama Head at the BBC, has called Jane Austen "the Quentin Tarentino of the middle classes" (Giddings, Selby 100). As the films appeared, articles in British newspapers, magazines and web sites associated the films with National Trust properties and even gave helpful advice to their readers about the locations of the great houses which appeared in the films. Saltram House near Plymouth (Norland in *Sense and Sensibility*), Montacute in Somerset (the Palmers' estate in *Sense and Sensibility*), Lyme Park in Cheshire (Pemberley in *Pride and Prejudice*) and others which appeared in the Austen adaptations became instant meccas for viewers who had seen them in the films. Lyme Park had 800 visitors during the first week after *Pride and Prejudice* was shown on television, yet only 86 in the same period in the previous year (Kelly 1). American audiences enjoyed the experience of being voyeurs not only of an alien lifestyle in the past but in a foreign land, yet a land enough like the United States so as not to be threatening and inhabited by people who actually speak English. Douglas McGrath, in England to film *Emma*, told a reporter that Americans "love that stuff." He amplified: "It appeals mainly to urban people—we're glad when these films open, because life in big American cities is quite harsh. It's a relief to see a film where the clothes, the houses, the landscapes are pretty and there's no graffiti" (Gritten 41).

Another factor at work, in both England and America, however, is that, even as viewers yearn for the good old days and good old places, they also congratulate themselves that, in many ways, our times are better. Thus they feel superior to Elinor and Marianne Dashwood because women today have more choices than the Dashwoods had. They do not have to stay home and wait for an eligible bachelor to appear; they do not have to marry in order to have status; they may even take an antibiotic and survive a putrid fever without being bled by a surgeon. They may not be able to afford, or even find, a reliable servant, but they have washing machines, dryers, microwave ovens, and electric lights.

Devoney Looser maintains that the recent Austen adaptations have been popular because they represent a "mainstreaming" of modern feminism. Often incorporating modern critics' interpretations of Austen's novels as embodying feminist principles, the adaptations of the nineties reflect modern feminism and are appealing to modern viewers for that reason ("Feminist Implications" 159). She has also expressed the opinion that Thompson remodeled the male characters in *Sense and Sensibility* to make them more acceptable as heroes to modern female viewers. She made Colonel Brandon and Edward Ferrars more sensitive to the feelings and opinions of their female love interests and even to the child, Margaret ("Men's Movement" 167). Giddings and Selby agree that the Austen adaptations of the nineties, like some other classic novel adaptations of the period, such as *Middlemarch* and *The Buccaneers*, appeal particularly to "socially, sexually and politically enfranchised women" (119–120).

Ironically, the viewers one might expect to be most pleased with the Austen adaptations—the readers who have made the novels their own—have often been the most critical of the films. Their complaints vary, but a common theme is that "It's not as good as the book." Fidelity to the story, the characters, the ideas, and the language is their main criterion. Some of them feel that since the film is not exactly the same as the book, it is not only inferior, but amounts to criminal trespass. Often readers have formed such strong visual conceptions of Elizabeth Bennet or Emma that no actress can live up to their expectations. They may object to new dialogue that the screenwriter has concocted, or to the moving of a drawing room scene outdoors, or to the possibility that Elizabeth Bennet seems not to be wearing underwear. Deborah Cartmell has suggested that canonical texts, such as Austen's novels, must be treated with more respect and with greater accuracy than contemporary ones (27). Her logic is that viewers will not tolerate many changes or additions to these well-known and revered novels. Since the most avid fans will never be satisfied, perhaps the better course for a filmmaker would be to make the best film that he can make and not worry about this group. In the case of the Austen films of the mid-nineties, a great many people have written about them, some praising them, some finding fault with the same elements that the others praise.

One of the best results of the new films is that they have inspired discussion of both the novels and the films, and discussion keeps a novelist alive. After the release of these films, the membership of the Jane Austen Society of North America almost doubled. Since heritage mansions were not within easy reach, American Janeites visited the Republic of Pemberley on-line. They participated in dialogues and arguments on-line; they posted information about all facets of eighteenth century customs, fashions, and music. Another happy result is that with the release of every new film, new editions of the novels appear and are scarfed up by new readers of the novels. During the week of January 15, 1996, the Signet paperback edition of *Sense and Sensibility* was No. 3 on the UPI's best-seller list (Winship). Teachers have testified that the films provide their students access to the novels so that they can better appreciate them. Hala Bentley, a teacher in a British comprehensive school, lamented some of the lapses from fidelity in the 1995 *Pride and Prejudice*, but found that the film provided her "semi-literate" students a bridge to the novel. She writes, "The stunning visual impact of this gorgeous, high-budget production, with its emphasis on vitality and sexual attraction, stimulated their interest in the characters and their fates" (143). An American college teacher, M. Casey Diana, reports a similar experience with *Sense and Sensibility*. She calls the film a "gateway" to the novel and says that her students were able "to grasp the plot more fully, to engage on a deeper level with the characters, and to remember a greater amount of detail" (147). However, I have discovered that a student who is assigned *Sense and Sensibility* to read may remember the details of the film, not of the novel. If he remembers how important and appealing a character Margaret is in *Sense and Sensibility*, he is remembering the film. A related problem implicit in showing these films to students is that they may not read the novels at all. Also, if the teacher uses a film only as a gloss on the novel, the student may not have an appreciation of the film as an independent work of art.

Brian McFarlane said in a paper presented to the Literature/Film Association in 1999, "Fidelity is obviously very desirable in marriage; but with film adaptations I suspect playing around is more effective" (165). He has criticized the 1995 *Pride and Prejudice*, calling it "the work of an industrious bricklayer rather than an architect, with one event from the novel remorselessly following another, without any sense of shape or structuring, without any apparent point of view on its material" (166). I think that he is being too hard on the mini-series, but I can appreciate his preference for *Clueless*, which he calls "a kind of commentary on its great antecedent, a new work" (166). He touches on a problem which I have mentioned above—that literary training may lead the viewer to see a film as valuable to the extent that it "approximates the precursor literary text." Furthermore, viewers with literary training want to find in the film what they liked in the novel and want to see there their own interpretation of the novel (164–165). Neil Sinyard asserts, " [...] [T]he best adaptations of books for film can often best be approached as an activity of literary criticism [...] a critical essay which stresses what it sees as the main theme. [...] [L]ike the best criticism, it can throw new light on the original" (117). A related possibility is that the screenwriter may be enough of a scholar to interpret a novel from the perspective of recent literary criticism. Clearly the recent adaptation of *Mansfield Park*, written and directed by Patricia Rozema, reflects the influence of scholars who have interpreted the novel as a reflection of Austen's abolitionist and feminist sympathies.

Geoffrey Wagner has divided adaptations into three categories: transposition, commentary, and analogy. A "transposition" follows the novel closely; a "commentary" alters the novel slightly, with a new emphasis or new structure; an "analogy" uses the novel as a point of departure (222–226). Most of the adaptations of Austen's novels have been transpositions. They include all or most of the characters in the novels, keep the main incidents of the novels, and use as much of the language as the screenwriter can manage, either as dialogue or voice-over narration. The BBC/A&E *Pride and Prejudice* is the prime example of this approach. Although Andrew Davies added some incidents and some dialogue, he did not deviate from the main course of action. *Mansfield Park* is an example of a "commentary." It reinterprets the novel, using the historical time and the characters of the novel but altering in significant ways their nature and their motivations. The third category, the analogy, is well illustrated by *Clueless*. This film moves the characters from the nineteenth to the twentieth century, changes their names, and has them talk in "mall-speak." The film was marketed for a youthful audience, most of whom did not connect the film to Jane Austen at all. It was appealing to this audience, but had an especial resonance for the viewer familiar with *Emma*. By making Emma/Cher a modern Valley girl, Amy Heckerling forced the informed viewer to recognize the relevance of Jane Austen's novel for the present day. At least one critic has called the film *Metropolitan* (1990) an analogy based on *Mansfield Park* (Young), but I feel that the connection to the Austen novel is too tenuous for the film to be included in a discussion of adaptations of Austen's novels.

Even the most "faithful" adaptation of a classic novel is not an exact reproduction of it. Film is, after all, a medium quite different from the novel. George Bluestone, the elder statesman of film criticism, said that the novel and film "belong to separate aesthetic genera," with "different origins, different audiences, different modes of production" (viii). In spite of this statement, Bluestone emphasized fidelity to the novel and to the intentions of the novelist as a chief criterion of the success of an adaptation. He felt that the film "leaves behind those characteristic contents of thought which only language can approximate" (viii). For this abandonment of language, some viewers disparage film as incapable of expressing complex ideas. It was this kind of thinking that led Anthony Burgess to maintain that films based on second- or third-rate novels are better than those based on good novels (Beja 85). Recent film critics have emphasized the advantages, rather than the disadvantages, of film for telling a compelling story—its immediacy, its strong sense of place and time. The two genres share the elements of characters, narration, and language, but these are revealed or expressed in different ways. The most important ways in which film differs from the novel lie in the additional elements of pictures and sound. The filmmaker may reveal theme and character and move the action forward by means other than language. A good director will find a way to make the visual image convey the ideas implicit in the story. Usually, the visual image conveys many ideas at once—contained in the expressions on the faces of the actors, in their wearing apparel, in the setting where they are seen, in the use of light, and in the editing of visual images. Bluestone stated, "Suffice it to say that dialogue, interior monologue, sound effects, music are ultimately determined by and therefore subservient to the demands of the visual image" (30). The choice of music is also important, as well as the way it is integrated into the film. I have always felt that music in films, except in musicals, is best when least obtrusive. If this is true, it is no wonder that many viewers are unaware of the way music creates mood and reinforces, or undercuts, the visual image in a film.

Bluestone stated that "[…] [C]hanges are *inevitable* the moment one abandons the linguistic for the visual medium" (5). Interpretation enters through the screenplay, through the choice of actors, through the actors' reading of a role, through the choice of settings, through the music, and through the photography. The screenwriter selects incidents and creates scenes. He may omit some characters and expand the roles of others. He may invent dialogue, or create dialogue from the narration; he may convey exposition through additional dialogue or through voiceover. He must also adjust to the form—whether a mini-series or a two-hour theatrical release—in deciding which scenes to select and how to structure the program. He may adjust to the anticipated audience—television viewer, art house crowd, multi-plex multitudes. He may have to explain certain customs and attitudes—as Emma Thompson does in *Sense and Sensibility*, when Elinor explains to Margaret why their half brother instead of their mother and her daughters inherits their home. This kind of interpretation may involve the portrayal of a character, as well. By developing the character of Margaret, Thompson conveyed the frustrations that a girl of our times might feel at the limitations facing her as a woman in the early nineteenth century. As Imelda Whelehan points out, "Gender, class and other social differences are inevitably reconstructed in our own image more often than with reference to the past." She refers to the "temptation to portray a scene from a late twentieth-century perspective in order, ironically, to sustain the adapter's sense of what is authentic to the text" (13). One of the greatest problems in adapting *Mansfield Park* is creating a sympathetic and believable Fanny Price. In the novel she is sickly, she is passive, she is judgmental, and she is boring. Readers of the early nineteenth century would have accepted her as a plausible heroine, but many readers of the present day cannot. Patricia Rozema did major surgery on this character in her recent film. She made her a satiric writer and a healthy, active woman, but retained the character's stubborn sense of her own rightness.

The choice of actors can be enormously important and may itself influence other aspects of a production. If a studio is going to invest in a star, it had better justify the expense by making a film which will appeal to a large or broad audience. MGM used heavy star-power in the 1940 *Pride and Prejudice*. Laurence Olivier and Greer Garson had proven box office appeal, and they were backed up by a group of screwball comedy veterans, such as Edmund Gwenn, May Boland, and Edna Mae Oliver. A more recent case in point is the star-power of Gwyneth Paltrow, which essentially carried the Miramax *Emma*. With this rising young actress in the title role, the studio also invested enough money in the production to create a highly polished film. The choice of actors for the BBC/A&E *Pride and Prejudice* was also a prime reason for that mini-series' success. One might think, however, that the audience appeal of Colin Firth as Darcy must have surprised the filmmakers as well as Firth, who had not evoked this much interest in anything he had played in before or has played in since. It is possible, however, that Firth will be offered better roles than the cuckolded husbands in *The English Patient* (1996) and *Shakespeare in*

Emma (Miramax 1996). Emma (Gwyneth Paltrow) dances with Mr. Knightley (Jeremy Northam). Harriet Smith (Toni Collette) dances behind them.

Love (1998) after his performance in *Bridget Jones's Diary* (2001). In the latter film, he plays a character named "Mark Darcy," thus participating in a self-referential in-joke taken from the novel.* The BBC/A&E *Pride and Prejudice* also benefited from the excellent supporting cast of actors frequently appearing in BBC productions.

Just as film viewers in South Louisiana register skepticism when an American actor raised in the concrete canyons of New York City or Los Angeles attempts one of the many South Louisiana dialects, so do British audiences and critics lie in wait for an American actress's rendering of a British dialect. Interestingly, Gwyneth Paltrow as the choice for Emma inspired skepticism in the British press prior to the film's release, but her performance in the role was generally praised. In England, criticism is just as apt to fall on an actor who is associated with modern working class roles but who attempts a character of the upper class—an actor like Ewan McGregor, a junkie in *Trainspotting* (1996), who plays Frank Churchill in the Miramax *Emma*.

The screenwriter particularly shapes the way the audience will see the adaptation. For some writers it is merely a matter of simplifying certain elements to enable audiences to accept them or of omitting others because they cannot easily be explained. On the other hand, Andrew Davies introduced both dialogue and incident to emphasize class difference in *Emma*.

*Helen Fielding claimed to have stolen the plot of Pride and Prejudice *for her novel* Bridget Jones's Diary *(Salber 1), but the similarities between the two lie primarily in the generic love triangle.*

This adaptation shows liveried servants moving cushions for the ladies who are picking strawberries, and introduces the concluding harvest dinner, at which gentry and tenants eat together and dance together, thus affirming a sense of community. Roger Sales postulates that American-made versions of classic British novels, which tend to emphasize romance and character, place less emphasis on "historical heritage detail" and less emphasis on class distinctions than do British films. He gives the 1940 *Pride and Prejudice* and the Miramax *Emma* as examples of these tendencies ("In Face" 196).

Another concern for the maker of either films or television serials based on English classic novels is the dialogue. Denis Constanduros* and Emma Thompson attest that language is important but that the screenwriter cannot use Austen's dialogue as it is. Constanduros says that the writer has to keep the dialogue "short and easy to speak and natural," yet retain the "flavour" of the novel. He also states that audiences are going to want to hear the famous lines as they appear in the novels. (Lauritzen 47). Thompson found the language of Austen's letters "very clear and elegant," "funny," and "much less arcane" than that of the novel. She attempted to capture these qualities in her screenplay (Hampshire 8). Andrew Davies, commenting on his approach to writing dialogue for *Pride and Prejudice*, says that he thinks that Austen's dialogue is not completely naturalistic, but rather "something like real speech, and alludes to it, but is more elegant and more pointed." He tried to make the dialogue "sound like something that could be spoken in the early nineteenth century, but also something you wouldn't think terribly artificial if it were spoken now" (Birtwistle, *Pride*, 13). Jennifer Ehle confessed to having difficulty with the dialogue, calling it harder to learn than Shakespeare's, "because the sense of the line comes at the end of it and also the lines are much longer" (Birtwistle, *Pride*, 13).

Other elements which create the image which the audience sees include the choice of settings—whether to film on studio sets or to use the buildings and the countryside which approximate those which Jane Austen knew and wrote about. Sue Birtwistle's books on the making of *Pride and Prejudice* and *Emma* are fascinating for their insights into the complexities of making a film—in particular about finding and using certain locations. It is difficult to find landscapes which do not show the impact of twentieth-century or even late nineteenth-century civilization. Apparently both McGrath and Birtwistle despaired of finding unspoiled

---

*Denis Constanduros *wrote the screenplays for the BBC's 1971* Sense and Sensibility *and the 1972* Emma. *He also wrote dramatizations of two Austen novels for radio—*Northanger Abbey *in 1962 and* Persuasion *in 1970.*

locations in Surrey for *Emma*, and chose rather villages in Dorset and Wiltshire. The list of great houses used for the BBC/A&E *Pride and Prejudice* and for *Sense and Sensibility* reads like the directory of National Trust properties. The makers of these films sought beauty and authenticity in their settings. Patricia Rozema was particularly interested in setting as symbol and, instead of choosing the modern (eighteenth-century) great house which the novel called for, chose sixteenth-century Kirby Hall because its ruined state would suggest the fragile moral and economic foundation of the Bertram family ("Place" 3). Michael Coulter, the cinematographer for both *Mansfield Park* and *Sense and Sensibility*, shows Kirby Hall as dark, barren, comfortless. He frequently uses helicopter shots to open up the perspective and to suggest a freedom contrary to that which the characters experience. In *Sense and Sensibility*, he also created highly pictorial images of the characters in the context of various natural settings. Marianne cutting reeds near Barton Cottage, or Marianne's small white figure in extreme long shot trudging up a green hill to view Willoughby's Combe Magna, or Edward and Elinor riding on the smooth green lawn of Norland—these are images that have emotional and visual appeal. Andrew Higson complains that the visual styles of these "heritage" films emphasizes the visual beauty of "heritage space" to the detriment of "dramatic goal-directed action" (117). However, since the action of Jane Austen's novels takes place primarily within the characters and since the temporal and spatial setting is integral to this action, I think that it makes sense for the filmmaker to show the kinds of houses and landscapes Jane Austen's characters inhabited.

Much more has been written on the art of making the feature film than of making the mini-series, a neglected and even despised form. The BBC has set the standard for the mini-series based on classic English novels. It might be said that if fidelity is the aim of the screenwriter and producer, it can best be achieved in a mini-series. In about 300 minutes or six fifty-minute episodes, the screenwriter may preserve all or most of a novel's characters and have ample time to develop relationships. Terrance Dicks, a script editor and later the producer of *Vanity Fair* (1987) for the BBC, said that he and his predecessor, Barry Letts, sought to "put the book on the screen as faithfully as possible" (Giddings 138). He contrasted Jane Austen's novels unfavorably with Thackeray's *Vanity Fair*, saying that their psychological emphasis and interior action render them problematic for the screenwriter. He said that dramatizations of Austen's novels tend "to come down to people standing in beautiful locations in beautiful frocks looking soulful!" (Giddings, Selby, Wensley 140). Monica Lauritzen, while researching the making of the 1972 *Emma*, interviewed both screenwriters and directors at the BBC regarding the making of classic serials. According to Lauritzen, those she interviewed expressed no reservations about the adapting of the Austen novels. They emphasized the importance of selecting a novel with "dramatic potential" or "conflict" (52). William Slater said that a six-part serial needs "six points of conflict" (52). Constanduros, stated, "You don't want something that comes to a dead stop. […] [Y]ou must set a problem […] have that carry-over of interest," especially into the second episode. He liked to accomplish this carry-over with a signature tune or with a series of vignettes (48–49). The makers of both the 1980 and the 1995 BBC *Pride and Prejudice* learned this lesson well. The former uses some clever water colors showing the characters in a comic manner involved in characteristic activities. The latter opens each episode with the distinctive pianoforte musical theme, while showing a hand sewing on a piece of fabric. All of these directors and screenwriters appear to agree with Bluestone's assertion of the "principle of Hollywood Aristotelianism": "that all elements of the film […] must be subordinated to plot, the prime arbiter" (103). As long as the makers of either feature films or television serials tell Austen's stories, they will not go far astray.

II

Sense and Sensibility

Sense and Sensibility is Jane Austen's first published novel. She started writing it in 1795 as an epistolary novel, first entitled *Elinor and Marianne*. In November 1811 it was published under its new title. It introduced situations which were to be typical of all of Austen's novels: women attempting to marry the men that they love, defying the social, personal, or economic barriers which would prevent them. In this novel, two sisters, their father having died, find themselves, their mother, and younger sister cast out from their home, Norland Park, where they had lived surrounded by all the comforts that wealth could provide. It is the situation that Mrs. Bennet, of *Pride and Prejudice,* feared for herself and her daughters. In *Sense and Sensibility* the uncle of Henry Dashwood left the property to him and specified that at Henry Dashwood's death, the estate would go to John Dashwood, the son of Henry Dashwood and half-brother to Elinor and Marianne, and then to John Dashwood's son. Little provision was made for the girls. The Dashwood women must now subsist on about 500 pounds a year, and the sisters will have dowries so small that their chances of finding suitable husbands are slight. Before they leave Norland Park, Elinor meets and develops a romantic interest in Edward Ferrars, the brother of her sister-in-law, Fanny. This young man's mother is wealthy, but she expects Edward to marry a woman of her choosing. As Fanny Dashwood tells Elinor's mother, he is entirely dependent on his mother's largesse. Thus he is not the free and eligible young man which he appears to be.

At their new home at Barton Cottage in Devonshire, the Dashwoods find their benefactor, Sir John, and his family far more kind than John and Fanny. Sir John's friend and neighbor, Colonel Brandon, a gentleman of about thirty-five, falls in love with Marianne. However, the seventeen-year-old Marianne considers Brandon a stodgy old man. Then, John Willoughby appears. He is visiting an aunt who lives in the area and happens upon Marianne after she has sprained her ankle. Marianne sees in Willoughby everything she wants in a man but has almost despaired of finding. He is a gentleman; he is young, handsome, active, and interested in music and literature. He seems to return her affection, but like Edward he is not free to make a commitment to Marianne. His financial situation requires that he marry someone who has a substantial dowry to maintain his self-indulgent lifestyle. He has also seduced and abandoned Colonel Brandon's ward, Eliza, a situation which temporarily causes Mrs. Smith, his wealthy relative, to change her mind about leaving him her estate, Allenham. Willoughby departs from Devonshire suddenly, leaving Marianne distraught.

When Edward comes to visit at Barton Cottage, although he is obviously still interested in Elinor, she finds him more reserved than he was at Norland. After she meets Lucy Steele, who is visiting at Barton Park, she learns the reason for Edward's reserve. Lucy reveals that she has been secretly engaged to Edward for four years. Because of a promise which Elinor makes to Lucy to keep her secret, Elinor cannot tell her family of Edward's prior commitment.

At this juncture, Sir John's mother-in-law, Mrs. Jennings, asks Elinor and Marianne to go to London with her. Although Marianne is delighted at this opportunity to see Willoughby again, Elinor dreads the thought of seeing Edward, but she yields to Marianne's desire to go. In London, Willoughby first ignores Marianne's letters, then snubs her at a party. When Marianne learns that Willoughby plans to marry an heiress, she is devastated. Meanwhile, Lucy Steele's sister tells Fanny Dashwood that Lucy is engaged to Edward, and Edward's mother tries to coerce him into breaking his engagement. After Edward refuses—even though he has long ceased to love Lucy—his mother disinherits him and makes his brother, Robert, her heir.

Colonel Brandon comes to the rescue. He tells Elinor about Willoughby's perfidy to Eliza and thus prepares the way for Marianne to realize that her hero is not the paragon she had thought him. Reacting against Edward's family's cruelty to him, Brandon also bestows a living on Edward. Ironically, when he asks Elinor to tell Edward of his offer, he does not realize that he may be enabling Elinor's rival to marry the man Elinor loves.

By this time Elinor and Marianne are eager to go home. When Mrs. Jennings and her daughter, Mrs. Palmer, set out for the Palmers' estate, Cleveland, they take the Dashwood sisters with them. Here Marianne becomes seriously ill. After Colonel Brandon leaves for Devonshire to pick up Mrs. Dashwood, Willoughby arrives at Cleveland, having heard of Marianne's illness. He explains his behavior and his motives to Elinor. When Colonel Brandon and Mrs. Dashwood arrive, Marianne is out of danger.

After the Dashwoods get back to Barton Cottage, Marianne sets out to reform her attitudes and behavior. She resolves to be more like Elinor both in the way she relates to others and in the way she governs her emotions. One day, they hear that Miss Steele is now Mrs. Ferrars, and naturally assume that Lucy has married Edward. Later, when Edward rides up to the cottage, they are surprised. They are even more surprised to learn that Lucy Steele has married Edward's brother. Edward has come to Barton Cottage to propose to Elinor. Thus, Elinor suddenly goes from hopelessness to happiness. After they are married they go to live at the Delaford parsonage; within two years Marianne marries Colonel Brandon and goes to live at Delaford manor.

Elinor and Marianne thus follow parallel courses. Both fall in love with men who will not or cannot commit to them. The different ways in which Elinor and Marianne handle their love and their disappointments in love—ways suggested by the title of the novel—constitute the main interest of the novel. Elinor's attitudes and behavior epitomize "sense," which can be defined as reason, decorum, and propriety. Marianne embodies the characteristics of "sensibility," which include the open display of emotion, spontaneity of action, and indifference to decorum. The more traditional critical treatments of the novel have generally presented Elinor as modeling behavior of which Jane Austen approved, and Marianne as exhibiting self-indulgent and even dangerous behavior. In recent years, however, some critics have maintained that Marianne's expression of her feelings is more healthy and admirable than Elinor's secrecy and restraint (Tanner 100). For those who value "getting in touch with your feelings," Marianne could be a role model. Elinor, on the other hand, has been criticized for her extreme, even unhealthy control of her feelings or even for lacking strong feelings. The problems for the critic are to decide first what Elinor's and Marianne's attitudes are and second to what extent these are admirable or blamable in the context of the novel.

My reading of the novel, looking at it in the context of Austen's other novels, is that Elinor models admirable behavior and that Marianne is in error. Elinor's behavior remains essentially the same throughout the novel. Since her conduct in her relationship with Edward, in her relationship with her family, and in her relationship with friends is irreproachable, there is no need for her to change. On the other hand, after pursuing a career of irresponsible and inconsiderate emotional self-indulgence, Marianne expresses the intention to reform and to become more like her sister. Roger Garis believes that Austen's best characters are those who change in some way and that the problem with *Sense and Sensibility* is that Elinor, the main character, does not change. He feels that she exists too much to illustrate "sense" (61). While it is true that she illustrates "sense" and is perhaps too good to be true, the reader remains intensely interested in Elinor's struggles to govern her emotions and to achieve happiness for herself and for those she loves.

Elinor, if not entirely in control of her emotions, is much in command of her expression of them. When Elinor meets Edward at Norland and begins to love him, she displays such a calm demeanor that Mrs. Dashwood is for a time unaware of her daughter's preference. However, when Marianne questions her about Edward, Elinor becomes enthusiastic in her praise of Edward's character, and the reader is told that she is "sorry for the warmth she had been betrayed into, in speaking of him" (*SS* 21). She goes on to say that she likes him and thinks highly of him, but that she is by no means sure of his affection (*SS* 21). Not only is she unwilling to admit love for a man who has not admitted love for her; at this point in time she will not allow herself even to think herself in love. There is a great deal of psychic self-protection in such a stance. When Edward visits the family at Norland, Elinor notices how melancholy Edward is, and when he visits them at Barton Cottage he is often in low spirits. After Marianne charges him with being reserved, he blushes in a guilty manner. At this point we may remember Mr. Knightley's and Emma's discussion of Jane Fairfax—their agreement on the value of an open temper, and their disapproval of "reserve." One must differentiate, however, between Jane Fairfax's, Frank Churchill's, and Edward Ferrars' reserve and that of Elinor. Jane, Frank, and Edward are operating under false credentials, pretending to be free when they are attached. Elinor is reserved as well, but her reserve is appropriate because she is not free to show her feelings for Edward until he makes clear his feelings for her. In spite of Edward's diffidence and reserve, and in spite of Elinor's resolve not to love him, by the time of his visit to Barton Cottage, Elinor loves Edward. She even convinces herself that the ring he wears contains a lock of her hair. The narrator states that when Edward leaves Barton Cottage, Elinor suffers greatly, but she makes an effort not to show her suffering. Although she does not retreat to her room to weep, she thinks about Edward and revolves over in her mind his conduct toward her. Marianne is astonished at Elinor's self control. She thinks that Elinor's feelings must not be strong if they can be controlled in this manner.

When Lucy Steele tells Elinor that she and Edward have been engaged for four years, Elinor is at first incredulous. She requires a great many supporting details to convince her that the man she loves could love this uneducated little schemer and that the man who had won her own affections could have been attached to another woman. Jealous of Edward's praise of Elinor, Lucy has sought out Elinor to confide in so that she might ascertain Elinor's attitude toward Edward. By the time Elinor goes to London, she knows that she has no chance of marrying Edward, but she has sufficient command of her emotions so that she can conceal her love and despair from Lucy Steele, who would enjoy seeing Elinor show disappointment.

Shortly after their settling at Barton Cottage, Marianne meets and falls in love with John Willoughby. "Falling in love" is the appropriate term for what Marianne experiences. After Willoughby finds Marianne suffering from a sprained ankle, he carries her home, and within a few days she is head over heels in love. By her unreserved behavior, Marianne reveals to everyone, including Willoughby, that she loves him. Willoughby later tells Elinor that, during his early acquaintance with Marianne, he thought only of his entertainment and had no "design of returning her affection" (*SS* 320). During daily visits to Barton Cottage, Willoughby ingratiates himself into the affections of the family but particularly into Marianne's affections. Elinor expresses concern that the pair are so little mindful of propriety. They are also often regardless of the claims of good manners so that in focusing on each other they slight their friends. Marianne refuses to heed Elinor's warnings that they know little about Willoughby and that her behavior will occasion gossip. She says that she knows Willoughby better than she knows her half-brother. She is convinced that she should follow where her feelings lead her and that if she behaves inappropriately, she will know it. Marianne is as extreme in her happiness, as later she is extreme in loss and disappointment.

After Willoughby leaves to go to London, Marianne makes no secret of her suffering. Even though she does not think that this parting is final, she is desolated. At first she goes to her room to weep. When she comes to dinner, she can eat nothing, and when her mother presses her hand, Marianne bursts into tears. We are told that she could not control her grief because "[...] she was without any desire of command over herself" (*SS* 82). Her behavior gives pain to her family, yet she indulges in tears, plays only the music that she and Willoughby had sung together, and reads only the books which they had read together. The narrator says, "Her sensibility was potent enough!" (*SS* 83). This behavior constitutes selfish indulgence in the pleasures of melancholy.

Later, she tells Elinor that she is ashamed of the way she acted, and that she realizes that she should have been more like Elinor. Both experience the same disappointments in love, yet when the sisters go to London, Marianne first pursues Willoughby openly by writing him letters and by approaching him at a party. Then, when rebuffed, she grieves openly, oblivious to the feelings of her family and friends and to the way she is feeding the gossip mills. Elinor deals with her disappointment by keeping it secret and by devoting her attention to her sister. It is apparent that Marianne's weeping, starving herself, and brooding over her lost love do not help her in any way. She may be venting her feelings, but this venting does not improve her mental or physical health. Indeed, she develops a "putrid" fever while at the Palmers' estate and comes close to dying. She admits to Elinor that her excesses brought on her illness.

Although not as often adapted as *Pride and Prejudice* and *Emma, Sense and Sensibility* has been presented on film and television four times. On June 4, 1950, NBC's *Philco Television Playhouse* featured a live hour-long adaptation based on a screenplay by H. R. Hays and directed by Delbert Mann (Brooks 865). Mann was an important director of early television drama and is particularly remembered for Paddy Chayefsky's play *Marty*, which Mann directed on television in 1953 and as a film in 1955. The film won Academy Awards for Best Picture, Best Director (Mann), and Best Actor (Ernest Borgnine). Madge Evans played Elinor in the 1950 adaptation of *Sense and Sensibility*, and a young Cloris Leachman played Marianne. Madge Evans had been a child star in silent films from the age of five and had made the transition to adult roles on Broadway and in Hollywood (Katz 430). Since Evans retired from both stage and screen in 1943, her appearances in the *Philco Television Playhouse* productions of *Pride and Prejudice* in 1949 and of *Sense and Sensibility* in 1950 represent something of a "star turn" for the veteran actress (Katz 430). In her early forties, Evans was somewhat old to play either Elizabeth Bennet or Elinor Dashwood. Cloris Leachman, of course, has had a busy career primarily on television but occasionally on film from 1948 to the present. My first memory of her was in the role of Ruth Popper in *The Last Picture Show* (1971), but others may remember her better as Phyllis in *The Mary Tyler Moore Show* from 1970 to 1975. Marianne was one of her earliest television roles.

According to the screenplay for the *Philco Sense and Sensibility*, it was presented on three sets: a living room in the Dashwoods' cottage, an outdoor set, and an elegant drawing room. This adaptation has omitted Margaret, Mrs. Jennings, Nancy Steele, Sir John Middleton and his family, and only mentions Fanny Dashwood. Instead of Mrs. Jennings, it introduces

Mrs. Fenner (Josephine Brown), who is the owner of the cottage in Devonshire which the Dashwood women rent and who invites Elinor and Marianne to her London townhouse.

Act I opens with John Dashwood (John Stephen) in the cottage speculating on the limited marital prospects of his impoverished step-sisters. Mrs. Fenner comes to call and introduces her friend Colonel Brandon (John Baragrey), a man with an income of five thousand pounds, to the Dashwoods. Another visitor, Edward Ferrars (Chester Stratton), tells Elinor that a friend of his "while still too young to know his own heart" gave his word to a certain young woman. Later he met the one "who possessed every attribute to make him happy." In this way, Edward reveals to Elinor that he loves her but that he is already engaged. He concludes, "Elinor ... please forgive me."

Outdoors, to the sounds of thunder, Willoughby (Larry Hugo) sees Marianne fall, goes to her aid, and carries her off stage. After a fade to the cottage, Elinor complains to her mother that Marianne is spending all her time with Willoughby. When Willoughby and Marianne enter, he announces that he must leave immediately for London. He leaves, and Marianne weeps. Toward the end of Act I, Mrs. Fenner brings Lucy Steele (Pat Hosley) to the cottage. Here Lucy informs Elinor that she is engaged to Edward.

In Act II, set in London in Mrs. Fenner's drawing room, Elinor urges Edward to introduce Lucy to his mother during a party given by Mrs. Fenner. Mrs. Ferrars (Cherry Hardy) rejects Lucy, and Edward leaves the party with her. Then Willoughby enters with a young woman, and Marianne faints when Willoughby snubs her. In Act III, still in Mrs. Fenner's drawing room, the recuperating Marianne responds to Brandon's attentions. Mrs. Fenner tells Elinor that Edward is married to Lucy. Then Edward arrives and tells Elinor that Lucy is married to his brother. His final words to Elinor are that he is "free of them all," meaning his mother, his sister, and Lucy. There is no mention at all of what Elinor and Edward are to live on. American audiences would probably assume that Edward could get a job (Hays, *Philco S&S* screenplay).

The *Philco* adaptation reveals the inevitable difficulty for the screenwriter and director of squeezing a novel into a fifty-minute time period. Even with the omission of the Barton Park family, the parade of all of the characters in Act I, followed by the swift resolution of their problems, must have made the story difficult for the ordinary television viewer to follow.

In 1971, the BBC presented a version of the novel, directed by David Giles, with a screenplay written by Denis Constanduros (who also wrote

Sense and Sensibility (BBC 1971). Center, Marianne Dashwood (Ciaran Madden); l–r, Edward Ferrars (Robin Ellis), Mrs. Dashwood (Isobel Dean), and Elinor Dashwood (Joanna David). (BBC Picture Archives)

the screenplay for the 1972 production of *Emma*). This production, recorded in color, was shown (probably in 50-minute episodes) on four consecutive Sunday nights—January 3, 10, 17, 24—and repeated on four consecutive Saturday nights—January 9, 16, 23, 30. The shooting script indicates that this version follows the novel closely, but it has omitted Margaret and introduced a chatty female servant to work for the Dashwoods at Barton Cottage. The chatty servant, Mary (Esme Church), is the one who tells the Dashwoods that Mr. Ferrars is married to Lucy Steele (Frances Cuka). In what must have been a funny scene, when Edward (Robin Ellis) proposes to Elinor (Joanna David) in the garden, as he starts to kneel, she places a handkerchief where his knees will touch the ground. He comments on how prudent she is, but surely not even Elinor could have had so much presence of mind at such a moment. Except for a few garden scenes, some transition shots showing moving carriages, and the scene where Marianne (Ciaran Madden) sprains her ankle, this adaptation was shot exclusively on studio sets (Constanduros, "*S&S*").

Only two adaptations of *Sense and Sensibility* are currently available for viewing. One of these was based on a screenplay by Alexander Baron and Denis Constanduros, directed by Rodney Bennett, produced by the BBC, and first shown serially, in seven thirty-minute episodes from February 1 to March 14, 1981. Perhaps because Constanduros, who wrote the screenplay for the 1971 adaptation, was co-author of the 1981 adaptation, this version differs only slightly in incident and dialogue from the 1971 adaptation. The main differences lie in on-location shooting and the greater use of outdoor scenes in the later serial. The 1981 adaptation was unusual for the times in that it was shot entirely on location—at great houses in Somerset, Dorset, and Bath. Irene Richards, who played Elinor in the 1981 adaptation, reports that Came House and Came Cottage near Dorchester, Dorset, were used for Barton Park and Barton Cottage. Cleveland's interiors and exteriors were filmed at Hatch Court, near Taunton, Somerset. Scenes in Mrs. Jennings' London house and the party at Woolcombe House in London were shot at Crowcombe Court, near Taunton. Bath provided the London street scenes, and Babington House, near Bath, the interiors and exteriors of Norland (e-mail 1/8/02).

The other, produced by Columbia/Mirage, was released to theatres in the United States in December 1995 and to theatres in the United Kingdom in February 1996. Ang Lee, the Taiwanese director of films so diverse as *The Wedding Banquet* (1994), *The Ice Storm* (1997), *Ride with the Devil* (1999) and *Crouching Tiger, Hidden Dragon* (2000), directed the theatrical release. It was produced by Lindsay Doran and was based on a screenplay by Emma Thompson, who won the Academy Award for the Best Screenplay Adaptation for 1995. The film was nominated for six Oscars, including Best Picture, Thompson for Best Actress as well as for Best Screenplay (not original), Kate Winslet for Best Supporting Actress, Best Cinematography, and Best (Original) Music. The British Academy of Film and Television Arts gave it the award for the Best Film, gave Thompson the award for the Best Actress in a Leading Role, and gave Winslet the award for the Best Actress in a Supporting Role. The film also won two Golden Globe awards for Best Film and Best Screenplay. With a sterling screenplay, a high-powered cast, a talented director, and a delightful soundtrack, this film is a winner in all respects.

The Mirage *Sense and Sensibility* stars Emma Thompson as Elinor Dashwood, and Kate Winslet as Marianne. Although Emma Thompson, at thirty-six, is considerably older than the nineteen-year-old Elinor, she conveys the air of maturity which the role requires. Kate Winslet, who first appeared on the big screen as a murderous teenager in *Heavenly Creatures* (1994), is convincing as the seventeen-year-old Marianne in *Sense and Sensibility*. She was to follow these roles with that of Ophelia in Branagh's *Hamlet* (1996) and that of Rose in *Titanic* (1997).

Thompson plays Elinor as having strong feelings, but as successfully concealing these feelings from her family and acquaintances. We see her walking and riding horseback with Edward (Hugh Grant) on the grounds of Norland Park. When Marianne attempts to get Elinor to reveal her feelings for Edward, Elinor uses the language of the novel, "like," "think highly of," "greatly esteem," to convey her feelings. Marianne registers indignation at such cold-heartedness. Elinor says, "Believe my feelings to be stronger than I have declared—but further than that you must not believe." While at Norland, Edward sees Elinor on the verge of tears as she listens to Marianne playing what Elinor says is her father's favorite tune. He gives her his handkerchief and allows her to keep it. Later, when Elinor is at Barton Cottage, we see her in her room alone caressing this handkerchief, with the monogram ECF embroidered in one corner.

In an obvious nod to viewers who might want explanations as to why the Dashwood women are in such desperate financial straits and are having to leave the family estate, Thompson has written several explanatory scenes. In one Elinor explains to her sister Margaret (Emilie François) why John (James Fleet) and Fanny (Harriet Walter), who have a house in town, are taking over Norland. Elinor explains that the law decrees that houses go "from father to son, not from father to daughter." This is a simplification of the situation described in the novel, in which the owner of the estate had left it to his nephew, the girls' father, and had required that he leave it to his son, John, and to John's son. We have earlier seen Henry Dashwood, on his deathbed, exact a promise from John that he "do something" for his sisters, and we have seen how John and Fanny whittle down that "something" to nothing. Thus, it is apparent that the Dashwood women will have little money to live on and that they will have to relinquish their home to their brother's family.

In another scene, while riding with Edward, Elinor says to him: "You talk of feeling idle and useless—imagine how that is compounded when one has no choice and no hope whatsoever of any occupation." Edward responds that their circumstances are the same. Elinor rejoins, "Except that you will inherit your fortune. We cannot even earn ours." Although Thompson's screenplay states that Edward is somewhat shocked at Elinor's boldness, this response is not apparent in the film. However, Elinor's statement reminds the modern viewer that respectable unmarried women had few options other than living with relatives or taking a position as a governess or lady's companion. Jane Austen would not have felt it necessary to have Elinor make such an obvious point or to make such a rude remark. In the film, the scene ends with Edward saying jokingly in an allusion to Margaret's plans to be a pirate, "Piracy is our only option."

Sense and Sensibility (Mirage 1995). Elinor Dashwood (Emma Thompson) and Marianne Dashwood (Kate Winslet). (MOMA)

Thus the seriousness of the commentary on women's lack of options is deflated by the insertion of humor. Devoney Looser refers to Claudia Johnson's term "depolemicized feminism" to describe Austen's critique of society's restrictions on women and sees the same "conciliatory feminism" in many of the recent adaptations (173). I find this "conciliatory" feminism conspicuously present in the Mirage adaptation of *Sense and Sensibility*.

In a scene at Norland which Thompson contrived to show the leave taking of Edward and Elinor, we see Elinor whispering to her horse, which the Dashwood women cannot afford to take with them. This sentimental situation is out of keeping with Jane Austen's portrayal of Elinor. Not even Marianne waxes emotional over animals, although trees and dead leaves inspire her to raptures. This situation is, however, primarily an occasion for Edward to approach Elinor away from other family members. Edward makes a joke that the horse could be put to work in the kitchen to earn his keep. Then he clumsily tries to tell Elinor about his engagement, but before he can do so, Fanny Dashwood appears at the stable door and insists that Edward leave for London at once. Elinor registers puzzlement, but does not give way to any emotional display. In her inclusion of this scene, Thompson not only shows Elinor as sentimental, but she attempts to make Edward less guilty of deceit by having him on the verge of confessing his engagement. In the novel, Edward at no time even hints of his engagement. However, Thompson also shows more interaction between Edward and Elinor, so that by enlarging Edward's role, Thompson makes Edward more vulnerable to the charge of giving Elinor false hopes.

In the 1981 BBC adaptation, Edward (Bosco Hogan) at Norland is much less attentive to Elinor (Irene Richards). In one scene, he carries Elinor's cushion and drawing materials but then abruptly leaves her to walk by himself. We see Marianne (Tracey Childs) coercing Edward into reading aloud one of Cowper's poems, and when she later criticizes his lack of passion and his stiffness, Elinor takes up for him. In another scene, Elinor is talking in an animated fashion about color and form in art while Edward listens. He then pauses to get the gardener to cut some flowers for her, asking whether they illustrate her ideas about color. We also see Edward apologizing for John (Peter Gale) and Fanny (Amanda Boxer) because they are not present when the Dashwoods leave Norland. He looks sad at their parting. This Edward could never be charged with irresponsible wooing. When he visits at Barton Cottage, again he is reserved, showing no more attention to Elinor than to other family members. Although he admits that he is not expected elsewhere, it is only with difficulty that they talk him into staying more than one night. When Mrs. Dashwood (Diana Fairfax*) and Marianne leave Elinor and Edward together, he immediately gives an excuse to leave the room as well. Later we see him walking with Mrs. Dashwood in the garden. When Sir John Middleton (Donald Douglas) arrives and issues his invitation to the Dashwoods and their guest to dinner at Barton Park, and mentions that the Miss Steeles are also going to be there, Edward announces that he will be unable to attend and must leave for London immediately. He says that he has recalled something that he had no right to forget—surely an allusion to his engagement to Lucy Steele.

The Mirage *Sense and Sensibility* omits Edward's early visit to Barton Cottage. Instead, Edward sends Margaret's atlas and a letter saying that he has business which detains him in London. Thompson's screenplay

---

Diana Fairfax played Emma in the 1960 BBC Emma.

states, "Elinor struggles to contain her bitter disappointment" (80). Margaret, however, is the one who expresses disappointment, so that Marianne takes her outside to spare Elinor Margaret's laments. When Mrs. Dashwood (Gemma Jones) attempts to assure Elinor that Edward loves her, Elinor says that she is not sure of his regard, and that even if he loves her, there may be "obstacles to his choosing a woman who cannot afford to buy sugar." When Mrs. Dashwood

Sense and Sensibility (BBC 1981). Marianne Dashwood (Tracey Childs) and Elinor Dashwood (Irene Richards). (BBC Picture Archives)

advises her to listen to her heart, Elinor says, "In such a situation, Mamma, it is perhaps better to use one's head." In spite of its omission of Edward's visit, this adaptation enables the viewer to see more of Edward and to see a more witty and charming Edward than is apparent either in the novel or the BBC version. Since Hugh Grant, an actor irrevocably identified as a tentative but ardent lover since *Four Weddings and a Funeral* (1994), is playing Edward, it is also much easier for the viewer to understand why Elinor can love him. In Donald Lyons' opinion, "When they know their love is impossible, their scenes together have a porcelain delicateness and a powerful undercurrent of blood pounding. Grant's droll manneredness fits perfectly in the decorum of this evoked world" (36).

In keeping with the novel's presentation of Elinor as the sensible member of the family, the Mirage adaptation shows Elinor keeping the family accounts and reproving her mother for her plans to renovate the cottage. Both BBC adaptations include a mention of the horse which Willoughby (Clive Francis, 1971; Peter Woodward, 1981) wishes to give to Marianne. As in the novel, it is Elinor who tells Marianne that the family cannot afford to accept the horse.

The two actresses who play Marianne are both young, pretty, and effective in conveying the character's sensibility. The greatest differences in the two most recent adaptations concern the staging of the scenes in

Sense and Sensibility (Mirage 1995). Willoughby (Greg Wise) gives the injured Marianne (Kate Winslet) a bouquet of wildflowers, while her sisters, l–r, Margaret (Emilie François) and Elinor (Emma Thompson) watch. (MOMA)

which Marianne appears. For instance, in the Mirage adaptation Willoughby's appearance is thoroughly dramatic and romantic. In this version, while Margaret and Marianne have been walking, it begins to rain, and they start running down hill toward their home. Marianne falls and is about to send Margaret for help when Willoughby (Greg Wise) appears at the top of the hill on a white horse. He is wearing a broad-brimmed hat and a long dark coat. Thompson's screenplay directions read: "Through the mist breaks a huge white horse. Astride sits an Adonis in hunting gear" (85). One can understand how a romantic like Marianne would respond to this image. As Willoughby lifts her up into his arms, she is surely seeing herself as one of the heroines of the novels and poems she loves. The BBC adaptations are tamer. Both show Elinor and Marianne climbing up hills in a wooded area. Marianne falls while going downhill. Willoughby, whom we have seen shortly before with his gun and dog, runs to assist her. Ignoring her protests, he picks her up and carries her home. This representation is closer to the incident described in the novel, except that in the novel, Margaret, not Elinor, is with Marianne.

The Mirage adaptation is superlative in the way in which it builds sexual tension and then dissipates it with humor. After Willoughby has deposited Marianne on a sofa, he excuses himself and asks permission to call on her the next day. After he has left, we hear the following comic exchange between Mrs. Dashwood, Elinor, and Marianne:

> Marianne: "He expressed himself well, did he not?"
> Mrs. Dashwood: "With great decorum and honour."
> Marianne: "And spirit and wit and feeling."
> Elinor: "And economy—ten words at most."
> [From below stairs we hear Margaret, wailing: "Wait for me!" She is afraid of missing any interesting conversation.]
> Marianne: "And he is to come tomorrow!"
> Elinor: "You must change, Marianne—you will catch a cold."
> Marianne: "What care I for colds when there is such a man?"
> Elinor: "You will care very much when your nose swells up."
> Marianne: "You are right. Help me, Elinor."
> Margaret: [Coming back with the bandages] "What has happened?"
> Elinor: "We have decided to give you to the Gypsies."

In both recent adaptations, the relationship between Marianne and Willoughby develops rapidly. In the Mirage film, on the second day of their acquaintance Elinor quips that Marianne and Willoughby have covered so many topics that soon they will have nothing more to talk about. Marianne says that she already knows Willoughby well. Elinor says, "Willoughby can be in no doubt of your enthusiasm for him." Marianne says, "Why should I hide my regard?" She continues, "If I had weaker, more shallow feelings perhaps I could conceal them, as you do." She immediately apologizes to Elinor, but certainly she does think that Elinor's feelings for Edward are shallow. Her own attitudes toward love have already been established. Early in the film she has told her mother, "To love is to burn—to be on fire, all made of passion, of adoration, of sacrifice! Like Juliet, or Guinevere or Heloise." Mrs. Dashwood reminds her that these heroines came to sad ends.

Another scene in the Mirage film which illustrates well the intrusion of the comic into the romance is that which occurs just after Colonel Brandon (Alan Rickman) has disappointed the party-goers. The Dashwood ladies and Willoughby are eating a picnic lunch on the lawn at Barton Cottage when Willoughby starts to criticize Colonel Brandon. Elinor chides him. Then Willoughby gets down on his knees, waddles about and says in imitation of Mrs. Jennings (Elizabeth Spriggs), "Come, come, Mr. Impudence—I know you and your wicked ways—oh!" He grabs Marianne's hands and twirls her around, as Margaret watches open-mouthed.

While they twirl, he continues to criticize Brandon and concludes, while slowing down, "[…] you cannot deny me the privilege of disliking him as much as I adore[…]." He and Marianne stop and gaze into each other's eyes. Then Willoughby breaks the mood by looking toward Barton Cottage, gesturing, and concluding his sentence with "[…] this cottage." He goes on to say that if he were rich enough he would tear down Combe Magna and rebuild it like Barton Cottage. Elinor quips, "With dark, narrow stairs, a poky hall and a fire that smokes?" Right after this exchange, Willoughby asks Marianne to see him alone the next day so that he may ask her "something very particular."

Thompson wrote into her screenplay at this point three more short scenes which were not included in the film but which would have furnished a striking contrast to both the humor and the romance. According to Lindsay Doran, Ang Lee had requested that she include these scenes, which would have shown Colonel Brandon in the London slums finding his ward, pregnant and surrounded by squalor. He wanted to show "the underbelly of this beautiful world" (Gray 82). These scenes would also have pointed up the moral contrast between Brandon and Willoughby—between the caring savior and the careless seducer. Apparently these scenes were shot but were later edited out of the film, as "too jarring" (Gray 81). As it is, we learn of Brandon's rescue of Eliza and of Willoughby's perfidy when Brandon tells Elinor about Eliza, and after Willoughby has publicly rejected Marianne.

The day after the picnic, Margaret and Mrs. Dashwood return from church to find Marianne in tears and Willoughby unable to explain why he must leave immediately. Marianne flees to her room as soon as her family come in. After he departs, first Mrs. Dashwood and then Margaret retreat upstairs to their rooms weeping. We see Elinor with the cup of tea which she had told Margaret to get for Marianne, and as we hear the others sobbing, Elinor sits down on the steps and resignedly takes a drink of the tea herself.

The BBC adaptations compress events so that Colonel Brandon's defection on the day of the planned picnic comes on the same day as Willoughby's departure for London. After Marianne drives off from Barton Park with Willoughby in his red curricle, Elinor and her mother go home and discover Marianne and Willoughby there. The young people have just come from Allenham, where Willoughby's aunt has cast him out. Marianne is devastated and dashes off to her bedroom weeping. Mrs. Dashwood, always sympathetic to Marianne's feelings, also weeps. Elinor's recommendation is that Marianne should be active and not dwell on her loss. Marianne ignores this advice and indulges in her sorrow.

The different ways in which the London ball scene is staged in the two recent adaptations also indicate vividly the more dramatic way in which the Mirage adaptation presents Willoughby's snubbing of Marianne. In the Mirage adaptation, when the Dashwood sisters, Lucy Steele (Imogen Stubbs) and Mrs. Jennings enter the grand ballroom, a great many people are milling about, some dancing, others talking and flirting. John and Fanny Dashwood are there and introduce Robert Ferrars (Richard Lumsden) to Mrs. Jennings and the girls. After Mrs. Jennings suggests that Robert dance with Elinor, he consents reluctantly, asking Lucy to reserve the allemande for him. This scene was shot in the magnificent Double Cube Room at Wilton House, near Salisbury. Tom Hoberg has observed that the effect of the huge ballroom and of the movements of the crowd of dancers is to emphasize the isolation of the individual dancers, in contrast to the use of dancing in films such as *Pride and Prejudice* (1995) and both *Emma*s (1996), where "[…] dance represents a social engagement, an act of community and harmony" ("Her First" 146).

While Elinor and Robert are dancing, Elinor finds herself facing Willoughby in the dance. He is evidently embarrassed, and much more so when, during the moment of quiet at the end of the dance, Marianne, across the room, sees him and shouts his name. Marianne rushes toward him, but he stands frozen, not even offering her his hand. Meanwhile we see that many curious people are watching them, including Lucy and Robert. With only a few evasive words, Willoughby excuses himself to go back to his party. After he goes into the next room, Marianne and Elinor follow and see Willoughby standing with a beautiful young woman (Lone Vidahl). Marianne tells Elinor to go to him and force him to come back. Elinor and Mrs. Jennings then lead the almost fainting Marianne from the room. The John Dashwoods look aghast; Lucy and Robert look smug. Robert offers to see Lucy home. It is noteworthy that in this adaptation the viewer is prepared for the eventual pairing of Lucy with Robert because of Robert's attention to Lucy. In the novel and in the BBC adaptation, their marriage comes as a complete surprise.

In the 1981 BBC version, the ball is a much smaller affair. Elinor and Marianne arrive with Lady Middleton (Marjorie Bland) and Sir John, who introduces Robert Ferrars (Philip Bowen) to the ladies. Marianne, looking haggard, with blue circles under her eyes, scans the room for Willoughby. When she sees him, although Elinor tells her not to display her feelings for all to see and tries to restrain her, Marianne runs over to speak to him. He mumbles incoherently and then moves in another direction with a young woman. Colonel Brandon appears and helps Elinor take the fainting Marianne to Brandon's carriage.

The immediacy of the film experience makes the confrontation between Willoughby and Marianne almost unbearably painful for a viewer, and certainly the Mirage adaptation brings home to the viewer the humiliation of Marianne's open solicitation of her lover and his cold rejection. When the camera pans to various people in the crowd, we see them looking at Marianne with wondering or scornful demeanors. The BBC version's treatment of this scene is mercifully shorter than that of the Mirage adaptation, but it must be remembered that in this scene in the novel, Elinor is continually cautioning Marianne about exhibiting her feelings and is trying to shield her from the view of others. Marianne may be oblivious to what others think, but Elinor feels the humiliation which Marianne ought to feel.

In both the novel and the BBC adaptations, after Marianne understands that Willoughby has forsaken her, Marianne chastises Elinor for expecting her to govern her feelings. She says that Elinor has no idea of her sufferings because Elinor has the love of Edward. Elinor must stand by, unable to tell Marianne about Edward's engagement to Lucy. Although the Mirage film omits this scene, it does have a striking scene in which, after Marianne learns about the engagement, Marianne says to Elinor: "Always resignation and acceptance! Always prudence and honour and duty! Elinor, where is your heart?" Thompson's screenplay says, "Elinor finally explodes. She turns upon Marianne almost savagely" (167). Elinor shouts at Marianne that she doesn't know about anything but her own suffering. Elinor says that she has had this secret pressing on her for weeks, unable to speak to anyone about it, enduring the exultation of the one who had taken Edward away from her. She concludes, "Believe me, Marianne, had I not been bound to silence I could have produced proof enough of a broken heart even for you." Marianne, chastened, bursts into sobs and Elinor tries to comfort her.

In the 1981 BBC adaptation, Elinor shows emotion after the visit when Edward and Lucy meet and leave together. She puts her head on her arms and weeps. Then, when the secret is out, and Marianne expresses guilt at having reproached her for being happy, Elinor confesses that she has suffered and seems about to cry. Irene Richards well conveys Elinor's characteristic serenity yet manages to reveal that this serenity masks intense feelings. In the novel in a long speech to her sister, Elinor says that had it not been for her promise, she would probably have shown to her family that she was suffering. She says that the composure which she now exhibits and the consolation which she has expressed have been the result of "constant and painful exertion" (264). These scenes go far to support the idea that, far from being without strong feelings, Elinor feels intensely both her love for Edward and her pain at being deprived of his love.

A topic which has incurred a great deal of discussion among those who have written about the 1995 film is the appropriateness of Elinor's various emotional outbursts. Rebecca Dickson laments Thompson's suggestion that Elinor needs these "cathartic outbursts" (53). One of these occurs when Elinor is watching by the bedside of Marianne. With Marianne on the verge of dying, Elinor sobs and begs her unconscious sister not to leave her. Moreland Perkins, writing about the novel, says that Elinor's love and concern for her sister which are manifested during her illness are Austen's most obvious indication that Elinor has deep feelings (91–95). It would appear then that this scene in the film is justified to support the characterization of Elinor as a woman of feeling. After all, it can hardly be said that Elinor breaks down in public, since her only audience is her sleeping or unconscious sister.

The next problematic scene occurs when Elinor discovers that Edward is free of Lucy Steele. Certainly Elinor's reaction to the good news is not handled as discreetly in the film as it is in the novel or in the 1981 BBC version. In the latter, Elinor turns and rushes outside onto the lawn, while Mrs. Dashwood and Marianne remain behind laughing hysterically. Edward says that he is just a joke to them and is about to leave, but Marianne advises him to follow Elinor. He does so and proposes to Elinor in the garden. In the film, Emma Thompson intended this scene to be dramatic, both in Elinor's reaction to the news and in Edward's proposal and their embrace. One feels that Jane Austen would have been dismayed at the unrestrained quality and public nature of Elinor's sobs, but the viewer may feel that Elinor was due an explosion. Modern viewers also expect to have proposals and embraces occur on stage rather than off. It is an entirely satisfactory climax for the film.

The novel ties up Marianne's story within two pages. Her marriage to Colonel Brandon is presented as inevitable, since that good man deserves to have her as his reward. We are told that Marianne, who "could never love by halves," "became in time, as much devoted to her husband, as [...] [she] had once been to Willoughby" (*SS* 379). I do not believe that Jane Austen is making the observation that Elinor's love for Edward turned out to be more deep and lasting than Marianne's love for Willoughby or for Brandon. It is obvious that Jane Austen felt, contrary to Marianne's beliefs when she was only seventeen that it is possible to love only once, that it is possible to love intensely more than one man or one woman.

The BBC adaptations show that Marianne is already beginning to

Sense and Sensibility (Mirage 1995). Colonel Brandon's gift of a piano has arrived. Standing l–r, Margaret (Emilie François), Marianne (Kate Winslet), Mrs. Dashwood (Gemma Jones), and Elinor (Emma Thompson). (MOMA)

depend upon Colonel Brandon from the time they leave Cleveland up to the time when he visits at Barton Cottage bringing her a box of books. In the 1981 BBC version, as the Dashwood women leave Cleveland, while in the carriage Marianne even quotes Brandon's praise of the "majestic Milton" and the "demi-god Shakespeare." The Mirage film shows Marianne beginning to weaken toward Brandon at Cleveland when she thanks him for bringing her mother. Then, at Barton Cottage Brandon reads to her lines from *The Faerie Queene* (5.2.39) appropriate to their experience:

> Nor is the earth the lesse, or loseth aught.
> For whatsoever from one place doth fall,
> Is with the tide unto another brought,
> For there is nothing lost, but may be found, if sought.

When he closes the book and announces that he will be away the next day, she appears concerned that he may not return soon. Not long after this day, a wagon arrives bearing a small pianoforte—a present from Brandon—and a piece of music. (In both the novel and the BBC adaptations, Marianne already has a pianoforte.) Shortly after this delivery, while Marianne is playing and singing the new song, Mrs. Dashwood sees a horse and rider approaching. She thinks that it is Brandon, but it turns out to be Edward. He reveals that he is free of Lucy Steele, Elinor explodes into joyful weeping, and the Dashwood women rejoice as Margaret reports from the tree house, "They're kissing."

The concluding scene features a wedding celebration. A band of children follow a man carrying a wedding cake atop a pole. We see a wedding party issuing from a church—the newly married Colonel Brandon and Marianne, Mrs. Dashwood and Margaret, John and Fanny, Mrs. Jennings, Sir John, the recently married Elinor and Edward, Charlotte and Mr. Palmer. The servants, villagers, and children throw flower petals as they watch the newlyweds approach and enter a waiting open carriage. After the newlyweds climb into their carriage, Colonel Brandon tosses handfuls of sixpences into the air for the children. The total effect is joyful and is highly reminiscent of the final scene of the film *Much Ado About Nothing* (1993)*, when flower petals fill the air. In a bit of comedy at the end, Thompson had written in the screenplay that Fanny would be hit in the eye with a coin and fall over into a bush. The actual scene showed her, instead, much in character, pointing out sixpences for John to pick up.

One of the most significant differences between the three most recent adaptations lies in the expanded or changed roles of the three main male characters. In the Mirage adaptation, as has already been pointed out, the character of Edward has been made more witty and amiable and his role expanded. Part of the problem was to make Elinor's lover appear worthy of her love. Hugh Grant, of course, comes with a guarantee for amiability. Also important in the revealing of Edward as a really good fellow is the way he interacts with Margaret, whose role has been much expanded. While at Norland, Edward manages to lure Margaret from under a table in the library during a funny interchange between himself and Elinor. Later Elinor sees him pretending to duel with Margaret on the lawn. When he looks up to acknowledge Elinor, Margaret pokes him in the ribs and he doubles over.

The character of Willoughby has not really changed except that in the Mirage adaptation his role has been diminished somewhat. Significantly, this version omits his visit to Cleveland while Marianne was ill. Critics have made much of his impassioned speech to Elinor and of her emotional response to him during this visit. Thompson asserts that she wrote numerous versions with Willoughby appearing at Cleveland, but that she thought his appearance "interfered too much with the Brandon

---

Thompson and Kenneth Branagh played the warring lovers Beatrice and Benedict.

love story" (272). Cheryl Nixon points out that Colonel Brandon, as a Willoughby substitute, is given many of Willoughby's appealing characteristics. Just as Willoughby carried Marianne to Barton Cottage, so does Brandon carry her, but with more difficulty, at Cleveland after she has trudged through the rain to get a glimpse of Combe Magna. As Willoughby recited poetry to her, so does Brandon read poetry aloud (41). Kathryn Libin has observed that Thompson has given Brandon the interest in music that in the novel Willoughby shares with Marianne. Brandon invites Marianne to play on his Broadwood grand, and he gives her a small square piano (191). Nixon states that for Brandon to be felt as the "emotional hero," Willoughby must disappear (42). Thompson does allow Willoughby one last romantic gesture, however, since he appears on a white horse at the top of a nearby hill observing the celebration of Marianne's wedding.

The problematic marrying off of Marianne to Colonel Brandon in the novel becomes much less problematic in the BBC adaptations. In these, Colonel Brandon is given opportunities to woo Marianne after she has been rejected by Willoughby. Robert Swann in the 1981 BBC version and Alan Rickman in the Mirage film are both good looking mature men, just the father figure Marianne is looking for in her physically and spiritually weakened state. Rickman conveys particularly well the saturnine melancholy of a man who has been disappointed in love but takes a chance on loving again. Terrence Rafferty observes of Rickman, "Although many English actors have taken a crack at portraying repression, Rickman may be the only one since Trevor Howard in *Brief Encounter* who has made it magnetic" (126). It is particularly delightful to see Rickman's Colonel Brandon, after over one hundred minutes of silent suffering, triumphantly tossing coins from his carriage following the wedding.

An important character in the Mirage adaptation is Margaret Dashwood, the thirteen-year-old sister of Elinor and Marianne. In the novel, Margaret receives little attention. The reader is told that she is "a good-humoured well-disposed girl," who has been infected with Marianne's sensibility without having her sense (*SS* 7). As in Austen's other novels, the younger girl does not manifest the sterling qualities of her older sisters. At the end of the novel we are told that Margaret is now old enough to be interested in dancing and young men. The BBC versions omit Margaret entirely.

In Thompson's adaptation, Margaret serves several purposes. She is the primary critic of the status quo and advocate of equal opportunity for women. As Kristin Samuelian points out, she expresses the resentment which her mother and sisters feel but cannot state. By her protests, she also is the occasion for her elders' explaining, for the edification of the viewer, the reasons for their predicament. Further, she practices a kind of freedom of action and speech that her sisters cannot. Samuelian calls her tree house a "symbol of [...] female mobility and independence" (149). Margaret's beloved atlas also functions symbolically in this way. Her interest in geography is the device which Edward uses to bring Margaret out of hiding. He and Elinor engage in a dialogue which purposely states errors about the location of the Nile so that Margaret, who is under the library table, will come out to correct their errors. Later, at Barton Park she pores over a map with the old soldier, Sir John. Since Margaret's plans for the future include a career in piracy, she obviously does not feel debarred from traditionally masculine activities such as the captaincy of ships and slaughter on the high seas. We see her practicing swordsmanship with Edward and hear him say that Margaret plans to take him along as a servant on her forthcoming expedition to China.

Although Thompson has essentially created Margaret from whole cloth, she is a delightful character. In addition to being a feminist, Margaret serves to reveal appealing aspects of Edward's character. I have already discussed how the favorable impression the viewer has of Edward owes much to his interaction with Margaret which we witness. Margaret is also a prime source of humor. Her behavior on the occasion of the dinner at Barton Park is typically amusing. Unlike Marianne, Margaret enjoys the joking give and take in which Mrs. Jennings and Sir John (Robert Hardy) indulge. When they are trying to "winkle" information about Elinor's beau, Margaret gives them hints. She tells them that he has no profession and that his name begins with "F." Mrs. Jennings torments Elinor with "Mr. F" for a long time after that. That evening as the carriage takes the Dashwoods back to Barton Cottage, Marianne chides Margaret for parading her "ignorant assumptions." Margaret protests that Marianne had told her about Edward and Elinor. Margaret also defends Mrs. Jennings. She says, "I like her! She talks about things. We never talk about things." Mrs. Dashwood intervenes to caution Margaret that, if she cannot think of anything appropriate to say, she should "restrict [...] [her] remarks to the weather." Much later, when Edward comes to see Elinor, and she thinks that he is married, we remember Mrs. Dashwood's advice when Margaret astounds her family by saying conversationally, "We have been enjoying very fine weather."

Several minor characters in the novel and in the two later films provide humor. Sir John Middleton and Mrs. Jennings are particularly funny. The interaction between Mrs. Jennings' giddy but goodnatured daughter, Charlotte, and her sarcastic husband is also a source of humor.

Thompson's screenplay, however, places much more emphasis on humor than does the BBC version. One of the reasons that Lindsay Doran asked Thompson to adapt the novel was that she was aware of Thompson's background of writing and performing comedy. Thompson had written most of the sketches for her comedy series, "Thompson," shown on BBC in 1988. Doran had seen some of her sketches and liked her approach to comedy (Sessums 143).

Although Sir John is a widower, Mrs. Jennings, his mother-in-law, is living at Barton Park. This jolly pair greet the Dashwoods as soon as they arrive at Barton Park. They arrive in an open carriage, calling out their welcome and accompanied by several dogs, who mill around the newcomers and help to create a sense of chaos. Thompson has Mrs. Jennings keep up a running commentary on everything and everybody, with Sir John chiming in and egging her on. The example given above of how they attempt to "winkle" out of Elinor the name of her beau is typical of their interaction. Good natured Sir John frequently makes remarks which Marianne finds offensive. For example, when he accuses her of "setting her cap at" Willoughby, she indignantly protests that she is not "setting her cap at anyone." He merely laughs at her indignation. On this occasion he is more interested in protecting Colonel Brandon's interests than in satisfying the women's curiosity about Willoughby. When Marianne asks him about Willoughby's tastes, passions, and pursuits, Sir John says, "Well, he has the nicest little bitch of a pointer—was she out with him yesterday?" Mrs. Jennings is a tease, a gossip, and a matchmaker, but she also is a kindly woman. She takes Elinor, Marianne, and Lucy Steele to London to stay in her town house, and later insists on staying with Marianne and Elinor during Marianne's illness.

Thompson also uses Charlotte Palmer (Imelda Staunton) and her husband (Hugh Laurie) effectively. Charlotte comes across as avid for gossip, good natured, and thoroughly silly. Mr. Palmer, however, is not merely the cold, disdainful husband of the novel and of the BBC adaptation (Christopher Brown). His interactions with Charlotte demonstrate well how mismatched this couple is. A typical scene shows Mr. Palmer holding his crying infant at arm's length while Charlotte rattles on about what a good father he is. However, Thompson's screenplay also shows him to be kind and considerate. When Brandon carries a soaking wet Marianne into the house, Mr. Palmer carries her upstairs, and when Elinor appeals to him in the middle of the night to get a doctor for her sister, he acquiesces without protest. He apologizes for having to leave Elinor and Marianne at Cleveland while he takes his wife and child to another house. Jane Austen's Mr. Palmer is a much less sympathetic figure, and

Mr. Palmer (Christopher Brown) in the 1981 adaptation is thoroughly obnoxious. One of the strengths of Thompson's screenplay is the way in which these minor characters come to life as multi-faceted beings. For habitual watchers of the BBC in Great Britain and of public television in the USA, many of the actors in Thompson's minor roles are familiar figures. For instance, they may associate Hugh Laurie with humor as they remember his portrayal of the absurd aristocrat in "Black Adder." American audiences may also recall Laurie as the benevolent foster father of the precocious mouse in *Stuart Little* (1999). They may even have seen Robert Hardy (Sir John) in the BBC/A&E *Northanger Abbey*, in which he plays the villainous General Tilney.

Thompson's omission of Lady Middleton is no loss to the film, but the deletion of Lucy Steele's sister, Nancy,* is a significant change. In the novel and in the BBC versions, Lucy's sister reveals to Fanny that Lucy is engaged to Edward. In Thompson's version, Lucy herself whispers this secret into Fanny's ear while they are sitting together. Lucy is holding Fanny's dog and Fanny is trimming a hat. This sets up one of the funniest and most satisfying moments of the film, when Fanny jumps up, tossing feathers everywhere, grabs the obnoxious Lucy's nose, and pushes her out of the house. In the BBC versions, Miss Steele is an amusing character, constantly asking impertinent questions and always wanting to be teased about her prospective beaux. When she mentions the engagement to Fanny, Fanny goes into hysterics as Lucy's sister stands quaking with fear. The novel does not dramatize this scene of discovery but has Mrs. Jennings report the news to the Dashwoods.

Setting plays an important part of Jane Austen's novel, and an even more important role in the Mirage film. One aspect of Marianne's sensibility is her response to the picturesque in nature. Austen makes clear that even Elinor appreciates naturalness in landscape scenes, but Marianne makes a fetish of the wild and untamed in nature. At one point in the novel, Mrs. John Dashwood brags that they have cut down a grove of trees and plan to install a Grecian temple. Elinor listens disapprovingly, glad that Marianne is not present to hear of this violation of her beloved Norland Park. The novel also expresses the pleasure of the Dashwood girls in the beauty of the downs at their new home in Devonshire.

As mentioned earlier, the 1981 BBC adaptation made use of many more outdoor scenes than had been used in the earlier adaptation. The scene in which Marianne falls and is carried home by Willoughby takes

---

Lucy Steele's sister is called Nancy in the novel, Nancy (Maggie Jones) in the 1971 BBC adaptation, but Anne (Pippa Sparkes) in the 1981 BBC adaptation.

place in a wooded area, whereas the novel clearly indicates that the girls have been climbing up the high downs in the open when it begins to rain and they run for shelter. Two scenes show Elinor and Edward walking on the lawn, near a large house (Norland) and a church. We also see Barton Hall in long shot and in a middle-range shot. Several scenes take place in the garden at Barton Cottage or in the lane leading to the cottage. Although the outdoor settings add some variety and beauty to the film, they have little symbolic or associative value.

By contrast, the Mirage film makes full and effective use of outdoor settings, to convey both beauty and meaning. It shows in striking contrast the domesticated order of Norland Park and the wild beauty of the countryside around Barton Cottage. At Norland Park, the great house is situated on an extensive manicured lawn with a lake nearby. In this scene of order and harmony, Elinor's and Edward's love flourishes. We see them walking on the paths and riding near the lake. Appropriately, Marianne and Willoughby fall in love in the wilder environs of Barton Cottage. We see Marianne and Margaret climbing up a green hill as they chase the sunshine. When the rain begins to fall, the girls run down the hill toward home, and Marianne falls. The rough terrain, the rain, and the romantic rescue suggest the disorder and wild emotions typical of the relationship between Willoughby and Marianne.

A striking scene in the Mirage film is that in which Marianne first wanders about the grounds of Cleveland, at one point framed against a deformed yew hedge, which Lindsay Doran called "the perfect background for Marianne's physical and emotional deterioration" (Thompson 287). Then she leaves the grounds at Cleveland and trudges across fields and up a high hill in order to look out on Combe Magna, Willoughby's estate. The viewer sees Marianne in a long shot, a small white figure against a broad expanse of green. Then in a medium shot we see her from the back, as enveloped in rain she looks down on a great house. Next we see her face in close-up as she recites lines from Shakespeare's Sonnet 116, which she and Willoughby had read together:

> ...love is not love
> Which alters when it alteration finds,
> Or bends with the remover to remove.
> O, no! it is an ever-fixed mark
> That looks on tempests and is never shaken....

In close-up, we see Marianne's face as she looks at Combe Magna and whispers, "Willoughby. Willoughby." The long shot emphasizes her ineffectuality in the face of the elements and of her loss of the man she loves. With the lines of the poem evoking memory of Marianne's earlier happiness, this scene conveys well her utter despair. The novel states that over the course of several days at Cleveland, Marianne sought out the wilder, less improved areas around Cleveland. There is, however, no dramatic walk in the rain to see Combe Magna, which is said to be thirty miles away from Cleveland. Rather, Marianne chooses not to go out in the rain, but even so, she becomes ill. In the 1981 BBC version we have barely a glimpse of the exterior of the house, and Marianne does not walk on the grounds. She faints and is carried off to bed shortly after entering the house.

In the Mirage film, after the Dashwoods have returned to Devonshire, in another long shot, we see Marianne and Elinor walking up a green hill, and in a middle-range shot, we see them sitting in the grass with the ocean behind them. The mood during this scene is resignation and tranquility. This scene is typical of how the film uses the wide screen to show the beauty of the natural scenery and to place the characters in this scenery.

The Mirage film also makes effective use of the exteriors and interiors of several great houses. Montacute House, an Elizabethan mansion near Yeovil, in Somerset, was the impressive house, with its gables, turrets, and obelisks, which served as Cleveland, the Palmers' residence. Both the grounds and the music room of Trafalgar House, near Salisbury, were used in the scenes set at Sir John Middleton's home, Barton Park. Saltram House near Plymouth (built and decorated by Robert Adam in the mid-eighteenth century and landscaped by Capability Brown*) provided the exterior and interiors for Norland. Mompesson House, on the north side of the Cathedral close in Salisbury, became the exterior of Mrs. Jennings' London town house, and Mothecombe House provided the drawing room. Barton Cottage is actually a beautiful Edwardian house on the Flete Estate in south Devon; the filmmakers showed only the unimpressive front view of the house (Thompson 286–287). Undeniably, the choice of both the interior rooms, the facades of the great houses, and their beautiful grounds adds greatly to the pleasure of the viewers of the film. In fact, the film has much the same nostalgic appeal that draws tourists to visit the great houses of England and envy the life styles of those who lived in these

---

*Lancelot "Capability" Brown (1716–1783), professional landscaper. His landscape designs were characterized by large expanses of smooth turf, with an irregularly shaped stream or lake in the middle distance which reflected groups of trees planted near the banks. He might situate a Greek temple near the water. The view from the house would be uninterrupted as far as the belt of trees surrounding the whole area (Malins 99).

mansions. Since the filming of *Pride and Prejudice* and *Sense and Sensibility*, National Trust properties such as Saltram House, Wilton House, Montacute, Belton (Rosings), and Lyme Park (Pemberley) have experienced a huge increase in numbers of visitors.

Another facet of the appeal of the Mirage *Sense and Sensibility* is the stunning soundtrack which accompanies the film. Patrick Doyle was responsible for selecting or composing the music. Director Ang Lee, commenting on the choice of the two songs which Marianne sings, emphasizes how they convey the "vision of duality" present in the novel and in the screenplay—a duality clearly expressed in the passage which Brandon reads from *The Faerie Queene*, which states, "[...] there is nothing lost, but may be found, if sought." The lyrics for the first song, "Weep You No More Sad Fountains," come from an anonymous poem in a seventeenth century collection by John Dowland. They express well both Marianne's innocence and her romantic attitudes toward nature as they compare the weeping of a person with the weeping of streams in nature. The song is pleasantly melancholy yet hopeful. An orchestral rendering of this tune opens the film and occurs at various transition points. This is the song that Marianne plays and sings at Barton manor. The second song, the one which Brandon sends her and asks her to learn, is based on a poem by Ben Jonson, "The Dreame." This song speaks of being surprised by love in a dream and feeling both guilt and desire. Lee feels that the lyrics and the melody, which Patrick Doyle wrote, express Marianne's "mature acceptance" but with "a sense of melancholy" for what has been lost (Notes CD). Marianne plays and sings the song, and later we hear Jane Eaglen sing it, to an orchestral accompaniment, as the credits run.

The adaptations of *Sense and Sensibility* discussed in this chapter illustrate clearly the great differences which may exist between adaptations. The *Philco* adaptation gallops through the story so rapidly that the viewer could have had little sense of the complexities of the sisters' feelings. The 1981 BBC mini-series is a pedestrian affair. It is competently acted, makes use of on-location shooting, and is faithful to the story-line of the novel. Calling this latter quality a merit is doubtful, since the problematic character of the novel's organization becomes all the more problematic when presented visually. Giddings and Selby call this the "dullest" of the Austen adaptations of the eighties (68). The Mirage theatrical release by necessity compresses much of the action to fit into a mere 135 minutes, but Emma Thompson has largely solved the organizational problems by selecting telling scenes and by developing the roles of Margaret, Edward, and Colonel Brandon. The fine acting of Thompson, Hugh Grant, Kate Winslet, and Alan Rickman make this a truly enjoyable viewing experience. Although one may find some adaptations of Austen's novels unsatisfactory when compared to the experience of reading the novels, Ang Lee and Emma Thompson have managed to create cinematic art from one of Austen's least successful novels.

III

Pride and Prejudice

Pride and Prejudice (1813) is the story of Elizabeth Bennet and Fitzwilliam Darcy, who begin by disliking each other and who spend the rest of the novel revising their opinions and falling in love. Like the title of *Sense and Sensibility*, the title of this novel indicates a ruling tendency in the two main characters. Mr. Darcy is proud of his social position and refinement; Elizabeth is prejudiced against him because he has disparaged and slighted her. Both behave badly, and both are ultimately chastened and reformed. Although *Pride and Prejudice* is not as complicated as some of Austen's later novels, it has the lightest touch. In Elizabeth and Darcy, it has two of Austen's most appealing characters, and its ironic narrator establishes an admirable distance from which the reader can observe and empathize.

The famous first sentence sets the ironic tone: "It is a truth universally acknowledged that a single man in possession of a good fortune, must be in want of a wife" (*PP* 3). What is more true, however, is that an unmarried woman of little fortune must be in want of a husband. Jane Austen makes gentle fun of the desperation of Mrs. Bennet to get her five daughters married. After all, the Bennet estate, Longbourn, is entailed, and upon Mr. Bennet's death, it will pass into the possession of Mr. Collins, a clergyman and Mr. Bennet's nearest male relative. The Bennet sisters will have only fifty pounds a year income apiece. When Mr. Bingley, an eligible bachelor with an income of five thousand pounds a year, rents a nearby house, Mrs. Bennet decides that Mr. Bingley will do for one of her girls, probably Jane, the eldest. When Mr. Collins comes for a visit, Mrs. Bennet's cup runneth over. Here is a man who wishes to marry Elizabeth, the second eldest sister. Very early Mrs. Bennet gives up on Mr. Fitzwilliam Darcy as a prospective mate for one of her girls, since he snubs Elizabeth and offends everyone by his arrogance. When Mr. Wickham comes to Meryton to join the militia, Elizabeth takes an immediate liking to him, a propensity intensified by their mutual dislike of Darcy. Wickham pours out to Elizabeth, and later to all who will listen, a tale of how Darcy deprived him of a clerical living which Darcy's father had promised him. Elizabeth eagerly believes the worst of Darcy.

Mrs. Bennet's plans for Jane and Elizabeth come to nothing. Elizabeth rejects Mr. Collins' proposal, and Mrs. Bennet is forced to watch while Charlotte Lucas attaches him. Then Mr. Bingley goes away, apparently on business, but his sisters and Mr. Darcy follow him to town. Miss Bingley writes to Jane that they may not return to Netherfield and that she and her sister anticipate that Bingley will marry Darcy's sister, Georgiana. Meanwhile, although Elizabeth becomes fond of Mr. Wickham, she is sensible enough to know that Mr. Wickham needs to marry someone with money. Thus, as fall passes into winter, the matrimonial prospects of the Bennet girls chill. Jane goes to London to visit Mrs. Bennet's brother and his wife, the Gardiners, and Elizabeth remains behind to listen to her mother's whining and her sisters' inanities. Her sister Mary spends her time playing the pianoforte and reading, while Kitty and Lydia trim hats and chase officers.

In the early spring, Elizabeth goes to visit Charlotte Lucas Collins at Hunsford, where they are much in the company of Mr. Collins' patroness, Lady Catherine de Bourgh. Since Lady Catherine is Darcy's aunt, Darcy and his cousin Colonel Fitzwilliam come to Rosings to visit. Thus, Darcy and Elizabeth find themselves seeing each other frequently. Although Elizabeth has retained her dislike of Darcy, he finds that the attraction which he had felt for her when he was at Netherfield is intensified by this proximity. To her great surprise, Darcy proposes to Elizabeth. To his great surprise and chagrin, Elizabeth rejects his proposal and accuses him of ungentleman-like behavior to her, of interference with her sister's happiness, and of cruelty to Mr. Wickham. This rejection prompts Darcy to write a letter to Elizabeth in which he justifies his remarks about her family and his part in preventing Bingley from proposing to Jane, but he defends and explains his behavior toward Wickham. He tells her how Mr. Wickham had forfeited his right to a living worth three thousand pounds, how he had squandered his money, and how he had attempted to elope with Georgiana Darcy. After Elizabeth reads this letter, she begins to see Darcy in a different light.

After Elizabeth returns home, she now looks forward to a summer trip with the Gardiners. Although they had planned to tour the Lake District, the Gardiners have had to limit their travels to Derbyshire, which happens to be the location of Pemberley, Mr. Darcy's estate. When Elizabeth and the Gardiners set out in July, she enjoys the rugged beauty of Derbyshire. Fearing to meet Darcy, Elizabeth yields reluctantly to Mrs. Gardiner's suggestion that they tour Pemberley. At Pemberley, the housekeeper gives a glowing account of Darcy's character while showing Elizabeth and the Gardiners the beautiful rooms. Then, after they leave the house and are walking on the lawn, Darcy appears. Both Elizabeth and Darcy are astonished to find each other at Pemberley. Darcy further surprises Elizabeth and the Gardiners by his courtesy and affability.

The next day Darcy brings his sister and Mr. Bingley to the inn where Elizabeth is staying. She perceives that he may still be interested in her. The following day Darcy comes again to call on Elizabeth at the inn but finds her distraught over news which has come in two letters from Longbourn. Her sister Lydia, who has been staying in Brighton, has run away with Mr. Wickham. When Darcy leaves her, Elizabeth is convinced that she will never see him again, and this thought pains her.

Like Elizabeth, the reader is unaware of Darcy's attitude toward Elizabeth or his immediate plans. Later we discover that he had immediately set out for London to try to locate Wickham and repair the damage to the family's reputation. Elizabeth and the Gardiners return to Longbourn, where the women wait and worry, while Mr. Gardiner follows Mr. Bennet to London. Both Elizabeth and Jane feel that they now share Lydia's loss of reputation and that no respectable man will be interested in them.

Then a letter comes from Mr. Gardiner explaining that Lydia is to be married to Wickham. Mr. Bennet, Jane, and Elizabeth feel that this is the best possible resolution to a bad situation. The simple-minded Mrs. Bennet is ecstatic that at last one of her daughters is married. She wants Lydia and Wickham to come to live in Merton, but it has been arranged that Wickham join the regular army and go to the north of England. During the newlyweds' visit to Longbourn, Lydia mentions to Elizabeth that Darcy was Wickham's best man at the wedding. Elizabeth immediately writes to Mrs. Gardiner to ask for an explanation. Her response reveals to Elizabeth that Darcy is the one who found the runaways and bribed Wickham to marry Lydia. This revelation makes Elizabeth wonder about Darcy's feeling toward her.

Soon after, Bingley and Darcy come to Netherfield, and Bingley, apparently with Darcy's blessing, proposes to Jane and is accepted. Having heard that Darcy may be interested in Elizabeth, Lady Catherine comes to Longbourn to get Elizabeth to promise not to become engaged to Darcy. When Elizabeth refuses to promise, Lady Catherine states that

Pride and Prejudice (BBC 1958). Elizabeth Bennet (Jane Downs) and Mr. Darcy (Alan Badel). (BBC Picture Archives)

she will take action to insure that Elizabeth will never "pollute" the woods of Pemberley. The immediate result of her actions is that Darcy comes to see Elizabeth to ascertain whether her feelings toward him have changed. Elizabeth assures Darcy that her feelings are quite changed, and she becomes engaged to him. The novel ends by assuring the reader that during their married life, Darcy was able to avoid the company of Elizabeth's less desirable relatives, such as Mrs. Bennet, Mrs. Philips, and the Wick-hams, but that the Gardiners, the Bingleys and Kitty were always welcome at Pemberley.

    Pride and Prejudice, of all of Jane Austen's novels, has been the most popular and the most often adapted for television and film. A theatrical release from MGM appeared in 1940. On January 23, 1949, a live hour-long adaptation was shown on NBC's *Philco Television Playhouse.** In 1952 and 1958, the BBC presented televised versions, each in six thirty-minute episodes. The 1952 version was adapted by Cedric Wallis and the 1958

Between 1940 and 1950, there were also eight presentations of Pride and Prejudice *on American and British radio (Wright 444–445).*

version by Wallis and Constance Cox.* The 1952 adaptation starred Daphne Slater as Elizabeth and Peter Cushing as Darcy. Cushing will be better remembered as Sherlock Holmes, in such films as *The Hound of the Baskervilles* (1959), and as the master of horror, in such films as *The Curse of Frankenstein* (1957). In the 1958 version, Jane Downs played the role of Elizabeth and Alan Badel, the role of Darcy. In 1967 the BBC presented a new adaptation of the novel, this one based on a screenplay by Nemone Lethbridge. Unlike most other adaptations at or before this time, at least some scenes of this version were shot on location. A record exists in the BBC Written Archives of location shooting in Bath, in Lacock Village, and at Dyrham Park in Wiltshire. This version was shown again on the BBC in 1969. Then in 1980 and in 1995, the BBC presented two new mini-series—the only BBC versions of *Pride and Prejudice* currently available for viewing.

The film adaptation which appeared in 1940 was based on a screenplay by MGM screenwriter Jane Murfin and British novelist Aldous Huxley. Jane Murfin was experienced in working in the genre of romantic and screwball comedy. With its warring lovers, witty dialogue, class differences, opportunity for elaborate costumes, and comic minor characters, the novel lends itself to the broadly comic treatment of screwball comedies. In keeping with the genre, the ad campaign warned, "Bachelors Beware! Five Gorgeous Beauties are on a Madcap Manhunt." This film was made during the great era of screwball comedies, such films as *It Happened One Night* (1934), *The Gay Divorcee* (1934), *Twentieth Century* (1934). Obviously Murfin had the success of such films in mind as she worked on the screenplay of *Pride and Prejudice*. The film's director, Robert Z. Leonard, was an experienced director of romantic comedy and musicals (*Ziegfeld Girl*, 1941; *The Divorcee*, 1930). Other MGM stalwarts involved in the production—costumer Adrian, cinematographer Karl Freund, and art directors Cedric Gibbons and Paul Groesse—were thoroughly familiar with these genres. Gibbons and Groesse won an academy award for Best Black and White Interior Decoration for their work on the film.

The collaboration of Murfin (*Alice Adams*, 1935; *The Women*, 1939) and Huxley (*Jane Eyre*, 1944) represents the meeting of opposite minds. Huxley, relatively new to writing screenplays, was primarily interested in conveying what he called "the diffuse irony in which the characters are bathed" (Clark 42). Jane Clark, in her book *Aldous Huxley and Film*, says,

---

Colonel Austen B. Knight wrote to the producer of the 1952 Pride and Prejudice *thanking him for the new series. He wrote, "I have never had so much pleasure from one of my great-great-Aunt Jane's romances before. Our present Jane Austen aged 7 has been allowed to sit up specially" (BBC Written Archives, February 1952).*

"[…] [W]e may assume that Huxley had a large part in the literate dialogue and the intelligent handling of Austen's ironic wit, while Murfin's Hollywood experience was a factor in determining the structure and pace" (42). Huxley apparently struggled to maintain the essence of the novel while having to compress the story and defend against efforts to sensationalize it. He stated in a letter, "I barely stopped my director from having Bennet fight a duel with Wickham!" (Dunaway 154). Another factor to be considered is that Helen Jerome's stage adaptation (1935–1936) was also given screen credit. Clark points out that "[…]there are really four texts here: Austen's novel, Jerome's adaptation, Huxley-Murfin's script, and the film itself—for the screenplay is not the movie" (41).

Some of the changes which have been made in adapting the novel may be explained in the context of screwball comedy as it developed during the 1930s and 1940s. For instance, the class difference between Elizabeth and Darcy has been accentuated. In the novel Elizabeth is essentially of the same class as Darcy, only less affluent. Although her mother comes from the professional class, her father is a gentleman. Darcy is more wealthy and is related to aristocracy. In the film, Darcy snubs Elizabeth at the first dance because he says he is in "no humor […] to give consequence to the middle classes at play." In the novel, he says, "I am in no humor to give consequence to young ladies who are slighted by other men," and in the Jerome play, his excuse is the same, that Elizabeth has been "slighted by other men" (Jerome 366). Thus, the film deviates from other early versions by indicating that Elizabeth is of a lower social class than Darcy.

True to the screwball comedy genre, the minor roles are played for broad humor. Since MGM had a large stable of well-known contract players, these roles were played by actors who were familiar to audiences from other screwball and romantic comedies—May Boland, Edna Mae Oliver, Edmund Gwenn, and Melville Cooper. For instance, Edna Mae Oliver, who plays Lady Catherine, is made to appear ridiculous when, in the scene in which she confronts Elizabeth, she sits on Kitty's music box and then must endure the squawks of Mary's parrot. However, according to Wright, Mr. Collins, Mrs. Bennett, and Lady Catherine were always played farcically in the Jerome play (431).

Commenting on the acting in the film, Huxley said, "The principals were *so* bad; the supporting cast was very good (Dunaway 154). His low opinion of Olivier and Garson was not that of most contemporary reviewers, and indeed it is difficult to understand how anyone could call Laurence Olivier's acting bad. However, it probably indicates Huxley's different conception of how Darcy and Elizabeth should be portrayed.

Pride and Prejudice (MGM 1940). Elizabeth Bennet (Greer Garson) and Mr. Darcy (Laurence Olivier). (MOMA)

Darcy's role is so underwritten that Olivier has little to do except react to Elizabeth's insults and to register disdain for her family's low behavior. Even so, Olivier may be the most expressive of those who have played Darcy on film and television. His handling of the proposal scene and of the reconciliation scene is particularly effective. His experience acting in sophisticated plays such as Noel Coward's *Private Lives* (Harvey 68–69) probably influenced his ultra supercilious rendering of the role; however, the role of Darcy is a far cry from that of Heathcliff in *Wuthering Heights* (1939), the role which brought him under consideration for the role of Darcy (Turan 141).

British actress Greer Garson plays Elizabeth Bennet broadly, with the bold looks and casual manners of a modern woman—like those of Carole Lombard or Rosalind Russell or other actresses of the screwball genre. Elizabeth in the novel may have been more forward and outspoken than is usual for an unmarried girl of twenty, but Garson was both too old and too knowing for this role. We may be able to blame some aspects of her performance on the director and on the script, which requires her to behave with extreme rudeness on more than one occasion. For example, at the ball she refuses to dance with Mr. Darcy, but immediately afterwards accepts Wickham (Edward Ashley) as a partner.

Whereas the novel emphasizes the difference in the manners of the two older sisters and the two younger, all of the sisters in this film lack decorum and restraint. Elizabeth is bold, and her sister Jane (Maureen O'Sullivan) is overtly flirtatious, very unlike the reserved character in the novel. She acquiesces willingly to her mother's plan for her to go to Netherfield in the rain so that she will have to spend the night at Netherfield, and when she is ill, she bats her eyelashes and shows her profile to Bingley (Bruce Lester). To contrast these two more admirable sisters with Kitty (Heather Angel) and Lydia (Ann Rutherford), the filmmakers have had to show the latter two behaving badly. At the party at Netherfield, Kitty becomes intoxicated and both sisters are shown laughing loudly. Kitty and Lydia are also shrieking while officers swing them high in the air.

The film does not concern itself that Mr. Bennet (Edmund Gwenn) is a failure as a father and husband or that Mrs. Bennet (Mary Boland) endangers her daughters' happiness. It uses them solely for comedy. Mr. Collins (Melville Cooper) has been changed from clergyman to Lady Catherine's librarian, but he is still the same ingratiating and officious toady that he is in the novel. As indicated above, Lady Catherine is also played as the comic villain, but with one surprising change. At the end of the film, when she has come to see Elizabeth to extract a promise from Elizabeth that she will not accept Darcy's proposal, she threatens to strip Darcy of all his wealth if he marries Elizabeth. After Elizabeth refuses to give such a promise, Lady Catherine leaves the house to rejoin Darcy, who has been waiting in her carriage. Lady Catherine gives her blessing to the match and sends him into the house. Lester Asheim suggested that

Pride and Prejudice (MGM 1940). Front right, Jane Bennet (Maureen O'Sullivan); center l–r, Elizabeth Bennet (Greer Garson), Mrs. Bennet (Mary Boland); back, l–r, Kitty Bennet (Heather Angel), Lydia Bennet (Ann Rutherford), Mary Bennet (Marsha Hunt), Lady Lucas (Marjorie Wood). (MOMA)

one possible explanation for this change in the character is that Edna May Oliver wanted to remain the gruff but good-hearted curmudgeon she was used to playing and that the public expected her to play (Bluestone 142).

Typical of the overall simplification of the plot and compression of the events of the novel so that its main events fit into a 117-minute time frame, Darcy goes in minutes from being disdainful of Elizabeth to being intrigued by and attracted to her. These alterations occur during the Assembly Ball, which combines material from the first sixteen chapters of the novel and compresses two dances into one. George Bluestone has pointed out that "[…] all the dramatic relationships are enunciated in terms of dance relationships" (127). Here we see Mr. Bingley dancing with Jane, Wickham dancing with Lydia, and Elizabeth dancing with Wickham. First Darcy slights Elizabeth by refusing to dance with her. Shortly after that, Darcy asks Sir William Lucas to introduce him to Elizabeth, and he asks her to dance. She refuses him, yet within minutes, and in front of Darcy, she accepts a dance with Wickham. By this time Darcy has become thoroughly intrigued with her.

Another scene which demonstrates how Elizabeth gains the upper hand in her relationship with Darcy occurs at a garden party at Netherfield. Darcy presumes to give Elizabeth an archery lesson. He demonstrates how to shoot and makes a bad shot. Elizabeth takes a turn and makes three bull's eyes. He says that henceforth he will not be so patronizing to young ladies. On this occasion she also bests the intrusive Caroline Bingley (Frieda Inescort) with her verbal arrows.

In the same scene, Elizabeth asks Darcy his opinion of a man who refuses an introduction to a poor man of no consequence. Her allusion is to Darcy's having refused introduction to Wickham. He responds that he would reserve his judgment until he knew the circumstances. Further admonishing Elizabeth for her judging him so harshly, he says that he expects people to give him credit for being a man of honor.

Shortly after this scene, Darcy attempts to comfort Elizabeth when she weeps at Caroline Bingley's unkindness. He says he admires the way she takes up for her friends. They appear to be on the verge of friendship. Then they overhear Mrs. Bennet gloating about Jane's prospective marriage to Bingley and how it will bring matrimonial possibilities to the other girls. Darcy looks displeased and immediately excuses himself from Elizabeth's presence. She will not see him again until they meet at Rosings Park.

Rapid pacing is a desideratum in a screwball comedy and credibility of action has never been a strong point in the genre, but in this film the rapid pacing has the unfortunate effect of reducing both the credibility of action and plausibility of characterization. After Elizabeth rejects Darcy's proposal and goes home to Longbourn, she finds that Lydia has eloped. Within minutes of her arrival, Darcy appears to offer his assistance in recovering Lydia. At this time he tells Elizabeth about Wickham's attempted elopement with his sister. After he leaves, she tells Jane of his earlier proposal, and she tells her that she loves him. This kind of swift reversal of feeling is not uncommon in screwball comedy, but it does represent a drastic change from the novel. Jane Austen shows the reader how Elizabeth's heart and mind undergo a gradual change over the course of several months. This compression, however, is also typical of the Jerome play, in which, as in the film, Darcy discovers Lydia's elopement when he comes to Longbourn to explain his treatment of Wickham to Elizabeth.

The film builds to a scene in which, just when the problems seem insurmountable, they are all resolved. The prospects of the Bennet family are bleak as they prepare to leave Longbourn in disgrace. Then a letter arrives announcing that Wickham is to marry Lydia, a carriage arrives bearing the newlyweds, and Lady Catherine arrives asking to speak to Elizabeth. Elizabeth reaches an understanding with Darcy, Bingley and Jane are reunited, and Mary and Kitty are seen entertaining beaux. The film concludes with Mrs. Bennet's remark to Mr. Bennet, "Think of it, three of them married and the other two just tottering on the brink."

In light of James Harvey's statement in *Romantic Comedy in Hollywood* that "[...] screwball comedy was a special kind of woman's game nearly always favoring the heroine to win" (287), it is easy to see that *Pride and Prejudice* is a natural for this kind of adaptation. In fact, all of Jane Austen's novels are "women's games." However, this particular film is the only adaptation which could be called screwball comedy.

Other aspects of the film which suggest the visual style associated with screwball comedy include elaborate costumes and scenes of the wealthy at play. According to Edward Maeder, Adrian (*Camille*, 1936; *Grand Hotel*, 1932), the costume designer, asked Leonard to place the film in a later time than the time of the novel so that the costumes might be more opulent than those of Austen's time (12). The dresses of *Pride and Prejudice* are in the style of those in *Gone with the Wind* (1939). They feature tight bodices, tight natural waists, huge puffed sleeves, and billowing hooped skirts. The women's hats are large shells which frame the women's faces. Maeder points out that in the costumes we see a mingling of 1830s and 1930s styles (14). Adrian created striking contrasts in the dresses for this black and white film. Caroline Bingley wears a black dress at the Assembly Ball—an unlikely color for a young single woman to wear to a ball during the nineteenth century. At the Netherfield garden party, Elizabeth wears a bouffant white dress and big white hat, but when Mr. Collins proposes to her, she wears a dress with a black waist, big black bows down the front of the light-colored skirt, and black zig-zag insets on the puffed sleeves. With two dresses, she wears black ties. Generally the effect is glamorous, especially in the dance scenes, but these full skirts also enabled the director to achieve comic effects. Early in the film, the five Bennet girls and Mrs. Bennet are walking rapidly down the middle of the street, their movements reminiscent of a covey of quail scurrying along. In a later scene, Mrs. Bennet gets out of her chair and knocks over several small tables with her skirts in her haste to look out the window. This latter example illustrates how Leonard took advantage of what could have been a problem—having actresses in the enormous skirts of early Victorian times moving about on a set with the small tables and delicate chairs of the Empire.*

Although in general the use of music in the film is unremarkable, the song "Sweet Afton" is used with good comic effect. It is first played as a theme in the scene in which Mr. Bennet can be seen reading in his study just before the arrival home of the Bennet ladies. It suggests that Mr. Bennet's peace and calm are soon to be shattered. Thereafter, it is a tune which Mary (Marsha Hunt) practices singing and playing on the piano. We hear her practicing at home, to the complaints of Kitty; then she plays and sings the song at Netherfield, missing the high note at the end, after which Mr. Bennet embarrasses her by asking that she "[...] give the other young ladies a chance to make exhibitions of themselves." At the end of the film, Mary again sings and plays "Sweet Afton," but this time with Mr. Witherington accompanying her on a flute. Unlike the other occasions, when she sang badly, this time she hits the high note, and she and the young man look pleased. The clear implication is that Mary's efforts at winning a man are also meeting with success. Other uses of music for comic effect may be cited; for example, strains from "Pomp and Circumstance" are heard early in the film to herald the appearance of Darcy and the Bingleys. At the point when Mr. Collins refers to himself as a gentleman, Elizabeth, at the harp, hits a sour note.

The film had both popular and critical success. When it opened at the Radio City Music Hall in August 1940, it drew the largest weekly audience during the month of August in the theatre's history. During its four-week run there, it grossed $1,849,000. Bosley Crowther, writing for the New York *Times,* and the critic for the *New Yorker* waxed ecstatic over Greer Garson as Elizabeth (Troyan 108–109).

The next adaptation appeared on NBC's *Philco Television Playhouse* on January 23, 1949. Presented live in black and white, this one-hour teleplay was directed by Fred Coe and based on a screenplay by Samuel Taylor. It featured Madge Evans (see Evans discussed in Chapter II) as Elizabeth Bennet and John Baragrey as Mr. Darcy. Baragrey had an undistinguished career in television, mostly in soap operas, such as *The Secret Storm,* and in crime dramas, such as *Assignment Manhunt* (McNeil 65, 739). Bert Lytell, who customarily introduced the dramas on the *Philco Television Playhouse*, introduced and had voiceover participation in this adaptation. Although two other actors are mentioned—Viola Roache and

---

*A press release stated that Cedric Gibbons, art director, and Adrian drew on "Ackermann's Repository of Art and Fashion," a monthly publication from the period 1820 to 1829, for fashions, furniture, draperies, and decorations. According to the press release, this source assured the film an "atmosphere of absolute reality."

Pride and Prejudice (NBC 1949). Elizabeth Bennet (Madge Evans) and Mr. Darcy (John Baragrey). (Photofest)

Louis Hector—the roles which they played are not identified in the screenplay. The most distinctive aspect of this version is the use of an actor playing Jane Austen to supply character analysis, transitions, and ironic perspective.

The screenplay calls for Jane Austen to appear, seated at a table writing. Lytell in voiceover asks her how her story begins. She says, "It is a truth universally acknowledged, that a single man in possession of a good fortune, must be in want of a wife." A dissolve takes us to Mr. and Mrs. Bennet, the latter announcing that Netherfield is let to an eligible bachelor. In voiceover, Miss Austen then characterizes both Mr. Bennet and Mrs. Bennet. She also mentions their three daughters, and a dissolve shows Elizabeth, Jane and Lydia wearing ball gowns. Austen in voiceover says that she will tell the story's beginning in terms of two balls. She comments on each of the girls as each appears in closeup. She calls Elizabeth, "the quick, the wise, the volatile." Then a dissolve reveals the ball—showing the Bingleys, Darcy, and others, with the three girls standing together.

Bingley asks Jane to dance, and Wickham, in uniform, dances with Lydia. Darcy slights Elizabeth in her hearing, saying that she is "tolerable" but "not handsome enough to tempt me." He declines to "give consequence to young ladies who are slighted by other men." When at Sir William Lucas's urging he asks her to dance, Elizabeth refuses. Miss Bingley and the Hursts disparage the Bennets for their low connections. As the scene fades to Miss Austen writing, in voiceover we hear her tell of the passage of time, during which Bingley becomes more and more interested in Jane, and Darcy in Elizabeth, although she is unaware of his interest. Jane and Elizabeth appear again, both preparing for the next ball. Lydia enters saying that Wickham will be there, calling him the "handsomest man that ever wore regimentals." The next scene, at the ball, shows Darcy and Wickham glaring at each other. Wickham retreats with Lydia. While Darcy and Elizabeth dance, Sir William Lucas stops them to comment on Jane and Bingley's possible "desirable event." Darcy also hears Mrs. Bennet talking loudly about the likelihood of Bingley's marrying Jane. After the dance, Darcy speaks to the Bingley sisters, who look concerned. As the dance breaks up, Miss Bingley informs the Bennets that they leave for London the next day.

In Act II, Miss Austen is seen writing again. Lytell in voiceover asks her to continue the story. She says that months have passed and that now it is April. A dissolve returns us to the Bennet sisters. Lydia tells Jane and Elizabeth that Darcy cheated and robbed Mr. Wickham of his rightful bequest. Elizabeth tells her father that she has rejected Mr. Collins' proposal. (Apparently Mr. Collins does not appear on screen.) As Mrs. Bennet rages over this refusal, Mr. Bennet offers to send Elizabeth to her aunt and uncle for a trip. In voiceover Miss Austen tells us that she will not describe all of the countryside which Elizabeth saw but will focus on one beautiful house. A dissolve takes us in long shot to a "stately English country home, complete with park." Austen's voice announces that this is Pemberley. Elizabeth and her aunt and uncle appear in an elegantly furnished room. We find that Elizabeth did not know to whom Pemberley belonged when she went there. Thus, she is surprised when the housekeeper mentions her master's name. Then Darcy walks into the room. Austen in voiceover tells of the days that follow, when Elizabeth on her walks frequently runs into Darcy. Then, after Elizabeth is shown alone in her lodgings, Darcy enters and proposes. His proposal repeats much of the language of the novel. In her refusal, she mentions his role in causing her sister's unhappiness and his mistreatment of Wickham.

Act III opens with Jane Austen chewing the end of her pen and looking at the camera with a worried expression. She tells of Elizabeth's consternation over the proposal, then of Lydia's elopement, and Elizabeth's return to Longbourn. After a dissolve Jane is telling Elizabeth that their father has gone to London to look for the runaways. Then Mr. Bennet comes back from London with the news that Lydia and Wickham are married. He tells the family that Darcy found the couple and paid the money. Austen appears again and reports that Bingley and Darcy have returned to Netherfield. When they call at Longbourn, Elizabeth thanks Darcy for assisting Lydia. He says that he thought only of Elizabeth, and he tells her that his affection for her is unchanged. He says, "You showed me how insufficient were all my pretensions to please a woman worthy of being pleased." She says, "You please me." Darcy approaches her but a dissolve intervenes before he can kiss her. Two comic scenes come near the end, in which first Bingley and then Darcy ask Mr. Bennet for permission to marry his daughters. In a really feeble last scene, Darcy says that he loved her for her "prejudice." She says "And I for your pride...." Then she asks his Christian name. He says, "Fitzwilliam." She says, "Ah, how nice" (Taylor, *P&P*).

As in the 1940 film, much as been omitted. Charlotte Lucas, Mr. Collins, Lady Catherine de Bourgh, Mary and Kitty Bennet, Mrs. Philips, Georgiana Darcy, Colonel Fitzwilliam, the Forsters, and Captain Denny do not appear at all. The visit to Hunsford has been dropped, and the first proposal comes while Elizabeth is visiting at Pemberley. Also, as in the 1940 film, not much time elapses between the first proposal and the second. There's a swift resolution of Lydia's elopement, followed almost immediately by the second proposal. One of the best things about the screenplay is the witty dialogue, much of which has been lifted from the novel.

The screenplay of the BBC 1967 adaptation provides an interesting comparison with both the 1940 film and the NBC version from the standpoint of compression and change. Divided into six thirty-minute episodes, it is longer than the 1940 film and the *Philco* teleplay but shorter than the later television versions. It was recorded prior to transmission primarily on studio sets, but according to Celia Bannerman, who played the role of Elizabeth Bennet, the cast also traveled to Somerset and other locations in the west country for various exterior scenes (Fax 9/24/01). The 1967 version omits the character of Mary Bennet entirely, but mysteriously retains young Edward Lucas (Stephen Grives), who exchanges quips with Mrs. Bennet (Vivian Pickles). Lady Lucas (Diana King) also has a prominent role, with emphasis on her rivalry with Mrs. Bennet. It also has Wickham (Richard Hampton) attend the Netherfield Ball but leave when Darcy (Lewis Fiander) threatens to have him removed. Elizabeth's visit

to Hunsford is much abbreviated. Darcy appears at the first dinner at Rosings, and his proposal follows almost immediately. The day after her rejection of him, he explains in person his dealings with Wickham and his role in Bingley's (David Savile) decision to desert Jane (Polly Adams). The period of uncertainty about Lydia's flight with Wickham is short, and Darcy is shown bribing him to marry Lydia (Lucy Fleming). The last scene places Darcy and Elizabeth, now married, in a barouche-landau, on their way to Pemberley. Pemberley appears (Dyrham Park, according to Bannerman), and the pair look at it from the top of a hill. Then, the carriage having arrived at the house,

Pride and Prejudice (BBC 1968). Elizabeth Bennet (Celia Bannerman) and Mr. Darcy (Lewis Fiander). (BBC Picture Archives)

Darcy says, "We are arrived. Welcome home, Mrs. Darcy" (Episode 6, 23).

The screenwriter, Nemone Lethbridge, recommended that the exterior of Wilton House be used for Rosings, since she thought that house cold and forbidding in appearance (Episode 4, p. 12). She suggested that Chawton Cottage, Jane's final home, be used as the exterior for Longbourn (Episode 1, 30).

The 1980 and 1995 adaptations were made as mini-series and are considerably longer than the Hollywood film, the *Philco* version, or any of the other BBC adaptations. The 1980 adaptation, which was shown on BBC-2, beginning on Sunday, January 13, runs 226 minutes on videotape. The 1995 version, which started its run on September 24 on BBC-1, is about 300 minutes on laserdisc and DVD, both formats including a few transition scenes which were not shown on A&E Television when the adaptation appeared in the United States beginning in January 1996. The DVD "Special Edition" (2001) is in wide screen, letterboxed, and includes several extras—a feature on the making of the film, a Jane Austen biography and bibliography, and biographies of actors. Having been digitally remastered, the DVD achieves striking clarity, depth, and color intensity. The laserdisc picture is beautiful, but the DVD is a revelation. Fay Weldon wrote the screenplay for the 1980 adaptation, and Andrew Davies (also the screenwriter for the Meridian/A&E *Emma*), the 1995 adaptation. The 1995 version was enormously popular in England and in the USA. An audience estimated at 10.1 million watched the final episode on the BBC (Thynne 1), and about 3.7 million households in the USA watched the adaptation on A&E (Kroll 66–67).

The 1980 adaptation opens with a series of water colors after the manner of Thomas Rowlandson, a famous satiric artist contemporary with Jane Austen. These show ladies and gentlemen in scenes drawn from the novel. For example, we see Mr. Bennet seated at the backgammon board with his wife and five daughters in the room. Another scene shows two girls, apparently Lydia and Kitty, dancing with two young officers, while a girl wearing glasses plays the piano. The titles run and the musical theme plays while these scenes scroll across the screen. The style of the water colors makes clear the satiric nature of the film to be shown. Each installment of the 1995 adaptation opens with a close-up of satin, brocade and lace fabric, fabric-covered buttons, and a female hand with needle and thread poised to embroider on the fabric. This introduction makes clear that we are about to enter a woman's world. The titles appear on this background to the music of the main theme, played on a pianoforte by Melvyn Tan. Carl Davis said that he used a popular Beethoven septet as his model for the sound he wanted. The pianoforte dominates the music in the more intimate scenes but is augmented by an orchestra of eighteen musicians in some of the longer scenes (Birtwistle, *Pride* 66).

Both versions are faithful to the novel, yet a close comparison of both with the novel reveals the different ways in which screenplay writers Weldon and Davies cut and pared the novel to fit the screen. Both drew much of their dialogue from the novel, but they often changed the speaker or the circumstance in which the dialogue is spoken. For example, the 1980 adaptation begins with Mary Bennet running out to the road to speak to a man leading a wagon, and then running back to the house with her report on the new residents of Netherfield, as Charlotte Lucas approaches the house. Inside the house, Charlotte speaks a variation of Mrs. Bennet's line in the novel regarding what a "fine thing" it is to have a single man in possession of a good fortune come into the neighborhood (*PP* 1).

Elizabeth responds with the first sentence in the novel, spoken by the narrator: "It is a truth universally acknowledged, that a single man in possession of a good fortune, must be in want of a wife" (*PP* 1). In the same conversation, Charlotte utters her opinion, which appears in Chapter 6 of the novel, that "Happiness in marriage is entirely a matter of chance," and "[…] it is better to know as little as possible of the defects of the person with whom you are to pass your life" (*PP* 23).

The 1995 adaptation begins with Darcy (Colin Firth) and Bingley (Crispin Bonham-Carter) on horseback galloping across a field. They pause to discuss whether Bingley will lease Netherfield. Elizabeth is watching the young men from a hill. The viewer hears Bingley ask for Darcy's approval and, when that is given, say to Darcy that he will take it. The men race off across the field. Elizabeth goes home to Longbourn, where her father is reading in his study and where Kitty and Lydia are quarreling over a bonnet. The next scene shows the Bennet family leaving church. Mrs. Bennet is reporting to Mr. Bennet that Netherfield has been taken by an eligible bachelor with five thousand pounds a year. This version retains having Mrs. Bennet speak the line, "What a fine thing for our girls." To vex her, Mr. Bennet pretends not to know what she is talking about. In the novel the girls are not present to hear these remarks or

Pride and Prejudice (BBC 1980). Elizabeth Bennet (Elizabeth Garvie) and Mr. Darcy (David Rintoul). (BBC Picture Archives)

their parents' subsequent comments. However, in this adaptation they are present, and Elizabeth says in a joking manner, "A single man in possession of a good fortune must be in need of a wife." Her mother, quite serious, agrees and urges Mr. Bennet to visit Mr. Bingley immediately. He refuses and urges that Mrs. Bennet go with the girls to visit him, but then he suggests that the girls go alone, since Mr. Bingley might prefer Mrs. Bennet because she is as handsome as any of them. Lydia laughs loudly at this remark and Elizabeth chides her for laughing. This scene effectively introduces Mrs. Bennet's foolishness, Mr. Bennet's lack of respect for her, Elizabeth's ironic intelligence, and Lydia's irrepressible nature. Charlotte's generalization that one should know as little as possible about one's future husband is directed, as it is in the novel, to Elizabeth at the party at Lucas Lodge, as they observe Jane with Mr. Bingley. As one might expect in a six-hour serial, the order of events and scenes in the 1995 adaptation is closer to that of the novel than is the order of the 1980 adaptation, and the 1995 adaptation also shows more variety and imagination in the way information is presented.

The actresses who play Elizabeth are good in both of these later film adaptations. Elizabeth Garvie (1980) effectively conveys the intelligence, humor, and stubbornness of Elizabeth Bennet. Until I saw the 1995 adaptation, I was convinced that no one could be better in the role. Then, Jennifer Ehle changed my mind. Her interpretation of the role of Elizabeth Bennet reflects not only her own manner of portraying the character but the way in which the screenwriter perceived the character. Andrew Davies' comments on the character indicate that he wanted a physically lively and active Elizabeth whose sexual energy captivates Darcy, who is not used to this natural, open kind of woman. Davies wanted to emphasize the "tom-boyish, gipsy-ish" quality in Elizabeth (Birtwistle, *Pride* 4). Thus, in addition to the scenes suggested in the novel in which Elizabeth walks three miles in the mud to see her sister, or walks in the woods and fields at Rosings, he inserted the opening scene in which Elizabeth runs down hill, various scenes in which she is walking, and a scene in which she climbs up on a big rock to gaze at the countryside in Derbyshire. Elizabeth Garvie's Elizabeth is more sedate, and, unlike Ehle's character, usually carries a parasol in her walks. Her physical appearance is also less sexual. Her sister Lydia (Natalie Ogle) may have difficulty keeping her lace tucker in place, but we need have no concern about the possibility of seeing too much of Garvie's bosom. Indeed, in most scenes she wears high-necked dresses. On the other hand, we do not see Jennifer Ehle wearing high-necked dresses or tuckers either in or out of doors. She exhibits décolletage in most of her costumes—day or evening. It would

be difficult for Mr. Darcy or the viewer to be unaware of Ms. Ehle's sexual appeal.

Critics have disagreed over the extent to which Elizabeth Bennet's conversation and manner deviate from what was considered decorous and proper during Austen's lifetime. Claudia Johnson says that today we may not realize how different Elizabeth's behavior was from that taught in the conduct books or from that demonstrated in conventional fiction of the day (*Jane* 75). In the novel Mrs. Bennet (herself no paragon of decorous speech) cautions Elizabeth about her "wild" manner of conversing with Mr. Bingley (*PP* 42), Caroline Bingley comments on her "self sufficiency without fashion" (*PP* 271), and Lady Catherine is shocked at Elizabeth's readiness to

Pride and Prejudice (BBC/A&E 1995). Elizabeth Bennet (Jennifer Ehle) and Mr. Darcy (Colin Firth). (Photofest)

state her opinion. Of course, it is precisely Elizabeth's difference from other women he has known which piques Darcy's interest. He has been exposed to feminine cattiness when Caroline Bingley and Mrs. Hurst criticize Elizabeth's muddy skirts, and he comments then on the "meanness in all of the arts which ladies sometimes condescend to employ for captivation" (*PP* 40). He may compare Elizabeth's witty irreverence to Caroline Bingley's clumsy flattery, as in the 1995 adaptation Caroline says of Darcy that "he is a man without fault." Not even Darcy can accept that flattering hyperbole, and Elizabeth, who sees irony in everything, will certainly not let it pass unchallenged. She hastens to point out that his fault is "a propensity to hate everyone." He counters with, "Yours is willfully to misunderstand them." To her chagrin, Miss Bingley's ploy to interest

Darcy in herself has turned into a verbal sparring match between Darcy and Elizabeth.

When we compare Elizabeth to Jane, we see that Jane is far less sure of the validity of her opinions about others. She attempts to find something good to say about everyone and is brought only with difficulty to decide that the Bingley sisters are not her friends. She tries to find a way to consider both Darcy and Wickham good men. She is reluctant to tell people the truth about Wickham because he may be sorry for what he has done, and exposure might make him desperate. She is so reserved and decorous that Bingley is unsure of her feelings for him. Jane's careful reserve is such that she could have been the heroine of one of Fanny Burney's novels, but Jane is not the heroine of this novel. However, Elizabeth looks mild-mannered indeed compared to the boisterous Lydia and the whining Kitty. These differences are clear in the novel and in the later film adaptations. Garvie and Ehle both convey Elizabeth's confidence in her own opinions and her willingness to express them. And both appear properly chastened when Elizabeth discovers that she has been unjust to Darcy regarding his treatment of Wickham and that she has been deceived by Wickham's lies. After she reads Darcy's letter she says, "Till this moment, I never knew myself" (*PP* 208). Thereafter she shows moderation in passing judgment on others and in trusting her first impressions.

There is no doubt that Colin Firth is the definitive cinematic Mr. Darcy. In an interview Firth called Darcy "rather inscrutable, very taciturn," and "used to keeping his emotions in check." He also stressed that "what Darcy *doesn't* say" is as important as what he says or does (Collin 3b). Through most of the first episode, Darcy says little. He looks disapprovingly at everyone who is not a member of his group. He spends a lot of time looking out of windows, as if to distance himself from people whom he considers his inferiors. However, he also spends time observing people, especially Elizabeth, whose disregard for him piques his interest. Later, while Elizabeth is playing the pianoforte at Rosings, Davies has provided Darcy lines from the novel in which he confesses to feeling inadequate to converse easily with strangers. Elizabeth chides him for not making more of an effort. It is a new experience for Darcy to receive instruction from anyone, especially a woman. He is used to the adulation of Miss Bingley (Anna Chancellor) and of his sister. When Elizabeth not only refuses his proposal of marriage but accuses him of wrongdoing, he defends himself in his letter to her, but the anger and hurt which he feels are well conveyed in the scenes in which he labors to write his explanatory letter to Elizabeth. He is in his shirt sleeves, his shirt open at the throat, his hair disheveled and his face drawn.

Of course, the character is much more fully presented in this adaptation than in any of the other versions. The role in the 1980 version reflects rather the meager proportions of this character's role in the novel. David Rintoul, who plays Darcy, reveals little variation in demeanor throughout the film. His expressionless face and the stiffness of his body language may be in keeping with the unbending nature of the character, but when the character finally is supposed to bend, Rintoul appears incapable of expressing any feelings. Since Rintoul is a gifted actor whose portrayal of Hamlet was much praised, it is possible that his emotionless portrayal of Darcy represents a directorial choice. One may note also that in the 1940 adaptation there is no mention of Darcy's feeling inadequate to converse easily with strangers. Laurence Olivier's manner demonstrates no diffidence in the presence of strangers, rather arrogance and indifference.

Davies added several scenes to give the viewer a sense of Darcy's life away from Elizabeth and to reveal him as a physically active and sensitive individual. His appearance in the first scene, where he and Mr. Bingley are on horseback and are looking toward Netherfield, furnishes various clues to his character. We see that Mr. Bingley defers to his judgment regarding the choice of the estate. Davies commented that he wanted to show them both as "two physical young men" (Birtwistle, *Pride* 3). Other scenes also emphasize Darcy's physicality. For instance, we see him bathing and getting out of a tub. We see him jumping into a lake in his underwear to swim. We see him fencing with a fencing master. This Mr. Darcy sweats. The spectacle of Colin Firth in a shirt open at the throat, a look of frustrated passion on his face, may have been responsible for the Darcymania that swept over England after *Pride and Prejudice* appeared on the BBC. However, Mimi Spencer, writing for the *Evening Standard*, asserts, "It was his button-front breeches and Irish-linen shirt that sparked off the contagion of Darcy fever" (19).

Another revealing series of scenes in the 1995 film occurs as Elizabeth reads Darcy's letter. We hear Darcy in voiceover speaking the words of the letter while a montage sequence shows Darcy in various roles during his past relationship with George Wickham (Adrian Lukis). We see Darcy and Wickham as children preparing to fish in a stream, then an older, disapproving Darcy in an academic gown entering a room to find Wickham with a half-naked girl on his lap and a quizzical expression on his face, and then a stern Darcy writing out a check which he gives to Wickham. Later, as Darcy tells how Wickham almost persuaded Georgiana (Emilia Fox) to elope with him, we see Darcy finding the pair together at Ramsgate and Darcy embracing his sister as Wickham leaves the inn. These scenes reveal him as morally superior to Wickham, as fair to Wickham, and as a loving brother to Georgiana. When Elizabeth finishes reading this letter, and has reflected on Wickham's behavior to her, she realizes that she has misunderstood Darcy's character, and the viewer also understands his character better.

Other scenes featuring Darcy are those which occur as Elizabeth reads the letter from Mrs. Gardiner describing Darcy's role in discovering Lydia and bringing about the marriage. As we hear Mrs. Gardiner in voiceover, we see Darcy in a coach, at a way station taking refreshment, and in London roaming the streets. Davies calls him "the Avenger on the trail" (Birtwistle 12). He buys information from a street urchin and knocks on a door, where Mrs. Younge can be seen within trying to deny him entrance. Then we see him looking at what is apparently an address on a piece of paper, followed by Lydia's comment on looking out the window,

Pride and Prejudice (BBC/A&E 1995). The Bennet family: front, l–r, Lydia (Julia Sawalha), Elizabeth (Jennifer Ehle), Jane (Suzannah Harker), Mary (Lucy Briers), Kitty (Polly Maberly); back, Mrs. Bennet (Alison Steadman) and Mr. Bennet (Benjamin Whitrow). (Photofest)

"Lord, what is he doing here?" Next we see him in a church standing next to Wickham as Lydia and the Gardiners arrive. Later, Mrs. Gardiner tells Elizabeth in a letter that Darcy insisted on bearing all of the costs relative to the marriage, and in a flashback we see and hear him doing so. In these scenes Darcy appears to be a man of action and authority. Unlike the ineffectual Mr. Bennet and even the well-intentioned but unsuccessful Mr. Gardiner, he gets things done.

Elizabeth's family is well portrayed in both recent versions. It is difficult to decide whether Alison Steadman of the 1995 version or Priscilla Morgan of the 1980 version is the better Mrs. Bennet. I am inclined to believe that Priscilla Morgan's Mrs. Bennet has the more unpleasant voice. Fay Weldon has given her even more opportunities to express her foolishness than has Davies. Morgan's Mrs. Bennet is particularly hard for the viewer and her family to tolerate when she calls Lydia "lucky" and "clever" for getting a husband, while her older sisters are still single. Both adaptations have Mrs. Bennet mingling concern that Mr. Bennet will fight Wickham, with anger at the Forsters for letting Lydia run away, and with concern that Lydia may not know the best places to buy her wedding clothes. In both adaptations, a clear parallel is made between Mrs. Bennet and her favorite daughter, who shows every sign of being as foolish and headstrong as her mother. In the 1980 adaptation, Mrs. Bennet criticizes Elizabeth for her talkativeness, saying, "In the company of young gentlemen, smile and hold your tongue. That's the way I won your father." These lines, which are not in the novel, help to explain how an intelligent man like Mr. Bennet could have wed such a ninny.

Mr. Bennet is also admirably played by both Moray Watson (1980) and Benjamin Whitrow (1995). Both Weldon and Davies reveal Mr. Bennet as lazy and irresponsible in his pursuit of his simple pleasures of books and wine. Whitrow is perhaps the more likeable of the two, since he does not bluster quite as much as Watson. Weldon's screenplay is less subtle than Davies' in making the point that Mr. Bennet, attracted by Mrs. Bennet's good humor and youthful beauty, had married unwisely. Weldon has Charlotte query Elizabeth concerning Mr. Bennet's knowledge of Mrs. Bennet before he married her, and Charlotte later reminds Elizabeth of the impropriety of her family's behavior.

The 1995 adaptation includes the scene described in the novel, but omitted in the 1980 version, in which Mr. Bennet meets with Elizabeth after she has become engaged. Here, Mr. Bennet is concerned that Elizabeth may have accepted a man she does not love. He says that he would hate to see her unable to respect her partner in life. This surely is an allusion to his own feelings about his wife. Elizabeth reassures him that she does love Darcy. She adds, "He is truly the best man I have ever known." In the 1980 adaptation, this meeting of Mr. Bennet and Elizabeth is omitted. Instead, Mr. Bennet and Mrs. Bennet discuss the prospect of having three girls married. Mr. Bennet says, "For what do we live but to make sport for our neighbors and to laugh at them in our turn." (In both the novel and the 1995 adaptation, he says this line in response to Mr. Collins's letter warning of Lady Catherine's disapproval of a match between Elizabeth and Darcy.) After this statement, Mr. Bennet says, "Mrs. Bennet, if any young men come for Kitty or Mary, send them in, for I am quite at leisure."

There is little to choose between Sabina Franklin and Suzannah Harker in the role of Jane Bennet, and Clare Higgins and Polly Maberly both perform well as Kitty. More interesting are the different ways Mary Bennet is portrayed. The novel presents Mary as something of a poseur. She claims to prefer reading a book to any other activity and reads mostly religious works, such as Fordyce's sermons, from which she draws edifying lessons with which to regale her sisters. Yet she is always alert to any opportunity to exhibit her talents in public. The least physically attractive of the sisters, Mary tries to draw attention to herself in other ways, but it is apparent that she is neither intelligent or talented. At the end of the novel we are told that Mary easily relinquishes her former pursuits in order to keep her mother company at home and abroad. She no longer has to compete with her more attractive sisters and may moralize without fear of reproach. Fay Weldon has chosen to emphasize Mary's hypocrisy. Mary (Tessa Peake-Jones) is shown to be much interested in gossip and ever ready to taunt Elizabeth about losing Wickham to Mary King. In both adaptations, Mary appears to admire Mr. Collins. In the 1995 version, Mary is the only one of the sisters who accepts Mr. Collins's condolences as sincere.

In both adaptations Mary is poised to leap into musical performance at every opportunity. In contrast to the uninspired but minimally competent performance at the pianoforte which Lucy Briers' Mary Bennet gives at Netherfield in the 1995 adaptation, Tessa's Mary Bennet hunches over the keyboard and sings wretchedly off key. This performance seems to belie her reputation for being accomplished. In the 1995 adaptation, Mary's choice of a familiar aria from Handel's *Xerxes* makes apparent to the viewer/listener how poor her singing and playing actually are, especially when contrasted to Mrs. Hurst's lively rendition of Mozart's "Rondo alla Turca" from his *Sonata No. 11 in A Minor*. Mrs. Bennet usually appears eager to have Mary display her talents, but at the party at Lucas Lodge, while Mary is playing a lengthy piece, Lydia appeals to Mrs. Bennet to get Mary to play some dance music. Mrs. Bennet says cruelly, "Oh, play a jig, Mary, no one wants your concertos here."

Mary is revealed in both adaptations as having a firm grasp of the obvious. Having called upon her sisters to pour the "balm of sisterly consolation" into "wounded bosoms," she observes that female virtue once lost cannot be regained. Her moralizing rubs salt, rather than balm, into the wounds of her listeners. We have more examples of Mary's moralizing in the 1995 version and hear her remark frequently that she would rather read a book than go to Brighton or to a dance. In this adaptation, we also see Lydia snort or otherwise show disdain for Mary's moralizing. Mary is usually right in what she says, but Mary is a bore.

Both actresses appear plain, but hair and make-up stylist Caroline Noble made Lucy Briers particularly ugly. She applied spots to her skin and chose an unbecoming hairstyle, made worse by the application of grease to give it an unwashed appearance (Birtwistle, *Pride* 58). Tessa Peake-Jones has big eyes accentuated with big round glasses and wears her hair in bangs, with the remainder pulled back in a bun. Both appear flat-chested and are dressed in plain high-necked dresses.

Lydia Bennet is the most openly sexual of the sisters and the one on whom the resolution of the plot turns. Both Julia Sawahla (1995) and Natalie Ogle (1980) convey well Lydia's pert outspokenness and her giddy thoughtlessness. Both also convey the sexuality of this character. One may protest that Jane Austen did not say anything about her characters' sexuality, but she was not blind to the existence of sex. In *Sense and Sensibility*, the subplot of Colonel Brandon's unfortunate first love and her daughter, who was seduced and abandoned, is as lurid as anything in the novels of Samuel Richardson. In *Pride and Prejudice*, Wickham certainly did not run away with Lydia because she was wealthy or intelligent. In the 1980 adaptation, Lydia's sexuality is pointed out particularly by there being much made of the "tucker" which Lydia is supposed to wear to conceal some of her bosom. Early in the film, prior to the Assembly Ball, as Mrs. Bennet is discussing Lydia's dress with Mrs. Lucas in the presence of the other girls, Mrs. Bennet says that Lydia will have to tuck a little lace around her bodice. When Lady Lucas agrees, Mrs. Bennet says snidely that Charlotte doesn't need to tuck any lace to conceal her negligible bosom. When Mary points out that Lydia's lace tucker has slipped, Mrs. Bennet says that she wishes that Mary looked as good as Lydia does. It is clear that Mrs. Bennet favors Lydia over Mary, who she says reads too much, and that she is rather proud of Lydia's physical assets.

Lydia in the 1995 adaptation also flaunts her sexuality. Her bosom is constantly on display and she thinks it hilarious when Mr. Collins catches her in the hall in her shift. He is shocked, and she can be heard giggling as he walks down the stairs. She and Kitty go to Meryton frequently to meet the officers of the regiment stationed there. At the breakfast table on the morning that Elizabeth walks to Netherfield, Lydia suggests that she and Kitty go to Meryton early and that perhaps they may catch Lieutenant Denny before he is dressed. They express enthusiasm for this possibility. Later Lydia and Kitty are in a swing being pushed high in the air, showing their petticoats and stockings. When Darcy writes to Elizabeth that the lack of propriety of her family, particularly of her two younger sisters, made him reluctant to ally himself to her, Elizabeth remembers Lydia's wild behavior at the Netherfield ball, as she ran around the room with Denny's sword. Considering Lydia's earlier conduct, it is hardly surprising that she would be so shameless as to run away with Wickham. When we see her lounging about in her gown and robe in their room in London, she seems quite at ease with her situation and totally unashamed. She says proudly to Wickham that she has done what none of her sisters has done, and she is only sixteen. Even he looks amazed at her. In both adaptations, when Lydia and Wickham return to Longbourn after their wedding, Lydia shows no shame at what she has done. Rather she parades her satisfaction with her handsome husband and suggests that Elizabeth must be envious.

Wickham's character is primarily revealed by Elizabeth's shifting attitudes toward him. She begins by liking him, finding him well-mannered and thinking him open and honest, but after Darcy tells her his version of Wickham's story, she gradually changes her opinion of him. George Wickham in the 1980 adaptation is played by Peter Settelen, and in the 1995 adaptation by Adrian Lukis. Both actors are good looking men, Settelen a blonde, and Lukis a brunette. Elizabeth appears to have a strong liking for Wickham in both adaptations, with perhaps more mutual attraction shown by Wickham and Elizabeth in the 1980 version. Here, while Wickham and Elizabeth are playing croquet, Elizabeth speaks warmly in sympathy with Jane, who has received word from Miss Bingley that her brother will probably marry Miss Darcy. Wickham says that because of her loyalty to those she loves, to be loved by Elizabeth would be a privilege. In this same version and in the novel, Mrs. Gardiner, Elizabeth's aunt, warns her against falling in love with Wickham. Elizabeth tells her that she is not in love but that young people seldom refrain from falling in love for lack of a fortune. In the 1995 version, this warning is omitted. When Wickham becomes engaged to Mary King, Elizabeth accepts the news calmly. She congratulates Wickham and says that "[…] handsome young men must have something to live on." In the 1980 version, she tells her sisters, who are more upset than she, that "Young men must have something to live on as well as young women." In this version it is more apparent that Lydia is attracted to Wickham than it is in the 1995 version. After it is revealed that Miss King will not marry Wickham, Lydia says that, if Elizabeth is no longer interested in Wickham, she will be nice to him. At the farewell party at the Philips's we see Lydia laugh to catch Wickham's attention. In the 1995 version, while Elizabeth is reading Jane's letter telling of the elopement, she remembers the way Wickham looked at Lydia at the Philips's party. This remembered scene was not shown earlier in the film. In this version, more emphasis is placed on Wickham's flawed character than in the 1980 version. In particular, the flashback scenes in Darcy's letter and the scenes shown as Elizabeth reads Mrs. Gardiner's letter reveal his greed and his lack of principle. The viewer sees him taking money from Darcy, sees him wooing Georgiana, and sees him running away with Lydia. In addition, we hear Mrs. Philips tell of his gaming debts, his seduction of the village girls, and his outstanding bills to local merchants. Upon her return home from Hunsford and after she has read Darcy's letter, Elizabeth has obviously relinquished her former favorable opinion of Wickham. At the Philips's party, after Wickham leaves her, she says *sotto voce,* "Yes, go, go. I would not wish you back again."

The ridiculous Mr. Collins is effectively portrayed in both adaptations. Malcolm Rennie plays this character in the 1980 adaptation, and David Bamber in the 1995 adaptation. The viewer's first sight of Malcolm Rennie at the Bennets' front door establishes an impression of Mr. Collins as an ungainly, storklike creature. This impression is achieved in part by the tall stature of the actor and in part by the black top hat, and tight black stockings and knee breeches which emphasize his skinny legs. Later, at Hunsford, we see Mr. Collins look even more absurd, wearing a tall beaver hat engineered to protect him from drowning. Since the detail of the hat is not in the novel, it obviously is included for visual impact. Both Charlotte and Elizabeth laugh at the thought of Mr. Collins wearing this hat.

David Bamber's appearance also suggests the ridiculousness of the character. Caroline Noble, in charge of make-up and hair design for the 1995 adaptation, said that she perceived Mr. Collins as being sweaty, with a "moist upper lip." She parted his hair low on one side to suggest incipient baldness and slicked down his hair with grease (Birtwistle, *Pride* 60). Since Mr. Collins is much in evidence in this adaptation, we see him in a great many foolish postures. While dancing with Elizabeth at Netherfield, he makes a misstep, runs into someone, and launches into a stream of apologies. At Hunsford, we see him simpering and waving to Charlotte just after he has told Elizabeth that he and Charlotte were made for each other. As he is about to set out to call on the Bennets, the servant starts the horses so suddenly that he is jerked back with a certain loss of dignity. At Rosings, Lady Catherine interrupts Mr. Collins almost every time he speaks.

In the 1995 adaptation we also hear a great deal of Mr. Collins's insipid conversation. At the first dinner at Longbourn, Mr. Collins regales the Bennets with the way he stores up compliments so that he may bestow them on appropriate occasions. Mr. Bennet urges him on to exhibit his folly, and Elizabeth tries not to laugh out loud. However, when Mr. Collins calls upon the Bennets to commiserate with them about Lydia, he reveals himself as not only foolish but morally unsound. He tells the Bennet sisters that it would have been better for the family had Lydia died—an opinion that provokes even good-natured Jane. Elizabeth points out to him that staying longer in proximity to such a depraved family might bring censure upon himself, whereupon he hastily takes his leave. In the novel and in the 1980 adaptation, he advises Mr. Bennet in a letter that Mr. Bennet should "throw off" his daughter to suffer the consequences of her crime.

Lady Catherine de Bourgh is played by Judy Parfitt in the 1980 adaptation and by Barbara Leigh-Hunt in the 1995 version. Each brings to the role her own special flavor. Judy Parfitt appears to be the younger of the two. Her Lady Catherine is considerably more active than Barbara Leigh-Hunt's character, who walks with a cane and whose hair is gray. The 1995 adaptation achieves a greater impact for the character by placing her clearly within a great country house and with the trappings of wealth. On the first evening when Elizabeth goes to Rosings with the Collinses, we see Lady Catherine ensconced in a large throne-like chair in front of a massive oil painting. From this chair she gives advice to the Collinses and questions Elizabeth. Later, when she goes to Longbourn to talk to Elizabeth, she arrives in a large closed carriage drawn by six horses, and with four liveried servants. The confrontation between them takes place in "a little wilderness" near the house.

Lady Catherine in the 1980 version is always elegantly dressed and projects the officious arrogance of the character. The screenwriter and director have made her even more free with advice than she is in the 1995 version. On Elizabeth's first visit to Rosings, Lady Catherine tells Darcy to eat more; then she asks him a question, but does not wait for an answer. She questions Elizabeth about her sisters. The next day, she bursts into the presence of Charlotte and Elizabeth at the parsonage to tell Charlotte that she should not have bought a whole leg of lamb. She says that she will exchange it for a half. At the next occasion for Elizabeth to visit Rosings, Elizabeth plays the pianoforte, while Lady Catherine talks about her loudly and incessantly. After Darcy walks over to the instrument to talk to Elizabeth, Lady Catherine brings her daughter, Anne (Moir Leslie), over to the pianoforte so that she may have "her part in the conversation." The confrontation between Elizabeth and Lady Catherine at Longbourn is set indoors. Lady Catherine is brought into the room by Mrs. Bennet. Elizabeth finally orders Lady Catherine to leave and holds the door open.

Like the novel, but unlike the 1980 adaptation, the 1995 adaptation includes Sir William Lucas (Christopher Benjamin) and Maria Lucas (Lucy Davis), Charlotte's sister, as Elizabeth's fellow visitors to Hunsford. Sir William is played largely for humor in this version. He is pompous but not unkind in the early scenes, as for example at the Assembly Ball, where Darcy rebuffs him when he praises dancing as "one of the first refinements of polished societies." At Rosings, he is awestruck and almost silent before the greatness of Lady Catherine. Maria furnishes a nice contrast to Elizabeth. Whereas Maria doesn't speak at all in Lady Catherine's presence, Elizabeth astonishes everyone by proffering her opinions freely. As she says when Darcy comes to the piano while she is playing, "My courage always rises at every attempt to intimidate me." It is not surprising that Lady Catherine could not coerce this Elizabeth into giving up Darcy. In the 1980 adaptation, Sir William, played by Peter Howell, has a minimal role, and Maria does not appear at all.

As in the novel, the two proposal scenes are focal points in the adaptations. The script and staging of Darcy's proposal at Hunsford are similar in both adaptations, but the 1995 adaptation is more effective because of Ehle's and Firth's acting. Ehle conveys well Elizabeth's simmering anger at Darcy because of what Colonel Fitzwilliam has revealed to her of Darcy's role in causing Bingley to reject Jane. Firth manages to suggest the intensity of Darcy's struggle between his love for Elizabeth and his proud reluctance to ally himself with her family. When Elizabeth rejects him, he appears hardly able to believe that she could turn down the great honor he does her. Firth said that he had to try to think himself into the time period in order to make this proposal sound at all reasonable. Most people at that time would have recognized the great honor which he was offering Elizabeth and would have understood his reluctance to connect himself to the Bennet family (Birtwistle, *Pride* 103). The scene is all the more effective because of the montage which follows, in which he agonizes over his letter to Elizabeth. Elizabeth's feelings afterwards—feelings of wonder and indignation—are also well represented. I particularly liked the scene in which she is in a carriage on her way back to Long-bourn. She looks out the carriage window, sees Darcy's face and hears him saying, "You must allow me to tell you how ardently I admire and love you." Then the face disappears and we hear the thunder of the carriage wheels. This scene helps to convey how much Darcy's expressions of love will stay with her until they overcome all of her resistance.

The scene in which Darcy asks Elizabeth whether her feelings are the same as they were in April, when he had proposed, differs significantly in the two versions. In the 1980 adaptation, Weldon combines dialogue from chapters 16 and 18 of Book III. After Elizabeth receives a note which evokes a smile, she is next seen outside walking with Darcy. They walk near some beautiful tall trees and are variously seen in two-shots, medium shots and long shots. She thanks him for his service to Lydia. He says that his thoughts were only for Elizabeth and then asks what her feelings are for him. After she tells him that her feelings are the opposite from what they were in April, he offers his arm to her. She takes his arm, and they walk together. A long shot places them among the trees. Then in a medium two-shot, she queries him about what attracted him to her in the first place. She explores his possible reasons in a playful manner. Next in long shot we see the couple walking. They stop, face each other, draw close, and the camera tilts up into the branches of a tree.

The 1995 adaptation follows more closely the situation and dialogue of the novel. Here Darcy calls at Longbourn with Bingley, and he, Elizabeth, Bingley, Jane and Kitty set out to walk to Meryton. Kitty turns aside to visit Maria Lucas, and Elizabeth and Darcy are far enough away from the other couple to talk confidentially. We see autumn foliage and a farm laborer with his cart. Elizabeth and Darcy, shown in two-shots or medium shots, look lovingly at each other, but they do not touch as they confess their feelings. The scene concludes with a long shot from behind Darcy and Elizabeth showing them walking at a short distance behind Bingley and Jane.

One of the most difficult problems facing the screenwriter who adapts one of Jane Austen's novels is that of writing a conclusion. Austen's novels typically do not close with a big scene. She likes to suggest something of the relationships of the various characters after the events of the novel. The last chapter of *Pride and Prejudice* tells that after only a year of proximity to his mother-in-law, Bingley and Jane left Netherfield and bought an estate near Pemberley. Kitty spent most of her time either with the Bingleys or Darcys. Mary Bennet became the sole companion of her mother; Mr. Bennet frequently visited at Pemberley. There was, however, no reformation for the Wickhams. Lydia often wrote to ask Elizabeth for money, and was even a guest at Pemberley when her husband was elsewhere. Georgiana lived at Pemberley and profited from observing Elizabeth's management of her husband. Lady Catherine was at length reconciled to the "pollution" of the woods of Pemberley not only by Elizabeth but by her whole family and deigned to visit the couple.

The 1980 adaptation closes with Mr. and Mrs. Bennet at home. She rejoices over the marriage of three daughters and exults over Lizzie's brilliant conquest, saying, "What pin money!" Mr. Bennet opines philosophically, "But for what do we live but to make sport for our neighbors and to laugh at them in our turn." He tells Mrs. Bennet, "[…] if any young men come for Kitty or Mary, send them in for I am quite at leisure."

The final scenes of the 1995 version show a double wedding, with Darcy and Elizabeth and Bingley and Jane standing before a beaming minister. The scene affords a striking contrast with the earlier wedding between Lydia and Wickham, where the minister, Darcy, and the Gardiners wear solemn expressions and the bride looks frightened. In this final scene, as the minister reads the marriage vows, the camera pans from left to right to show Bingley, Jane, Darcy and Elizabeth, then pulls back to show all four. Then the camera picks out members of the congregation, their expressions indicating their attitudes toward the wedding or toward their own circumstances. Caroline Bingley wears a particularly sour expression. As the minister says that one purpose of marriage is for the procreation of children, we see an unhappy Lady Catherine, at home, with her sickly daughter. As he reads that marriage serves as a remedy against sin and fornication, we see Wickham and Lydia on a bed. When he states the third purpose, to provide mutual society, we see the two couples looking lovingly at each other. In this final scene, we see Colonel Fitzwilliam, the Collinses, the Gardiners, Miss Bingley and the Hursts, the Philipses, Mr. and Mrs. Bennet, Kitty and Mary, as well as others from the village. Then, outside of the church Darcy and Elizabeth get into one carriage and Bingley and Jane get into another. As the carriages pull away from the church, Mrs. Bennet comments to Mr. Bennet that they are blessed to have three daughters married. In the final frames Darcy and Elizabeth exchange a chaste kiss.

One of the appeals of the 1995 adaptation is the beauty of the great houses and the English countryside and the attention to detail in the uses of settings. Gerry Scott, who was in charge of the design of the film, said "[…] [We] wanted to use the English landscape as a player in the film" (Birtwistle, *Pride* 37). He even preferred to show real exteriors outside of windows (37). It is likely that reasons of economy dictated that most of the 1980 adaptation be set indoors, and the little scenery that appears is without distinction. In this version there is little or no effort to indicate that the events of the novel cover about a year. It is autumn when the novel begins, winter when Jane is in London, early spring when Elizabeth goes to Hunsford, summer when she visits Pemberley, and fall when Bingley returns to Netherfield. In the 1995 adaptation, we have a clear sense of the passage of time and the seasons, both from the appearance of the landscape and from the characters' wearing apparel. In the early part of the film, Darcy and Bingley shoot birds, and Elizabeth, wearing a long-sleeved spencer, walks amidst autumn foliage. During Mr. Collins' visit, the girls wear cloaks when they walk to Meryton. In winter, Elizabeth is wrapped in a shawl as frost coats the window of her room. At Hunsford, with Elizabeth still dressed for cool weather, she mentions the beauty of the spring vegetation. In the summer, Elizabeth and Jane wear short-sleeved frocks and pick flowers in the garden. In the fall, Elizabeth puts on a long-sleeved spencer before going outdoors with Lady Catherine into an area strewn with dead leaves.

Setting also helps to define Elizabeth Bennet as a person who appreciates natural beauty. From early in the novel the reader knows that Elizabeth likes to take walks and that she considers walking three miles to Netherfield in wet conditions no difficulty. At Rosings, she likes to walk by herself along paths unfrequented by others. She looks forward to a trip to the Lake District with the Gardiners, and is disappointed when this excursion must be canceled. In particular, we find her pleasure in Pemberley derives from the harmony of the great house in its natural setting. We are told, "She had never seen a place for which nature had done more, or where natural beauty had been so little counteracted by an awkward taste" (*PP* 245). Elizabeth likes to see a mingling of the wild and the domesticated. She prefers the natural and the picturesque to the restructuring of nature favored by landscape designers such as Humphry Repton.

The 1995 adaptation also makes extensive use of landscape to support the characterization of Elizabeth as an energetic, active creature. I have mentioned earlier her running down hill in the opening sequence, her three-mile walk to Netherfield, her walks at Rosings Park, and her climbing up a big rock to gaze out at the countryside. But Elizabeth is not the only character associated with particular landscapes. Setting also functions to reflect the character of others in the film. The scenes at Rosings were filmed in Lincolnshire, at Belton House (Birtwistle, *Pride* 25). Our first look at Rosings comes when the Collinses, Elizabeth, Sir William Lucas, and Maria approach the house by a formal avenue. The shrubberies on each side are trimmed into uniform shapes, suggestive perhaps of Lady Catherine's efforts to control everything and everyone within her domain. In contrast, the setting of Pemberley, which was filmed at Lyme Park on the Cheshire/Derbyshire border, reflects that blending of the wild and domesticated which Elizabeth in the novel so much admired. As in the novel, she associates the master of Pemberley with the good taste which she sees there, and she says *sotto voce,* "Of all this I might have been mistress."

As in the novel and in the 1940 film, singing, playing the pianoforte, and dancing are important, not only for showing the culture of the times but for revealing character and for showing relationships between characters. In the 1980 adaptation, Elizabeth sings twice—once at Lucas Lodge and once at Rosings. She sings simple sentimental ballads. At Lucas Lodge her performance contrasts favorably with that of Mary, who also sings a sentimental ballad but sings it out of key. Mary is at the additional disadvantage of competing with violins in the background. When she is about to sing again, her mother tells her, "You have delighted us long enough." Darcy, who has walked near to the piano to get a closer look at Elizabeth, shows disdain when Mary begins to perform.

In the 1995 adaptation, Elizabeth sings and plays at both Rosings and Pemberley; Georgiana plays at Pemberley. The episode at Pemberley is particularly effective. Here, in the presence of the Gardiners, Bingley, Caroline Bingley, Mr. and Mrs. Hurst, and Darcy, Elizabeth performs first. She plays and sings "Tell Me What Love Is" from Mozart's *The Marriage of Figaro.* Darcy watches and listens intently as she performs this passionate love song. Georgiana asks not to be made to sing as well as play. The relationship between Elizabeth and Georgiana seems almost that of sisters. Darcy is at first alarmed and then pleased as Elizabeth intercedes to cover for Georgiana when she is startled at Caroline Bingley's mention of Mr. Wickham. At that moment, a high degree of intimacy between Darcy and Elizabeth exists as she looks sympathetically toward him. Later that night, as he stands in the same room looking toward the pianoforte, he recalls, in flashback, that look and he smiles.

All in all there are fifteen different dances in the 1995 adaptation (Birtwistle, *Pride* 70). These occur at the Assembly Ball, with a trio of musicians playing a flute, a violin, and a cello; at Lucas Lodge, where Mary plays for the dancers; at the Netherfield Ball, with an eight-piece orchestra; and at the Phillips's Christmas party, where Mary plays. The most important dance is that which occurs at Netherfield, where Darcy and Elizabeth dance and talk. This dance, called "Mr. Beveridge's Maggot," is a line-dance. (This is the dance which Emma and Mr. Knightley dance in the Miramax *Emma.*) In this elegant dance, the dancers weave around each other, clasp hands, with each stationary at times, as they progress down the line. Thus, it exhibits well the grace of the dancers and enables them to converse with each other. Andrew Davies compared the dance to a fencing match. He said, "It echoes a tango or a *pasa doble*. There's a lot of stamping feet, they come together and they part, and some turns they make are like the turns of a matador. You get a sense of combat as well as dancing" (Birtwistle, *Pride* 71). Colin Firth felt that this dance scene visualizes the couple's relationship. He said, "We see an honesty and playfulness in Elizabeth, while there's something slightly comical about Darcy trying to maintain his formal manner while holding up his end of the repartee. She'll say something that stings him, and he has an entire eight-step circle to do before he is permitted to respond" (Birtwistle, *Pride* 102). In the 1980 adaptation, the presentation of Darcy's dance with Elizabeth at Netherfield is not so effectively staged. Here the focus is on what the pair say to each other and the expressions on their faces. In both versions, Sir William Lucas interrupts the dance to praise the dancers and to remark to Elizabeth how common such dances will be when Jane and Bingley are married. This comment triggers Darcy's interference in his friend's romance with Jane Bennet.

For a novel with such a complicated plot and a variety of settings, it is not surprising that *Pride and Prejudice* has found its best treatments in the mini-series format. The 1940 film has its charms, primarily deriving from the performances of Laurence Olivier and Greer Garson, but it suffers from its severe compression. Before the 1995 mini-series appeared, I felt that the 1980 adaptation was superior to all other adaptations of Austen's novels and certainly an adaptation faithful in story-line and spirit to the novel. In the BBC/A&E adaptation of *Pride and Prejudice*, however, we find a faithful rendering of the story, charismatic actors and excellent performances in all of the main roles, and effective use of both indoor and outdoor settings. Can it be done any better?

IV

Mansfield Park

Following the popular *Pride and Prejudice*, Jane Austen published *Mansfield Park* (1814). Critic and recent editor of the novel Claudia Johnson calls it "Austen's most controversial novel" (Introduction xii). Certainly it is different from the more "light and sparkling" *Pride and Prejudice*, but Austen was confident that it would be well received and unhappy when it was not. One of the problems with the novel for the modern reader is its protagonist. Fanny Price is modest, retiring, decorous, and prudish. Moreover, she is said to be physically unattractive and weak. Except for her stubborn resistance to Sir Thomas Bertram's insistence that she marry Henry Crawford, she is essentially passive. She waits patiently for the man she loves to realize that he loves her. *Mansfield Park* is also the least witty and satiric of Austen's novels. Fanny herself is without humor, and Mary Crawford, the only character who is full of wit and clever repartee, is unsympathetic.

Until recent years, modern critics (Trilling 136, Duffy, Mudrick 157) characterized Sir Thomas Bertram as an honorable man—one who has high principles and good intentions. Although he made mistakes in the raising of his children and in his harshness with Fanny, he has been called the only really admirable father in Austen's novels. During the 1980s and 1990s, critics (Johnson, *Jane Austen* 107; Fleishman 7–8; Lew 283; Kirkham 117; Said 87; Stewart 113) pointed out that Sir Thomas is a slave-owner and that the prosperity of Mansfield Park depends on the labor of slaves on his Antiguan plantation. They found his values warped by his connection with slavery and found even his mistreatment of Fanny connected to his ownership of slaves.

The protagonist of the novel is Fanny Price, the impoverished niece of Sir Thomas's wife, who is sent to Mansfield Park to enjoy the advantages of being associated with this prominent, wealthy family. As usual in Austen's novels, *Mansfield Park* is about money and social status. Although Fanny's mother, Mrs. Norris, and Lady Bertram are sisters, they represent three different social levels, defined chiefly by money. Lady Bertram is the wife of a baronet and mistress of a grand estate and large income. Fanny's mother married a common Lieutenant of Marines and has an income of only 400 pounds with which to sustain a large family. Mrs. Norris became the wife of a clergyman with the living at Mansfield Park worth 1000 pounds. After her husband's death, she is much at Mansfield Park. Although all contact between Lady Bertram and Mrs. Price has ceased, Mrs. Norris convinces Sir Thomas to bring ten-year-old Fanny Price to live at Mansfield Park. Although Mrs. Norris declines the financial responsibility for Fanny, she willingly undertakes to keep Fanny in a position subordinate to the Bertram sons and daughters. Among the Bertram children, only Edmund, the younger son, is sympathetic and helpful to Fanny. She comes to love him more than anyone, except perhaps her favorite brother, William.

In Chapter Three, Sir Thomas sails for Antigua, with his elder son, Tom, to look after affairs in his holdings there, leaving Edmund and Mrs. Norris in charge. When he finds that he cannot return by the end of a year, he sends Tom back to England. By the summer of the following year, Fanny is eighteen. In July, Mary and Henry Crawford come to pay a visit to their sister, Mrs. Grant. Dr. Grant had taken over the living at Mansfield Park after the death of Mr. Norris. Thus, two attractive and eligible young people enter the limited society of Mansfield Park. Maria Bertram, the elder daughter of the house, has recently become engaged to Mr. Rushworth, who has a fine estate and 12,000 pounds a year. However, when Henry Crawford comes on the scene, both Maria and Julia are attracted to him. Mary comes to Mansfield Park intending to make a marital play for Tom Bertram, but when Tom shows more interest in his horses than in her, she finds herself attracted to Edmund. Through much of the narration up to this point Fanny has little part. Edmund arranges for her to have a horse to ride, and although she is left out of the dances and parties which the others attend, she is present at Mansfield Park when the Crawfords visit and is included in an outing to Sotherton, Mr. Rushworth's estate. She is in the background, observing and listening, but too humble to feel slighted at her neglect. She watches as Edmund and Mary grow more attracted to each other, and as Henry Crawford flirts with both sisters.

When Tom convinces the others that they should put on a play, Fanny and Edmund speak against the enterprise. After Edmund defects to the other side, Fanny alone resists the pressure to take part in the play. She thinks that Sir Thomas would not approve of these theatricals and she sees that Henry Crawford, for whom the play provides opportunities for flirting with Maria, is coming between Maria and her fiancé. Meanwhile, Julia feels jealous and rebuffed. Lady Bertram and Mrs. Norris are oblivious to these emotional currents, the former too indolent to take notice and Mrs. Norris wholly concerned with economy and management.

At this point, Sir Thomas returns home. He sets out to banish all signs of the theatricals and to restore his house to its original state. When Henry Crawford announces that he is going to Bath, Maria realizes that he is not really interested in her. She urges her father to allow her to marry Rushworth within a few weeks. After the newlyweds and Julia leave Mansfield Park, Fanny begins to receive more of Sir Thomas's attention. He had commented on the day that he returned that she had improved in looks. Mary Crawford also turns to Fanny for companionship. When Henry Crawford returns to the parsonage, he decides to amuse himself by making Fanny fall in love with him.

When Fanny's brother William returns to England from sea duty, Sir Thomas invites him to Mansfield Park. Noticing Henry Crawford's interest in Fanny and wishing to compliment Fanny and William, Sir Thomas decides to give a ball in their honor. Edmund, meanwhile, is conflicted because Mary Crawford does not see herself as the wife of a practicing clergyman. Fanny sees with distress that Edmund would like to marry Mary Crawford. Henry, having perceived that his best way to Fanny's favor is by getting preferment for her brother, manages to acquire a second lieutenancy for William. With this news in hand, he proposes to Fanny, who is delighted at William's promotion, but astonished and displeased at the proposal.

The next day, Henry tells Sir Thomas of his desire to marry Fanny. Pleased with this news, Sir Thomas goes to Fanny's room to give his permission to the match. He is amazed and angry when Fanny refuses to marry Henry. Mindful that Henry has already helped William and is wealthy enough to assist others in her family, he accuses her of selfishness and ingratitude. This match is far above what she might be expected to make. Even Edmund urges Fanny to accept Henry. She tells him that she objects to Henry's character and mentions his careless behavior toward Maria. Edmund decides that Henry has been too precipitous in his suit but feels that if he persists he will succeed. He convinces his father to give her time. Sir Thomas agrees, but he sends Fanny home to Portsmouth with William, thinking that she will soon tire of the privations of her home and better appreciate what Henry has to offer.

Once Fanny is home she finds herself little valued in her parents' home, a place where confusion and noise reign. Her mother is much like Lady Bertram in her inability to manage anything, except having children. She does not discipline her children or control her servants. Fanny's father makes coarse jokes at Fanny's expense or ignores her. Fanny sorely misses the order and decorum of Mansfield Park.

About four weeks after Fanny has come to Portsmouth, Henry Crawford appears at the family's dwelling. After a visit of two days, Fanny begins to see him in a more favorable light than before. He is kind and considerate to her family and seems to have reformed his morals as well. He also has the advantage of reminding her of the world of Mansfield Park, which she misses.

Fanny now expects to be sent for around Easter, but letters from Mansfield Park report that Tom has been brought home very ill and that Edmund is tending him. Mary, apparently not desolate at the possibility of Tom's death, writes to assure Fanny that Henry is faithful to her. Then Mary sends a letter warning Fanny not to believe any rumors she may hear about Henry. She hears no more until her father reads from a newspaper that Mrs. Rushworth has run off with Henry Crawford. She is shocked and horrified, but not surprised that Mary would prefer that the affair be hushed up. Fanny worries about the impact on Sir Thomas and Edmund. Then she receives a letter from Edmund telling that Julia has eloped with Mr. Yates. Edmund plans to come after Fanny immediately and invites her sister, Susan, to come to Mansfield Park, as well.

At Mansfield Park, Fanny learns the whole story of Maria's affair and the elopement with Henry Crawford. Edmund, meanwhile, realizes that Mary Crawford's morals are defective. He tells Fanny that Mary looks upon the affair as merely an indiscretion and that the detection of the affair is what she laments. She thinks that if Henry can be convinced to marry Maria, all may yet be smoothed over.

The novel concludes with Tom's recovery and reformation, Julia's contrition and reconciliation with her father, Sir Thomas's realization of his errors in raising his daughters, Mrs. Rushworth's going into seclusion with only Mrs. Norris as her companion, and finally Edmund's realizing that he has loved Fanny all the time. Sir Thomas gladly consents to their marriage, realizing that Fanny is the daughter that he had wanted. After Mr. Grant's death, Edmund and Fanny end up at the parsonage at Mansfield Park.

The first adaptation of the novel, based on a screenplay by Ken Taylor, was produced by ITV for BBC television in 1983. It was directed by David Giles, who has made several mini-series based on adaptations of literary classics for the BBC, including *Sense and Sensibility* (1971). In November 1999, another adaptation was released by Miramax, first to theatres in the United States, and in April 2000, to theatres in Great Britain. This film was written and directed by Canadian director Patricia Rozema. In spite of some rather sensational subject matter, the film was a financial failure and received mixed critical reviews. Most Janeites were horrified at the very thought of this most moral of novels being made into a film which exhibited nudity and emphasized slavery, drug use, and madness.

Sylvestra Le Touzel plays Fanny Price in the 1983 BBC adaptation. Le Touzel continues to perform on British television, as in the BBC's *Vanity Fair* (1998). Reading about this physically unattractive heroine in the novel is not painful for the reader, who forgets about her unattractiveness and focuses on her thoughts and actions. But to have to watch a really plain actress portray a character whose primary virtues express themselves in resistance rather than action verges on torture. This is the case with Le Touzel. She is small, she is plain, and she has no physical grace. She even affects some small nervous mannerisms. Amanda Root, who plays Anne Elliot in the 1995 *Persuasion,* is not a beautiful actress, but she has charisma, and even projects a kind of beauty toward the end of the film. Le Touzel acquires some curls toward the end, but these are not enough to compensate for a crooked nose and a square chin. Let's face it. Television and film are visual media. The choice of Sylvestra Le Touzel for the role of Fanny was fatal to the success of this adaptation. Ironically, the child who played Fanny as a ten year old (Katy Durham-Matthews) was pretty, and it is unlikely that she would have grown up to look like Le Touzel.

The other characters are generally well-cast, but with no really outstanding performances. Nicholas Farrell plays Edmund Bertam with a kind of strong-jawed resoluteness. Farrell has had a lengthy and respectable acting career. He was in *Chariots of Fire* (1981), performed in several BBC productions of Shakespeare's plays (e.g., played Horatio in the 1996 *Hamlet*), and appeared in 2001 in the big Hollywood production *Pearl Harbor.* His character is actually more appealing on film than it is in the novel. Robert Burbage plays Henry Crawford appropriately as a Regency dandy. At one point he wears a pink top hat and a pink waistcoat under a pale gray suit. He is affected in manner and does a lot of posing. Anna Massey is convincingly obnoxious as Fanny's Aunt Norris. Bernard Hepton plays a rather young looking Sir Thomas Bertram. (Hepton may be recalled as playing Emma's hypochondriac father in the BBC's 1995 *Emma.*) The witty Mary Crawford is well portrayed by Jackie Smith-Wood, who is far easier to look at than Le Touzel. Maria Bertram is played by another actress familiar in Austen adaptations—Samantha Bond—who plays Miss Taylor, Emma's former governess, in the 1996 A&E *Emma.*

In dramatizing *Mansfield Park,* Ken Taylor followed the story-line of the novel closely. For many Janeites, this faithfulness to the novel makes up for other deficiencies. The liberties which Patricia Rozema, as director and writer, took with the novel have incurred the wrath of this coterie. One must bear in mind, of course, that Rozema's film, at about 112 minutes, is much shorter than the television mini-series, which ran serially for about 261 minutes, but the omission of much of the content of the novel is by no means their chief complaint. Rozema has, to use her own term, "reinterpreted" the novel

Mansfield Park (BBC 1983). Fanny Price (Sylvestra Le Touzel) and Edmund Bertram (Nicholas Farrell). (BBC Picture Archives)

(DVD Commentary). In this reinterpretation she has been much influenced by recent critics, such as Claudia Johnson, who have emphasized the importance in the novel of the issues of slavery and the oppression of women, particularly as they relate to the character of Sir Thomas Bertram and his treatment of Fanny Price. Rozema sets the film clearly in the context of a specific social and political milieu—the chief events of the story-line occurring in 1805 and 1806.* She said that she is just pointing out social and political realities which would have been obvious to contemporary readers (DVD Commentary). The BBC mini-series, on the other hand, focuses mainly on the costumes and manners of the times. A comparison of the two versions is revealing about two entirely opposite approaches to adaptation and to filmmaking.

Rozema's *Mansfield Park* opens with young Fanny (Hannah Taylor-Gordon) about to leave her home in Portsmouth to go to Mansfield Park.

Critics disagree on the dates of the chronology in the novel. See <http://mason.gmu.edu/~emoody/mp.calendar.html> for a summary of the discussion.

We see her pregnant mother (Lindsay Duncan) with a child in her arms (Rozema's infant) and five other young children around her telling Fanny goodbye. Young Fanny is poorly dressed and her hair disheveled. She asks her mother to write to tell her when she is to come home, but her mother turns away, not answering.* This child-actress, with her big dark eyes, conveys well Fanny's uncertainty and unhappiness as she realizes that she has been given away. However, in keeping with Rozema's recreation of Fanny's character, we see even in young Fanny a bright intelligence. Indeed, the film begins with Fanny telling her sister Susan a story of her own invention. In contrast, in the BBC mini-series, young Fanny is well-dressed, in a red cloak and a hat, and too shy to speak unless spoken to.

Mansfield Park's house and grounds are also presented differently in the two adaptations. Rozema used Kirby Hall in Northhamptonshire for both the exterior and some of the interior scenes of the Bertrams' great house. This mansion dates from the Elizabethan period and thus is not the "modern" house mentioned in the novel. The house is imposing, but its disrepair enabled Rozema to suggest that the Bertram family fortunes are on the wane. She said that she wanted to show something "grand and majestic, but worn and faded" (DVD Commentary). The set design for the interior of the house also gives the impression of coldness and age. Furnishings are minimal, and the floors and walls are mostly bare. When Fanny takes her first tour of the house, she walks up bare stone stairs and down bare halls, finally ending up in what looks like an attic storage room, full of castoff furniture and toys. The BBC adaptation, on the other hand, presents a beautifully furnished and decorated interior. This style is much more in the "heritage" tradition, with careful attention given to period decor. The exterior of the house is of the "Adam"† style, which would corroborate the novel's statement that the house was "modern." Unlike most of the other BBC adaptations, many scenes are filmed out of doors. Obviously, more money has been spent on the production of this mini-series than the BBC spent on mini-series in the 1970s, yet the outdoor scenes are filmed with little design rather than to permit opportunity for characters to walk and to converse in a variety of settings.

The Miramax film exploits the outdoors for both beauty and sym-

---

*The published screenplay includes a short scene in which Mrs. Price, in her kitchen after parting with Fanny, bursts into tears (14). In the film she shows no emotion at losing Fanny, nor any when Fanny returns. The novel says only that Mrs. Price was surprised that one of her fine boys was not the one sent for (MP 11). When Fanny returns with William, her mother meets her with "looks of true kindness," but she immediately turns her attention to William (MP 377–378).

†Named for Robert Adam (1728–1792), architect and exponent of architecture based on Greek, Roman and Renaissance Italian models. It was characterized by free use of ornamentation, delicate colors, Venetian windows, and smooth or scored stucco fronts (Watkins 65).

bolism. In one particularly evocative scene, as Fanny and Edmund come back to the house when Tom Bertram is desperately ill, Mansfield Park appears with the early morning fog enveloping it like a shroud. It is a scene of beauty, yet of foreboding. Another scene of spectacular beauty is an aerial shot showing the chalk cliffs near Durdle Door, with a tall ship just off shore.

In the Miramax version, Fanny arrives at Mansfield Park at 5:00 a.m. and waits in the darkness until Mrs. Norris (Sheila Gish) comes to take her inside. Tom Bertram, who was drinking on a balcony when Fanny arrived, had told the coachman to leave her there. Sir Thomas Bertram (Harold Pinter) welcomes Fanny, and when Mrs. Norris reveals that she has no intention of taking Fanny into the parsonage, Sir Thomas reconciles himself to keeping Fanny at Mansfield. Mrs. Norris gladly accepts his charge that she never let Fanny forget her second-class status at Mansfield Park. In both versions, he states that Fanny is inferior to his own children and he wants her to be aware that she is not their equal. In the BBC version, he expresses this opinion out of Fanny's hearing, but in the Miramax version she hears him say this while she stands in the hall outside the room where Sir Thomas is talking to Mrs. Norris, his wife, and daughters. Thus, it is established that Fanny understands her status from the beginning. In both versions, Mrs. Norris assures Sir Thomas that there is no danger that his sons will see Fanny as other than a sister.

An important difference between the two versions is that Rozema has made Fanny a budding writer, a young Jane Austen. Claudia Johnson asserts that Rozema's film "[...] gives us what many of us love about Austen in the first place, what other movies never deliver: Austen's presence as a narrator" (*TLS* 16). Often, as Fanny reads to Edmund or speaks in voiceover what she has written, we hear passages taken from Jane Austen's juvenilia. For example, when the film opens, young Fanny is reading to her sister from a story she has written. The story comes from Austen's *Love and Freindship* (sic), but Rozema has combined parts of sentences and omitted passages. In Austen's story, in "Letter the 13th," Sophia is "majestically removing" (that is, stealing) a bank note from Macdonald's desk drawer when Macdonald catches her in the act. Sophia chides him for interrupting her and denies that she was stealing anything (*MW* 96). Her friend Laura (not Eliza) is not present at this time. In the film, Fanny reads:

> ...and just as Eliza was majestically removing a fifty pound note from
> the Drawer to her own purse, we were suddenly, most impertinently
> interrupted by old Macdonald himself. We called up all the winning dig-
> nity of our sex to do what must be done: Sophia shrieked and fainted

> and I screamed and instantly ran mad. For an Hour and a quarter did
> we continue in this unfortunate situation—Sophia fainting every
> moment and I running Mad as often.

Rozema has drawn some of this material from a passage occurring later
in Letter 13, in which Laura and Sophia see their husbands lying dead in
the road. This passage reads in part:

> Sophia shreiked (sic) and fainted on the Ground—I screamed and
> instantly ran mad.—.We remained thus mutually deprived of our Senses
> some minutes, & on regaining them were deprived of them again—.
> For an Hour and a Quarter did we continue in this unfortunate Situa-
> tion—Sophia fainting every moment and I running Mad as often. [*MW*
> 99]

It is apparent from Rozema's film that Fanny is a precocious child with a
head full of romance novels and an eye for the absurd. Jane Austen was
apparently fifteen when she wrote *Love and Friendship* (*MW* 1). Much
later in the film, just before Sir Thomas informs her of Henry Crawford's
marriage proposal, the mature Fanny reads aloud to herself from what she
has written: "From this period, the intimacy between them daily increased
till at length it grew to such a pitch, that they did not scruple to kick one
another out of the window on the lightest provocation." This passage,
which substitutes "they" for "the families of Fitzroy, Drummond, and
Falknor," comes from Austen's *Frederic and Elfrida: A Novel* (*MW* 6), which
Austen wrote when she was between twelve and fifteen (*MW* 1). Ironically, the lines which Fanny was supposed to have written at eleven and
the lines which Fanny was supposed to have written at twenty-one were
both written by Jane Austen as a teenager.

Rozema shows young Fanny becoming older Fanny as she reads from
Austen's juvenile work *The History of England.* First she looks at the camera and reads: "It was in this reign that Joan of Arc lived and made such
a row among the English. They should not have burnt her but they did...."
Following a dissolve, Fanny continues to read: "Henry the 7th. His majesty
died, and was succeeded by his son Henry whose only merit was his not
being quite so bad as his daughter Elizabeth." (The Fanny in this scene is
seen only indistinctly, but she is older than the first speaker.) After another
dissolve, Fanny (Frances O'Connor) looks at the camera and reads: "And
then that disgrace to humanity, that pest of society, Elizabeth, who, Mur-
deress and Wicked Queen that she was, confined her cousin, the lovely
Mary Queen of Scots for 19 YEARS and then brought her to an untimely,
unmerited, and scandalous Death. Much to eternal shame of the Monar-
chy and the entire Kingdom." At this point, we also see the older (about

26) Edmund (Jonny Lee Miller*) for the first time. He has been Fanny's audience for her reading from her history of England.

This Fanny is also more assertive and much more physically active than the Fanny of the novel. After the child Fanny turns into a young woman, she can be seen chasing Edmund as they run downstairs toward the stables. Later, she actually rides her horse, Mrs. Shakespeare, at night in a rainstorm. There is never any mention of her feeling ill or weak. She is reminiscent of Elizabeth Bennet in the 1995 *Pride and Prejudice*—obviously in robust health and something of a tomboy. Fanny, however, is on a more familiar footing with a male friend than any of the other Austen film characters, except perhaps Cher in *Clueless*. At one point we see Fanny lying on her stomach on her bed, kicking her feet in the air, while Edmund listens to her read aloud. This scene, like many others, presents Fanny as having a twentieth century girl's ease with the opposite sex.

An important omission from the Miramax adaptation is Fanny's brother William. William is Fanny's correspondent and the dearest member of her family. He is particularly important because Henry Crawford's successful efforts to get him a commission complicate Fanny's reaction to Henry's proposal. In addition, the BBC film often has Fanny in voiceover reading the letters she writes to him, and thereby reporting events at Mansfield Park. In the Miramax version, Fanny's letters to her sister are read in voiceover to convey information to the viewer. William is also important as a reason for the ball's being given, since Sir Thomas wishes to honor both William and Fanny. In the Miramax film it is given solely for Fanny's benefit, to show her off to prospective suitors.

The issue of slavery enters the Miramax film early and pervades it. As Fanny is on her way from Portsmouth to Northhamptonshire, the coach pauses on the road overlooking a bay where a tall ship lies at anchor. She hears a plaintive song coming from the ship. The coachman says, "Black cargo" and he explains that perhaps a captain or ship's doctor is bringing some "darkies" home for his wife. This song will be heard again when Fanny is on her way back to Portsmouth and again during the credits. Rozema explains in her commentary on the DVD that the lyrics of the song, "Djongna" (slavery), tell how a young African has been taken from his home. He sees a bird and asks it to take a message telling of his plight first to his mother, then to his father and then to the elders of his village. When this song is first heard it can easily be associated with Fanny, who, like the slaves on board the ship, is being taken far from home.

An interesting bit of trivia: When Jonny Lee Miller was ten, he played the role of Charles Price, Fanny's brother, in the 1983 adaptation of Mansfield Park.

In the novel slavery is mentioned only one time—Fanny tells Edmund that when she brought up the subject of slavery in the presence of the family, nobody said anything. In the BBC film, the topic is not mentioned. In the Miramax film, slavery is mentioned again when, after Sir Thomas has chided Fanny for her boisterous behavior, she tells Edmund that Sir Thomas is sorry that he ever took her in. Edmund tells her that he speaks harshly because he is troubled over "problems with the plantation." He adds, "The abolitionists are making inroads." Fanny responds, "That's a good thing, isn't it?" Edmund points out that they all live off the profits from slavery, even Fanny.* Edmund appears to be justifying his father's manner and even his role as a slave-owner, but in a later scene he rebukes his father for his mistaken ideas about mulattos. Rozema commented that she had intended to show Sir Thomas reading a ledger which listed the slaves who had died on the plantation, but in the final cut the viewer cannot see what he is reading (DVD Commentary).

The handling of the character of Tom Bertram (James Purefoy) in the Miramax film is also significantly different from both that in the novel and that in the BBC version. In both the novel and the BBC adaptation, Sir Thomas takes Tom into his study and chastises him for his reckless expenditures, which have caused Sir Thomas to have to sell a benefice meant for Edmund. Tom is penitent and says that he hopes to have better fortune. However, he does not intend to give up gaming and horse racing. He just hopes for better luck. In the Miramax film, Tom is not just the indulged elder son. He is also a deeply troubled young man. We have earlier seen him drinking as a teenager. On the day that Fanny arrived at Mansfield Park, Mrs. Norris points out to her one of Tom's paintings— a self-portrait showing himself holding a canvas in one hand, with his other hand palm outward to the viewer, and the figure of Death with its hand on his shoulder. When we next see Tom, he and his father are raging at each other. Sir Thomas says to him, "You will do as I say." Tom says, "And do as you do? Even I have principles, Father." As will become clear by the end of the film, Sir Thomas is to blame for his son's self-destructive and rebellious behavior. It is interesting that Tom, who has only a minor role in the novel, takes on the role of his father's conscience in this film. Edmund, who is so right-thinking in the novel and in the BBC adaptation, seems untouched by the family's ownership of slaves. The ambiguity of Edmund's attitude toward his family's ownership of

---

*Omitted from the film but present in the published screenplay are Edmund's comments about a load of slaves from Loanga, West Africa, which Sir Thomas had bought. Edmund says that these slaves are unhappy, and Fanny observes that the slaves must miss their families. Edmund reminds her that Mansfield Park "is entirely dependent on the profits of that operation... It's not, it's not ... clear" (33).

slaves is problematic in the film, and makes the viewer unsure that a person so indecisive and complacent really deserves to win Fanny.

When Sir Thomas goes to Antigua to attempt to improve his income from his plantation, he takes Tom along. The BBC adaptation devotes considerable time to showing how Mrs. Norris manages to get Maria engaged to Mr. Rushworth while Sir Thomas is gone. We also see the introduction of Mary and Henry Crawford to the family, and the important episode in which Fanny, Mrs. Norris, Henry, Mary, Maria, and Julia visit Sotherton. On this outing, we see the jealous maneuvering of the two sisters to win Henry Crawford's affection, and we hear Maria say to Henry that, although engaged to Rushworth, she anticipates feeling restrained in her marriage. She compares herself to the starling in Laurence Sterne's *A Sentimental Journey*, who laments, "I can't get out." Henry suggests that, just as they may go around the gate, to which Rushworth has the key, so may she evade the confinement of marriage.

The Miramax film omits the visit to Sotherton. However, Rozema effectively stages the introduction of the Crawfords to the bored inhabitants of Mansfield Park. When the butler announces the pair, we first see only their backs as they face the family. Then, in slow motion, at thirty frames a second instead of the usual twenty-four, Rozema shoots the reactions of Maria (Victoria Hamilton), who drops her cards, Rushworth (Hugh Bonneville), who gapes, Julia (Justine Waddell) and Lady Bertram (Lindsay Duncan), who smile widely, and Fanny, who has a quizzical look on her face. Then she shoots the Crawfords from the front. The camera tilts up to show Mary Crawford (Embeth Davidtz) from feet to head; then the camera starts at the boots of Henry Crawford (Alessandro Nivola) and tilts up his body to his face. The family is so stunned by the appearance of this elegant pair that Henry sarcastically calls them a "dreary lot." Recovering their wits, Maria and Julia both vie for Henry's attention. As the Crawfords walk back to the parsonage they discuss their visit. Henry says that he prefers an engaged woman because she is more "safe" than an unmarried girl. Mary laments that Tom, the elder son and heir to Mansfield Park, is away from home.

The film makes clear the fascination the Crawfords have for the Bertrams. The Crawfords are like aliens visiting from another world, their world being the fashionable society of Regency London. In the novel and the BBC adaptation we are told that they have imbibed in their uncle's home and from their fashionable friends a laissez-faire morality. Some critics have said that the novel is about the conflict between the town and country, and that Sir Thomas represents country virtues (Mudrick 173; Trilling 136). Edmund blames Mary's uncle for her occasional lapses of decorum. When asked about whether she knows William's captain, Mary indicates that she meets only the higher level naval officers. When she puns that she is familiar with "rears" and "vices," Edmund and Fanny are shocked. In the film, she is even more indiscreet. She plays billiards with the men, and she takes a drag from Henry's cigarillo. In the novel, she asks the question, "Who is to be Anhalt? What gentleman among you am I to have the pleasure of making love to?" (*MP* 143). The BBC adaptation places no particular emphasis on this speech, but in the Miramax version, it is a show stopper. Here Mary leans back against the billiard table and addresses this speech to the men. They react with astonishment. Rozema obviously expects the viewer to interpret "making love" as the carnal act, its twentieth-century meaning, rather than as wooing, its nineteenth-century meaning.

The costumes which the women wear in the two adaptations reflect the directors' different approaches to filming the novel. In the BBC version, Fanny's clothing is plain and unadorned, in white or pastel colors. Mary also wears mostly pastel colors, but her clothes are more elegant and more tailored. On several occasions she wears a crimson velvet spencer over her dress. Her bonnets are far more elaborate than Fanny's. We are

Mansfield Park (Miramax 1999). Edmund Bertram (Jonny Lee Miller) and Mary Crawford (Embeth Davidtz). (Photofest)

told that the white dress that Fanny wears to visit the parsonage and that she wears to the ball is the one which she was given to wear to Maria's wedding. Neither Fanny, Mary, nor the Bertram girls, shows much décolletage. In the Miramax version, Fanny wears dark nondescript jumpers of a heavy material over long-sleeved blouses as her everyday clothing. Troost and Greenfield, citing a press release, state that Andrea Gale, the costume designer, in her choice of clothing for Fanny, "went for simplicity of dress coupled with strength" ("Mouse" 191). Fanny's clothing is in keeping with the wardrobe of a girl who is not concerned about how she looks, and her dresses are loose and full enough that she can ride her horse without changing into a riding habit. However, the dress she wears to the ball is white with embroidered flowers on it, a frock suitable for Cinderella. Indeed, the contrast between her previous clothing and this dress make her seem to be a Cinderella. It is in the empire style, with a shaped bodice and décolletage. In the scenes following the ball, Fanny continues to wear dark loose dresses, but she now shows a great deal of bosom. (Perhaps this is what is meant by "coming out," a term much discussed in the novel.) Fanny wears a form-fitting red coat and no hat when she travels to Portsmouth. Apparently, Rozema felt that hats were not appropriate for Fanny, even for traveling. Given the obsession with hats manifested by the women of the period, Fanny's hatlessness represents a significant disregard for period fashion on the part of the director.

The most striking apparel is that worn by Mary Crawford. In her first appearance at Mansfield Park she wears a mannish hat, a dark skirt, a blouse with a high white ruff, and a form-fitting long-sleeved jacket. In her two most shocking scenes (the scene in the billiard room and the scene in which the family hears of Maria's disgrace) she wears the same flowing black velvet dress—with décolletage and long perforated sleeves. She never wears pastels. Mary's apparel is darker than one would expect for 1806, when young unmarried women wore mostly light colors. The clothing of the Bertram girls is more typical of period clothing. Mary exudes sophistication and, perhaps, decadence. The women's costumes are just one more area where Rozema modernized the look of the film and attempted to suggest qualities of character through costume. She generally operated on the principle that visual impact is more important than authenticity.

In the treatment of the play we also see entirely different sensibilities and purposes at work. As usual the BBC version follows the novel closely. Tom and his friend Yates (Charles Edwards) are the prime instigators, but Henry is also eager to act. When Henry urges Julia not to play the role of Agatha, she sees clearly that he favors Maria. Julia declares that she will not play any role. When Tom calls on Fanny to play the cottager's wife, she vehemently refuses, saying that she cannot act. Mrs. Norris chides her for not being willing to assist her cousins. Fanny has two reasons for refusing. For one thing, she does not want to exhibit herself. It is also clear in the novel and the BBC version that she agrees with Edmund that the play, Mrs. Inchbald's *Lovers' Vows*, is not suitable for them to present, especially given Maria's situation as an engaged woman. Mrs. Norris, instead of seeing the unsuitability of the play, concentrates her efforts on saving money on the green cloth that must be bought for a curtain. Lady Bertram is, as usual, swayed by whoever talks to her last. The outcome is that Edmund is too much tempted by the thought of playing a key role opposite Mary Crawford to sustain his resistance to the scheme. Fanny is uncomfortable when both Mary and Edmund come to her to rehearse their lines, forcing her to become a reluctant observer of their courtship.

Reviewers were agog over what they interpreted as lesbian overtones in the Miramax film, particularly in the scene in which Mary rehearses her lines with Fanny. In this adaptation, Fanny does not refuse to play a role in the play. Rather, when Henry asks her opinion of the project, Aunt Norris embarrasses Fanny by telling her to go about her work. She apparently fears that Fanny is being looked upon as the equal to the privileged young people. Fanny sheds tears of frustration as she stands outside the room and hears Henry discussing with the others whether Fanny is "out" in society. When the plans go forward for the play, Edmund comes to Fanny's room to complain that an outsider is to be brought in to take part. Then, Mary, wishing to rehearse with Fanny, comes into her room. Edmund decides to play Anhalt only after he watches Mary reading her part with Fanny. This scene is profoundly suggestive. The camera circles Mary and Fanny as Mary stands close to Fanny and puts her hands around Fanny's waist. Using one of her favorite camera techniques, Rozema enables the viewer to look beyond the girls in the foreground to Edmund, who is watching them.

In this scene, Mary is obviously doing more than practicing her role. She is also flirting with Edmund, and perhaps even with Fanny. Fanny is quite passive at this time, as she is when Mary later removes her wet clothing after finding Fanny outside the parsonage in the rain. Rozema says of the latter scene that Mary's chief interest is in finding out from Fanny what Edmund says about Mary. She calls Mary "Machiavellian" (DVD Commentary). Some reviewers have suggested that Fanny willingly participates in Mary's lesbian advances (Serpico, Kantrowitz). They might legitimately suspect Rozema had included scenes with suggestions of les-

Mansfield Park (Miramax 1999). L–r, Henry Crawford (Alessandro Nivola) and Edmund Bertram (Jonny Lee Miller). (MOMA)

bianism, since her earlier films (*When Night Is Falling*, 1995, and *I've Heard the Mermaids Singing*, 1987) include lesbian characters, but the director, in her comments about the making of the film, says only that Fanny is fascinated by Mary (DVD Commentary).

In the Miramax version, Sir Thomas arrives home to find his house in turmoil: Julia is drinking, Rushworth is preening before a mirror, and Maria, her make-up and clothing awry, is standing close to Henry Crawford. The BBC adaptation does not include such unseemly discoveries, but emphasizes Sir Thomas's displeasure with Yates, whom he finds declaiming in his billiard room, and with Aunt Norris for her cooperation in the play-acting scheme. In both versions, after the dust has settled, Maria realizes that Henry Crawford is not in love with her and asks her father to allow her to marry Rushworth as soon as possible.

The Miramax adaptation includes an effective scene in which Maria watches through a half-open door as Henry Crawford reads to Fanny from Laurence Sterne's *A Sentimental Journey*. Maria realizes that Henry is wooing Fanny. The camera circles Henry and Fanny as he reads about a captive starling. The narrator has heard the bird say, "I can't get out," and he tries to open the cage but cannot. The circling camera and the different views we get of Fanny's apprehensive expression indicate that Crawford is trying to ensnare Fanny and that Fanny is at least vaguely aware of the fact. Rozema introduces the image of the caged starling in order to apply it to both Maria and Fanny, and to the various kinds of captivity which they experience. Rozema points out, however, that the image does not simply suggest that women are locked into cages by men. Maria chooses her cage—marriage with Rushworth (DVD Commentary).

In a telling scene in which Sir Thomas talks freely to his assembled family, he speaks about his slaves. He praises the beauty of mulattos. He says, "The mulattos are in general well-shaped and the women especially well-featured. I have one so easy and graceful in her movements as well." The enthusiasm with which he praises the beauty of his female slave is disturbing to the viewer. He goes on to say that mulattos are like mules, in that two mulattos are unable to produce children. Edmund exchanges a look with Fanny and then chides his father for speaking nonsense. Sir Thomas advises Edmund to read Edward Long's *History of Jamaica* to learn the truth. He says that he is thinking of bringing a slave back to England to work as a servant. At this point Fanny chimes in, saying that if he did so, the slave might have to be freed. She says that she has been reading Thomas Clarkson. No part of this scene appears in the novel. However, in one of Jane Austen's letters she professed admiration for Thomas Clarkson (*Letters* 198). He was a key figure, along with William Wilberforce and Granville Sharp, in the fight which resulted in the abolition of slave trading in the British colonies in 1807. On the other hand, Edward Long, a Jamaican plantation owner, defended the use of African slaves on the sugar plantations in the West Indies and compared mulattos to mules (Long II 335–336). Rozema's addition of these details fits neatly into the time period of the film. Regarding the novel, Avrom Fleishman has pointed out that Jane Austen's contemporaries would have been well aware of the novel's historical context—the economic situation in Antigua resulting from the French embargo which impeded the marketing of the produce of the British-owned sugar plantations and of the abolitionist efforts which led to the Abolition Act (7–8). Since neither the modern reader nor the film viewer would have such awareness, perhaps we can see some justification for Rozema's foregrounding the subject of slavery.

It is surprising, given Sir. Thomas's irascible nature, that he does not take offense at Fanny's comment about slaves. Instead, he reiterates his praise of her improved appearance and speaks of the beauty of her complexion and figure. In the novel, he also notices improvement in Fanny's appearance, but in the Miramax film, Rozema has associated his praise of Fanny with his praise of the beauty of his mulatto slave. When Edmund attempts to focus his father's attention on Fanny's intelligence and upon her writing style, Sir Thomas ignores his remarks. He proposes that he give a ball in Fanny's honor and says, "Surely some young man of good standing will sit up and take notice." Overwhelmed by this unwelcome attention, Fanny leaves the room hastily. When Edmund follows her, she tells him angrily, "I'll not be sold off like one of your father's slaves." She has understood that Sir Thomas perceives that her improved beauty makes her a more marketable product.

Since dances are so much a part of most adaptations of the other Austen novels, it is interesting to contrast their use in these two. In the BBC version, Fanny is horrified when Sir Thomas tells her to lead off the first dance. Fanny looks as attractive as this actress can look, with her hair in curls and wearing her white dress and the cross that William brought her. We see Fanny dancing first with Henry, then with William, and next with Edmund, in a variety of period dances. Her dance with Henry is slow and stately; with her brother she dances a lively jig. When she dances with Edmund, the dance is elaborate and formal, but the dancers hold hands and move close together. Fanny obviously enjoys this dance more than any other. As in the novel, Sir Thomas is the benevolent despot who is pleased with his benevolence toward his poor relations and who finally orders Fanny to bed for her own good. In the Miramax adaptation, the dances are period dances which, according to Rozema, have been adapted to make them more intimate (DVD Commentary). Rather than the over-all patterns or movements, Rozema shows close-ups of hands clasping, hands on waists, laughing faces. She shoots part of the dancing in double time (48 frames per second). When Crawford rejoices that Fanny has complimented his dancing, Fanny says to him, "Keep your wig on." After recovering from shock at this most outrageous modernizing, I was pleased at both Rozema's and Fanny's audacity. The viewer's general impression of the ball is of Fanny's delight in the dancing and of Henry's and Edmund's appreciation of Fanny. Fanny leaves the dance of her own accord, wine glass in hand, to go to her room.

A strong subtext in the Miramax film is the similarity of the situation of women in that time to the captivity of slaves. Women moved from their parents' control to their husbands' control. Those who were not able to find a husband found themselves enslaved by poverty or by the whims of relatives. Jane Austen experienced, if not poverty, living with only a small income and sometimes was embarrassed because she was unable even to tip the servants appropriately at her brother's mansion when she stayed there (Myer 120). Marriage could bring a woman a measure of independence and security, but marriage was a terminal state. As Maria Bertram discovers after she has married Rushworth, she is like a bird in

Mansfield Park (Miramax 1999). Sir Thomas Bertram (Harold Pinter) reminds Fanny Price (Frances O'Connor) of her duty. (MOMA)

a cage. She can't get out. Only death or disgrace will deliver her from her marriage. Fanny feels bound by gratitude and material obligations to Sir Thomas, who has been her surrogate father. After all, he has supported her and educated her for ten years. Sir Thomas is more dictatorial to Fanny, his wife's niece, than to his daughters. He tells Maria that she does not have to marry Rushworth if she does not love him. After Henry proposes to Fanny, Sir Thomas insists that Fanny marry him, even when she says that she does not love him.

In the BBC version, as in the novel, Sir Thomas is not so ferocious to Fanny as he is in the Miramax version. He does not understand her reluctance to marry a man who has helped her brother and could help her family. He thinks it extraordinary good luck for this penniless girl to have made such a good catch. Even Edmund thinks that in time Fanny will accept Henry, and he encourages his father in this belief. After Sir Thomas gets over his outrage, he calms down and speaks kindly to her. He invites Crawford to frequent the house so that he may further his suit. Finally, however, Sir Thomas decides to send Fanny with William back to Portsmouth, thinking that being deprived of the luxuries of Mansfield Park might make her more ready to accept Henry.

Harold Pinter as Sir Thomas shows great severity in his manner to Fanny. His language is essentially that of the novel, but presented as if in a harangue delivered over the space of several days in different places in the house. We get close-ups of Pinter's dark, frowning countenance as he accuses Fanny of ingratitude to him, selfishness, and "wilfulness of temper, self-conceit, and every tendency to that independence of spirit which prevails so much in modern days. [...]" Although this accusation is taken directly from the novel (*MP* 318), in the context of the film, it associates Fanny with the perverse voices of the times which were calling for freedom for all enslaved peoples.

The portrayals of Fanny's home in Portsmouth mainly differ in that Rozema emphasizes the extreme poverty of Fanny's home. The BBC portrayal, and that of the novel, emphasize the lack of order and quiet. These are the qualities of Mansfield Park which Fanny chiefly misses. It is made clear that nobody appears to care whether Fanny is there or not. Her mother, father, and brothers are much more interested in William than in Fanny. Fanny is an outsider in her own home. Rozema says that she tried to make the poverty of Fanny's home "visceral" (DVD Commentary). She conveys vividly the smallness, the congestion, and the darkness of the rooms. She shows dirty dishes and maggots on the table. When Crawford visits, he surreptitiously wipes off a fork and reluctantly takes a bite of what Rozema describes in the published screenplay as "a glob of grisly meat in a vomitlike sauce" (112). Fanny is also shown cutting up vegetables and tending the fire. In the bed which she shares with two sisters, Fanny scratches in her sleep, obviously fending off a bed-bug or other insect.

Some reviewers of the Miramax film objected to having Fanny accept Crawford's proposal and then reject him. They find this vacillation out of keeping with Fanny as Austen portrayed her. Rozema justifies this deviation from the novel by saying that she based the incident on Jane Austen's own acceptance and next-day rejection of Harris Bigg-Wither (DVD Commentary). It is also possible to justify it from the novel itself, since we are told that had Henry not dallied with Maria, then Edmund would have married Mary, and Fanny would probably have married Crawford. A particular reason for Rozema to have Fanny accept Crawford at Portsmouth is that it shows Fanny, after she thinks that Edmund is going to marry Mary Crawford, yielding to the temptation to escape the poverty which appears to be her only other choice. Henry Crawford is very attentive. He offers to assist her parents. He realizes that Fanny loves Edmund, and he comforts her when Edmund's letter tells her that he can see himself marrying no one except Mary Crawford. The present which he has delivered to the door one morning is symbolic. A boy delivers a crate of white pigeons on a cart. As another boy plays an hand organ, the first boy lights fireworks and releases the pigeons. They soar into the air and thus express the freedom which Fanny desires—a freedom from poverty which Henry Crawford can supply.

This film makes Henry Crawford a more sympathetic figure than that in the BBC film. Whereas in the novel and the BBC adaptation Henry Crawford sets out to amuse himself by making Fanny fall in love with him, in the Miramax film he appears really to fall in love with her. We come to empathize with Crawford as he tries to win Fanny, and to feel sorry for him when she tells him that she has changed her mind. He comes into the kitchen the morning after she accepted him, bearing a bouquet of daisies, sneaks up on Fanny who is facing the fire, and sings out, "Good morning, Miss Price." When she turns and rebuffs him, we cringe in empathetic embarrassment.

Mrs. Norris in the BBC adaptation is presented as an officious busybody, parsimonious and very much a toady when it comes to ingratiating herself with Sir Thomas. Anna Massey is effective in this interpretation of the character. She has a pinched, narrow face and rushes about talking incessantly. Rozema states, however, that she sees Mrs. Norris as one who thought that she should have been the mistress of Mansfield Park, instead of her indolent, beautiful sister (DVD Commentary). Thus Rozema chose a different type of actress, one who still has the vestiges of good looks. Sheila Gish as Mrs. Norris is a sour and envious woman who cannot endure seeing Fanny the recipient of the kind of marriage offer that she would like to have had. We glimpse her personal vanity when, like Maria and Julia, she primps in front of a mirror in preparation for the arrival of the Crawfords.

In another daring characterization, Rozema presents Lady Bertram as a laudanum addict. In both the novel and the BBC film, Lady Bertram (Angela Pleasence) is an indolent and slow-witted couch potato, who cares more about her pug dog than about her children. In the Miramax film, she is indolent and oblivious. We see her dozing in the background of several scenes. When Sir Thomas returns from Antigua, she greets him happily, but gives the impression that whether he had been gone a year or a day would have been all the same to her. Ironically, she is the only one really happy to see him. Lindsay Duncan, who plays this role, also plays Mrs. Price, Lady Bertram's sister. Having the same actress play both roles suggests to the viewer that Lady Bertram in a hovel would have been as slatternly and as poor a housekeeper as Mrs. Price.

Rozema has remarked on the novel's ambiguous sexuality. On the

DVD, she comments on the brother/sister relationship of Fanny and Edmund, and the film shows them struggling to deal with their growing sexual love for each other. In particular one recalls the scene where Edmund's head falls over on Fanny's bosom as they ride in the carriage toward Mansfield Park. Later, when Edmund is attempting to comfort Fanny after she has found Maria and Crawford together, they nearly kiss each other on the mouth. The marriage of first cousins was much more common and acceptable in Jane Austen's time than it is today. Sir Thomas in the novel was apprehensive about the possibility of one of his son's being interested in Fanny mainly because he considered his sons worthy of a better match. Rozema's treatment of this romance suggests something of a modern disapproval of it. Her suggestion that a father may have a sexual interest in his daughter is, however, even more typical of modern attitudes. Rozema shows Fanny's father (Hilton McRae) as overly enthusiastic about his daughter's appearance as he greets her upon her homecoming and embraces her, while shots of her mother's and Susan's reactions suggest an uneasiness perhaps deriving from their own experience. Even the scene in which Sir Thomas dwells on Fanny's improved beauty makes the viewer squirm with discomfort.

In the novel and in the BBC film Fanny learns about Henry and Maria's flight while in Portsmouth. She also learns of Tom's illness and yearns to be summoned back to Mansfield Park. Edmund comes to take both Fanny and Susan back to Mansfield. In the BBC adaptation, the family, including the invalid Tom, greets them. Sir Thomas is in London. Later, as Edmund and Fanny sit alone together, with rain falling outside the window, Edmund tells Fanny about his last meeting with Mary in London. A close-up of Edmund's face fades to show in a flashback Mary receiving Edmund in the library. She condemns Henry and Maria, not for the sin of adultery, but for their lack of discretion. She says that Fanny is to blame for the affair, because she did not return Henry's affection. In her opinion, had Fanny married Henry, the relationship between Henry and Maria would have ended in a kind of "regular standing flirtation." She says that they must urge Henry to marry Maria and it may yet all turn out well. They can invite the couple to dinners and gradually reintroduce them to good society. She says that fortunately there is "more liberality" about such things nowadays. While she is speaking, Edmund looks shocked. He finally says to her, "To be detected in a folly is the greatest crime you know." He says that he is appalled at her indifference to morality and to feeling. He realizes that the woman he has loved is a creature of his imagination. She retorts that he is preaching to her. He excuses himself and leaves. As he goes out into the hall, she follows him and calls to him, but he resists the temptation to go back to her. Following the flashback, he tells Fanny that, even though he regrets his loss, he knows he did the right thing. We see Fanny in profile, as she listens to him call her his "dearest Fanny" and as he takes her hand. He says, "What shall I do if you ever go away?" She says, "I shall never."

The Miramax film picks up considerable speed following Fanny's return to Mansfield Park. Four big scenes fall like thunderbolts on the viewer. In the first one Fanny finds Tom's sketchbook, full of drawings of slaves being abused. Although the viewer may feel that such explicitness is unnecessary to make the point that Sir Thomas's wealth derives from the blood of slaves, Rozema said that this scene is the reason that she made the film (DVD Commentary). She said that she wanted "to show the disregard for human dignity that must have been the case" (DVD Commentary). Thus, we see in one sketch Sir Thomas whipping a slave and in another a female slave kneeling in front of Sir Thomas, perhaps to perform a sexual act. One drawing, done by William Blake, a contemporary of Jane Austen, shows a slave bound with ropes and hanging on a hook. In another, a woman is being gang raped by several young men; this sketch is ironically titled "Our Neighbors." While Fanny is looking at these images, and while the sound of groans and screams merge with the music in the background, Sir Thomas comes into the room, grabs the sketchbook, and begins to feed the pages into the fire. He says, "My son is mad." Indeed, the viewer does not know whether the sketches showing Sir Thomas represent reality or Tom's fevered imagination. The viewer wonders how Sir Thomas could have any redeeming qualities if he is as bad as Tom thinks him.

The second shocker occurs later that evening. Earlier that day, Maria and Julia have come home, and later Henry Crawford calls at Mansfield Park. We see Crawford with Maria in the library. She says that she wishes that he could feel about her as he does about Fanny. That night we see a shadowy figure approaching Mansfield Park. Fanny, hearing noises, gets out of bed to go to Tom's room. Her candle having gone out, Fanny goes into Maria's room rather than Tom's. She finds Henry Crawford in bed with Maria. She staggers out into the hall and into Tom's room, where Edmund asks her what is wrong. Sobbing, she can only point down the hall. Edmund goes in that direction and finds Henry Crawford, now with his pants on, and Maria in bed with a sheet pulled up to cover her nakedness. Henry doesn't speak, but Maria attempts to justify herself by saying, "I can't get out," reiterating the refrain of Sterne's caged bird. Edmund goes back to Fanny to comfort her.

After this, a comic interlude provides some relief. Maria's husband arrives with a newspaper reporter in tow. He has already been to the parsonage looking for Henry and has not found him. Now he is looking for Maria to brag about how the newspaper will carry an article about the improvements to his estate. The reporter is obviously much interested to find that Mrs. Rushworth, as well as Henry Crawford, has disappeared.

The third big scene shows the family gathered in a salon, with Mary Crawford also present. Sir Thomas asks Fanny to read an item in the newspaper reporting that Mrs. Rushworth has run away with Henry Crawford. When Fanny finishes reading, Mary tells the family that they must make the best of Henry and Maria's indiscretion. They must do nothing, but hope that Henry will marry Maria. Then, if the Bertrams receive the couple, all may be well. She says that she and Edmund will give good dinners and large parties and enable Henry and Maria to reenter society. Wearing her slinky black dress, she walks back and forth in front of her mostly silent audience. Fanny asks her how she and Edmund will be able to afford these dinners and parties. Mary shocks everyone, even the befogged Lady Bertram, by saying that she expects Tom to die, thereby making Edmund the heir. She says to Fanny that "it could all be construed as your fault" for not marrying Henry. Mary says that if Fanny had accepted Henry, he would not have run off with Maria. They could merely have had a "regular standing flirtation" when they met in society. When she has finished her monologue, Edmund stands up and says, "You are a stranger to me." He tells her that he does not know her, and that he does not want to know her. She leaves the room. This scene is much more dramatic than either the novel's presentation of Edmund's conversation with Mary or the BBC's. It includes the whole family, except Tom, and contrives to show both Mary's amorality and her callous and mercenary hope that Tom will die.

The final scene before the epilogue is set in Tom's bedroom, where Sir Thomas, holding the hand of his sleeping son, hears the doctor say, "Time can do anything." Sir Thomas says that he knows Tom will recover. He reminisces that as a boy Tom liked to pretend that he was Tom the Knight. He would ask his father to give him a noble mission. The implication is that as Tom grew up he realized that Sir Thomas was no King Arthur, but a slave-owner. Sir Thomas accepts responsibility for the psychological problems which have led Tom so near the death that he had anticipated as a youth. He says to Tom, "I'm sorry, Tom. So sorry." In the novel Sir Thomas experiences awareness of his failings, mainly regarding the education of his daughters. In this film, his sins of omission and commission are much greater. They are perhaps too great to justify as happy an ending as Rozema provides.

The BBC film ties up the loose ends by having Fanny read in voiceover her letter to William. Here we learn that Mr. Rushworth gets his divorce. Mrs. Norris, who has left Mansfield Park to set up a home for Maria, is seen traveling in a carriage. Julia and Yates, who had eloped shortly after Maria had run off with Crawford, are married and come home to make peace with Sir Thomas. Then we see Fanny's mother, children, and father in church. Fanny in voiceover tells William that today she is to be married to Edmund, and we see Edmund and Fanny standing before a clergyman in the church. Fanny also tells William that since Dr. Grant is leaving, she and Edmund will live in the parsonage, "within the view and patronage of Mansfield Park." The final shot is of Fanny and Edmund sitting on a bench on the parsonage lawn, with Pug (or an offspring of Pug) in front of them.

In the Miramax film, Fanny in ironic voiceover tells the viewer that things might have turned out differently, but they didn't. Swooping flocks of computer-generated starlings and a soaring camera separate the episodes of the epilogue. As the narrator tells us that Henry Crawford did not marry Maria, we see Mrs. Norris and Maria in a cottage by the sea, both looking regretful. Next, a soaring camera shot shows Henry and Mary Crawford with a pair of stylish young people taking tea on a lawn. There's a freeze-frame shot of Henry and Mary looking off in opposite directions, while their companions look slyly at each other. Apparently the Crawfords have found kindred spirits with whom to pass the time. More swooping starlings, and the camera soars again to come to rest at Mansfield Park, where Edmund and Fanny sit by a pond. Edmund declares his love to Fanny. He says that he has loved her all of his life— "as a man loves a woman. As a hero loves a heroine." They embrace and Fanny smiles confidingly at the viewer over Edmund's shoulder. Behind them Sir Thomas and Lady Bertram may be seen strolling on the lawn, she making a witticism about Fanny and Edmund—"It looks as if they're finally getting someplace." The narrator says that Susan (Sophia Myles) has come to live at Mansfield Park. We see her reciting a history lesson to Julia, who is much interested in a letter which she has received from Mr. Yates.* We also see Tom seated in a chair on the lawn, sketchbook in hand.

The voiceover tells us that Sir Thomas gave up his interests in Antigua and decided to pursue "opportunities in tobacco." In the published screenplay this voiceover statement is present, but in the earlier, unpublished screenplay the voiceover states that he chose some "exciting

---

*There's no sight or mention of Julia in this scene in the published screenplay.

new opportunities in India" (165). Apparently Rozema was uncertain about how Sir Thomas could give up being a slave owner yet support Mansfield Park. If Sir Thomas divested himself of his plantations in Antigua, he probably sold the land and slaves to someone else. If Sir Thomas invested the money gained from the sale of his slaves, he would still be living off money earned by slave labor, and to invest in tobacco doubles the likelihood that the labor of slaves would be generating the interest on his investment. Had Sir Thomas been truly sorry for his exploitation of slaves, he might have liberated his slaves and have paid them wages to operate his plantations. Susan Morgan states that after 1802 it was frequently argued in Parliament that planters could actually improve their profits by turning to wage labor. She cites Henry Brougham's pamphlet "Inquiry into the Colonial Policy of the European Powers" (1803), which supported the abolition of slavery partly on this basis (90). If, as Alistair Duckworth asserts, Rozema's purpose is "to depict the moral ruin of Mansfield Park's inhabitants" (565), she backs away from any real penance for Sir Thomas. If Sir Thomas were as bad a man as he is portrayed in the film, a greater sacrifice, and not only of money, would have been necessary to redeem him—perhaps the death of his elder son.

Finally, as we see Fanny and Edmund walking toward the parsonage, he tells her that a publisher is interested in her writing. The conclusion is vaguely nostalgic and whimsical, as the narrator reiterates that it might have turned out differently, but it didn't. Claudia Johnson points out that this refrain, which accompanies the vignettes of the epilogue, reminds the viewer of the "benign yet unblinking intervention" of Fanny's art (Rozema *Final Shooting Script*, Introduction 9).

The cover of the videotape, of the DVD and of the published screenplay of the Miramax *Mansfield Park* shows a smug-looking Frances O'Connor looking directly at the viewer. She holds a large key close to her bosom. At the bottom of the picture is a great house in the Adam style. The implication appears to be that Fanny has the key—spiritually and physically—to Mansfield Park. With her intelligence, her keen sense of morality, and her persistence, she has emerged triumphant over those who have sought to corrupt Mansfield Park and, by reforming even the master of the house, has established herself as the true daughter of the house. This is indeed very much the point of the novel and of the BBC mini-series. However, Rozema has stated that Fanny has escaped from the "decay" and "rot" at the heart of Mansfield Park. "Fanny Price finally escapes with, yes, her true love to another place: a parsonage!" ("Place" 3). Troost and Greenfield, in another twist, which makes even better sense than Rozema's interpretation, argue that Fanny's writing constitutes her key to freedom, a freedom not dependent on Mansfield Park or her marriage to Edmund ("Mouse" 201). I feel that in some ways the conclusion to the Miramax *Mansfield Park* exemplifies the problems implicit in Rozema's radical reinterpretation of the novel—the problem of Sir Thomas's penance, the problem of Edmund's acceptance of the family's dependence on slaves, the problem of Fanny's love for Mansfield Park. Perhaps the reinterpretation was not radical enough.

V

Emma

Jane Austen's *Emma*, published in 1815, represents Jane Austen at her complicated best. In style, organization, and character development, this novel represents the high point of her literary accomplishment. Having at its center Emma Woodhouse, a character whom Austen said nobody but herself would like (Austen-Leigh, *Memoir* 157), the novel reveals Emma's passage from immature girl to mature woman. Emma is "handsome, clever ... rich, and ... twenty-one" (*E* 5). Like Marianne of *Sense and Sensibility* in her tendency to let her imagination or sensibility run away with her, but like Elizabeth in *Pride and Prejudice* in her over-confidence in her own judgment, Emma fantasizes about those around her and is convinced of the rightness of her opinions. Unlike these other heroines, however, Emma attempts to manipulate others into or out of love relationships. The novel is primarily about her path to self-knowledge, learning from her own mistakes and from the loving guidance of a good man.

The novel is remarkable among Jane Austen's novels both for its limited setting and its sense of community. Although some characters come to Highbury from the outside world, and others leave for brief periods, Emma never leaves the close environs of her little village where she reigns as undisputed queen. The rank and respective status of the inhabitants of Highbury are quite clear. Mr. George Knightley, master of Donwell Abbey, is the most respected and influential man in the area. He is in many respects the ideal country squire, taking an active part in running his estate and extending his benevolence to those in need. He does not keep carriage horses, preferring to walk, and when he wishes to use his carriage to pick up the Bateses and Jane Fairfax, he rents horses at the Crown Inn. Emma is one of two daughters of Mr. Woodhouse, the owner of Hartfield and the second most prominent man in the neighborhood. His

107

estate is small but he has an ancient name and a fortune little inferior to that of Mr. Knightley. With her fortune of 30,000 pounds, Emma is a matrimonial prize, comparable to Georgiana Darcy in the marriage mart. Emma is the only one of Austen's heroines who is wealthy and who does not have to marry in order to be comfortably independent. Having been the sole mistress of the house since she was sixteen, she caters to her father and dominates him. Her chief disadvantage is that her field of operation is so limited. Her sister, Isabella, is married to John Knightley, the brother of Mr. George Knightley and a lawyer in London. Isabella, who visits her father with her children and husband at Christmas, appears to be much like her father in her tendency to worry about her own and her children's health. It is no wonder that Emma thinks so well of her own ability and judgment when she compares them to the weakness and indecisiveness of her nearest relatives.

The Knightleys and Woodhouses represent high society in the little pond that is Highbury. One level down we have the Westons. Mr. Weston is of good family and has been in the military, but he has made his money in trade. The vicar and his wife, the Eltons, also may be included in this level. We have no knowledge of Mr. Elton's origins, except that he is "without any alliances but in trade" (*E* 136). Because he is a clergyman and has a modicum of social skills, he is invited to the homes of the Woodhouses and Westons. His bride's family made their money in trade, and Augusta comes into her marriage with a substantial dowry of about 10,000 pounds. She offends Emma's sense of propriety with her frequent references to the Sucklings, her sister's family, who have a large estate near Bristol and a barouche-landau. Mrs. Bates, having been the wife of a vicar, has a courtesy connection with this level of society. She and her unmarried daughter live in rented rooms above a shop in Highbury. They have little income and depend upon the kindness of the Woodhouses and Mr. Knightley for luxuries such as apples and pork loin. Mrs. Goddard, mistress of the village school, also forms a part of the social circle on which Mr. Woodhouse depends for card games and company.

Beyond these we find those in the village who are rising in status because of their economic success. The Coles have prospered in trade and are able to invite even Miss Woodhouse to dinner. Extremely aware of social differences, Emma is reluctant to go until she finds that the Westons and Mr. Churchill are going. As members of the emerging class, the Coles' offspring may soon find themselves acceptable marriage partners to sons and daughters of the Westons or Knightleys, as the Bingleys are to the Bennets in *Pride and Prejudice*. Others on the rise, but not as successful as the Coles, include Robert Martin, a farmer on the Donwell

Abbey estate, and the Coxes, country lawyers in Highbury. Apparently, Mr. Perry, the apothecary, is prosperous enough to speak of setting up a carriage, which would represent a considerable expense, but would give his family a certain prestige. There is also a passing reference to Dr. Hughes, who as a physician would rank above Mr. Perry.

Below these we find Mr. and Mrs. Ford, who keep a shop where gloves and ribbons may be purchased, Mrs. Wallis, the pastry cook's wife, and Mrs. Stokes, the landlady of the Crown Inn. We also hear of William Larkins, steward of Mr. Knightley, and of Miss Nash, Miss Prince, and Miss Richardson, who teach at the school. Harriet Smith might also have figured at this level had Emma not taken her up as her friend. Harriet is the illegitimate daughter of a merchant, who has placed her with Mrs. Goddard but has made no further provision for her. In spite of Emma's fantasizing that she is the daughter of a gentleman and thus worthy of marrying a gentleman, Harriet is fortunate to attract the interest of a prosperous farmer. We also hear of servants—James, Mr. Woodhouse's coachman, Mrs. Hodges, Mr. Knightley's cook, and Patty, the Bateses' maid. Emma and Harriet also pay a visit to a poor family who live a little way out of Highbury. As in other Austen novels, the members of the servant class or lower have little importance in *Emma*.

Characters who come from outside Highbury act as catalysts which change the complexion of the quiet life of the community. When Jane Fairfax comes to visit, she becomes a rival of Emma, superior to her in her musical skills and an object of Mr. Knightley's admiration. She is followed by Frank Churchill, who stirs the pot vigorously. Mrs. Elton, who snubs Harriet and tries to manage Jane, much as Emma has managed Harriet, also makes a contribution. Even the gypsies have an impact on the plot.

The way Austen weaves a tapestry of community relationships is particularly evident in her use of and frequent reference to the Bateses and Mr. Perry. Mrs. Bates and Miss Bates intermingle with both the Knightley/Woodhouse/Weston faction and the Coles, Coxes, and others on that level. Miss Bates is a good, unpretentious, gregarious woman, liked by everyone and received by everyone. She and her mother make a kind of comic pair. The mother is somewhat deaf; the daughter extremely talkative. Emma is impatient of Miss Bates's talk, especially when her topic is Jane Fairfax. Miss Bates's conversation is a disjointed mishmash of trivial gossip, personal revelations, and expressions of gratitude. However, anyone who listens closely to Miss Bates could learn a great deal about what is going on in Highbury—often more than Miss Bates realizes that she is revealing.

A primary emphasis in the novel is Emma's snobbishness. One can imagine that had she been situated in London, rather than in a village, Emma would not have socialized with people such as the Coles, Bateses, and Mrs. Goddard. However, if she does not extend her social interaction beyond her own class, she will be lonely indeed. Having committed to the necessity of this interaction, Emma finds it difficult to avoid continued socializing. As Oliver MacDonagh has pointed out, "[...] [In] so compressed a society personal preference could not safely be indulged" (134). Yet this necessity does not prevent her from being constantly aware of social differences. Her attention to social distinctions contrasts with Mr. Knightley's mode of evaluating people. He does not deny social distinctions, but he gives respect where he feels respect is due. He considers Mr. Martin superior to Harriet Smith, calling him a "respectable, intelligent gentleman-farmer" (*E* 62). Whatever Harriet's parentage, she is only a simple girl with little information and no connections. Mr. Knightley does not despise her, but recognizes that, in spite of her beauty and sweetness, she cannot aspire to better than Mr. Martin. In contrast, we see his opinion of Jane Fairfax, whose father was in the military but who left her no money. She may not have a dowry, but she is intelligent, beautiful, and accomplished. He sees Jane as the appropriate companion for Emma.

Emma, on the other hand, is very conscious of rank. She feels that although Mr. Knightley is the model of a gentleman, he does not always conduct himself in a manner to make people mindful of his rank. She does not like to see him arrive at social occasions on foot. She also thinks that Mr. Elton should not have thought himself good enough for her. She considers herself generous to withhold judgment upon Mrs. Elton until she can see her, but she is already predisposed to find her lacking in manners and accomplishments. The reader is apt to agree with her when she finds the new Mrs. Elton vain, self-important, and familiar. In response to Harriet's query whether she had seen Mr. Martin, Emma says,

> A young farmer, whether on horseback or on foot, is the very last sort of person to raise my curiosity. The yeomanry are precisely the order of people with whom I feel I can have nothing to do. A degree or two lower, and a creditable appearance might interest me; I might hope to be useful to their families in some way or other. [*E* 29]

She later tells Harriet that she is pleased that she refused Mr. Martin, because she "could not have visited Mrs. Robert Martin of Abbey-Mill Farm" (*E* 53). Indeed, at the end of the novel, it is made clear that the intimacy between Emma and Harriet will decline as both assume their new roles as Mrs. Knightley and Mrs. Martin.

The question naturally arises as to what extent the novel reflects Jane Austen's view of class distinctions. In *Emma*, Austen is by no means attacking the assumption that desirable values, information, manners, and accomplishments are more likely to be found among the upper classes than among the lower. There is no example of a really boorish squire—no Squire Western—in the novel. However, in her last novel, *Persuasion*, Austen does show effete and corrupt gentlemen, and portrays self-made men who are superior to these gentlemen.

The history of television dramatization of *Emma* began on Sunday, May 23, 1948, with a production by BBC TV. This adaptation was shown live in black and white from 8:30 p.m. to 10:15 p.m., with a repeat performance at the same time on Thursday, May 27. Judy Campbell wrote the screenplay and acted the role of Emma Woodhouse. Michael Barry is cited on the screenplay as the producer, but there is no credited director. The screenplay reveals the inevitable limitations of live television and the additional limiting factor of the 105-minute period in which the adaptation was presented. The story is slightly compressed—the John Knightleys are omitted, the gypsy attack on Harriet (Daphne Slater, who played Elizabeth Bennet in the BBC's 1952 *P&P)* occurs offstage so that Frank (McDonald Hobley) carries her into the street of Highbury, Mr. Elton (Richard Hurndall) proposes to Emma just after he has delivered the framed picture to Hartfield, Emma insults Miss Bates (Gillian Lind) at the strawberry picking party at Donwell, and there is no trip to Box Hill—but the essentials are there. Oddly enough, Mr. Perry (Victor Platt) has a larger role than usual in the adaptations, but there is no mention of his plans for a carriage. The last scene, at Hartfield, shows the married couple, Emma and Mr. Knightley (Ralph Michael), exchanging a kiss. The adaptation was shot on two studio sets: Studio A—the interior of Hartfield, Mrs. Bates's parlor, Mrs. Ford's shop, a street in Highbury, and a grotto with two oak boughs; Studio B—Donwell, a roadside grotto, and the Crown Inn (Campbell, "*Emma*"). Thus, it can be seen that this adaptation attempted to represent many of the settings mentioned in the novel.

The first television dramatization of *Emma* in the United States was presented in November 1954 by NBC's *Kraft Television Theatre*. The *Kraft Theatre*, an hour-long dramatic program that ran on Wednesday nights from 1947 to 1958, often presented original live drama and was a training ground for actors who went on to become Hollywood stars—actors such as Paul Newman, Anthony Quinn, Grace Kelly, Charlton Heston (Brooks and Marsh 550). "Emma" was a live presentation, in black and white, dramatized by Martine Bartlett and Peter Donat, both of whom had minor roles in the adaptation. It starred Felicia Montealegre as Emma and Peter Cookson as Mr. Knightley. The best performance in the show was that of Roddy McDowall, who played Mr. Elton. During the thirties, McDowall had been a child actor in British films, and after leaving London in 1940 to escape the blitz, he starred as a juvenile in *How Green Was My Valley* (1941) and other films. During the fifties he moved into adult roles on Broadway and on American television, before heading back to Hollywood (Katz 868). His role in this production of *Emma* was much expanded, compared to Mr. Elton's usual role. In fact, this adaptation omits entirely Miss Bates, Mrs. Bates, Robert Martin, Mr. Churchill, Jane Fairfax, the John Knightleys, and the gypsies. It focuses entirely on Emma's mistaken efforts to match Harriet to Mr. Elton. The character William Larkins, instead of Robert Martin, is the "gentleman farmer" who loves Harriet and eventually wins her.

A live, studio-bound adaptation, this version of *Emma* differs from the earlier BBC version in its limited setting. Most of the scenes take place at Hartfield, with several different interior perspectives, including a fireplace and a staircase. There is also a "garden," with an artificial tree and a potted plant. The viewer's impression is of grandeur, beauty, and wealth. Two other scenes—the church and a room in Mr. Knightley's house—are shot in such close quarters that the background cannot be clearly distinguished. The emphasis on elegance apparent in the sets extends to the costumes. The women's costumes appear to have been influenced by the costumes in the 1940 *Pride and Prejudice*, or perhaps, like the costumer for that film, the costumers for *Emma* thought Regency dresses not sufficiently glamorous. Emma's dresses have enormous puffed sleeves, a natural waist, and full skirts. The men, however, are wearing the short-waisted coats with tails and pantaloons typical of the Regency. The servants wear powdered hair and full livery. William Larkins, on the other hand, looks out of place coming in the front door of Hartfield with Mr. Knightley, since his apparel is that of a farm worker, not of a "gentleman farmer."

Typical of television plays of this period in the United States, the adaptation is divided into three acts, with advertisements appearing between. Act I begins with the wedding between Mr. Weston and Miss Taylor, followed by the reception. Mr. Elton conducts the ceremony and at the reception he regales the ladies with the charade from the novel, which concludes, "Woman, lovely woman stands alone." After Mrs. Weston tosses the wedding bouquet and it lands at Harriet's feet, Emma decides that Mr. Elton is the one meant for Harriet (Sarah Marshall). In

the next scene, the following day, Harriet is at Hartfield singing and playing the pianoforte. Mr. Knightley enters, attended by William Larkins
carrying a basket of apples. Mr. Knightley expresses the opinion to Mrs.
Weston that Harriet's singing is "caterwauling," and at her suggestion
they retreat to the garden for tea. William Larkins greets Harriet by lift-
ing her off her feet and then hugging her. He tells her that "her" sow,
Polly, has just had a litter of pigs, and he invites her and Emma to come
to see them. His dialect is reminiscent of that of a denizen of the West
Virginia hills. After Larkins departs, Emma alludes to his obvious lack
of culture and tells Harriet that he will probably marry a farmer's daughter. She also expresses the opinion that by the time Larkins is forty he
will be thinking of nothing but "profit and loss."

In the second act, a few days later Mr. Elton praises Harriet's performance at the pianoforte and gladly sits by Emma to hold her yarn. He
encourages Emma to sketch Harriet and reads aloud Byron's poem "She
Walks in Beauty" while Emma sketches. Elton insists upon taking the picture to London for framing. Emma is delighted that her plans for the
match are going so well. In the next brief scene, Mr. Knightley encourages William Larkins to propose to Harriet. Later, Emma is in her room,
in corset and petticoat, when Harriet shows her the proposal of marriage
from William Larkins. Emma says that she will not advise her, but she
does so indirectly by disparaging Larkins and by suggesting that Mr. Elton
is interested in Harriet. After Mr. Knightley learns that Harriet has refused
Larkins, he comes to Hartfield to chastise Emma for causing Harriet to
reject Larkins and for encouraging her to think of Mr. Elton as a marital prospect. While they are talking, Harriet runs in to report that the
bull is out and that Larkins has him by the tail. Mr. Knightley leaves hurriedly to rescue Larkins. (Shades of *The Beverly Hillbillies!*) When Mr.
Knightley comes back in, he and Emma reconcile, Mr. Knightley agree-
ing with Emma that they are closer now than they were when he was sixteen and she was an infant. His glance indicates that he feels much closer.
When Harriet comes in, Mr. Knightley leaves. Harriet seems to be in a
daze, apparently in love. Emma assumes that her object is Mr. Elton and
encourages her to anticipate a higher match than she had previously hoped
for. Harriet leaves as Elton arrives with the framed picture. Elton,
delighted to be alone with Emma, proposes to her and leaves in a huff
after she rejects him. When Mr. Knightley comes in, he laughs at Emma's
surprise that Elton loves her. She is preoccupied with concern about what
Harriet will say when she learns of the proposal so that she does not
notice Mr. Knightley's loving interest in her.

In Act III, after the passage of several days, during which both Mr.

Knightley and Mr. Elton have gone to London, Harriet rushes in to report that Elton has returned from London with his bride. Now Emma learns that Harriet loves Mr. Knightley. Emma asks whether Mr. Knightley returns this affection and is distressed to find that Harriet believes that he does. In the next scene, Mr. Elton comes to call on the Woodhouses with Mrs. Elton (Martine Bartlett). She chatters non-stop, mentions her fondness for music, nuzzles her husband, and refers twice to their barouche-landau. Mr. Woodhouse (Stafford Dickens) suggests that Emma needs a basin of gruel to bolster her spirits. In the next scene, Mr. Knightley enters, having just returned from London. Emma is at first reluctant to hear his news of a coming wedding, but happy to hear that Larkins and Harriet are to be married. Then, standing behind Emma he tells her that he has fallen in love with her. Although we see her joyous reaction, he cannot see her face. She reminds him of the time when she called him "Henry" (not George) but says that she did not repeat the freedom when he seemed not to mind. He begs her to call him by his Christian name again. He looks downcast as she tells him that she will never call him by his Christian name. Now we see only Emma, standing, looking toward Mr. Knightley, and partly concealing her face with her fan. She concludes her statement, "…except once and you may guess when." We do not see his face.

The *Kraft Television Theatre* adaptation can hardly be considered among the best cinematic presentations of *Emma*. Felicia Montealegre plays Emma broadly, exaggerating every response, and Peter Cookson, although an amiable presence, stumbles over several speeches. The adaptation gives little indication of the novel's core of ideas. It exploits only the most superficial elements of the novel. The introduction of William Larkins as a country bumpkin makes for an incongruous kind of low comedy that is typical of American television of that time. A peculiarly American twist to the handling of Larkins' character resides in the emphasis on his cultural and intellectual inferiority, rather than class difference. Larkins, however, reveals no sense of his inferiority nor shows any marked deference to either Emma or Mr. Knightley. As for Harriet, there is no reference to her being of low origins. Her inferiority resides in her silliness and her lack of polished manners.

The next American presentation was on CBS's *Camera Three* on August 26, 1960 (Wright 449). During the sixties, *Camera Three* was a Sunday morning hour-long program which varied in content, presenting drama, concerts, and interviews (McNeil 139). "Emma" was directed by John Desmond and was based on a screenplay by Clair Roskam. Nancy Wickwire played Emma Woodhouse (Wright 449). Wickwire was a regular on several soap operas of the 1950s and 1960s, including NBC's *Days of Our Lives*, NBC's *Another World*, and CBS's *As the World Turns* (McNeil 50, 60, 204).

The BBC TV's next production of *Emma* appeared in 1960 in six half-hour installments, from 8:00 p.m. to 8:30 p.m. on consecutive Fridays, from February 26, 1960, through April 1, 1960. Like the 1948 version, it was shown live in black and white. Vincent Tilsley wrote the screenplay, and Campbell Logan was the producer. Diana Fairfax played Emma Woodhouse, Paul Daneman played Mr. Knightley, and a very young David McCallum played Frank Churchill. Gillian Lind, who played the role of Miss Bates, had also played this role in the

Emma (BBC 1960). Emma Woodhouse (Diana Fairfax) and Mr. George Knightley (Paul Daneman). (BBC Picture Archives)

1948 version and had played Mrs. Bennet in the 1952 adaptation of *Pride and Prejudice*. The screenplay for this adaptation, like the earlier BBC adaptation, omits the John Knightleys and merges the events of the Box Hill picnic into the strawberry picking at Donwell. It shows the gypsies pursuing Harriet (Perlita Neilson), emphasizes Mr. Knightley's suspicions about Jane's (Petra Davies) secret correspondence, mentions Perry's plans for a carriage, and lets Harriet overhear Emma talking to her father about her plan to marry Mr. Knightley. After Emma accepts Mr. Knightley, he kisses her hand. The film ends with Emma and Knightley in a carriage, immediately following their marriage, discussing what name she is to call him. She says that he will always be Mr. Knightley to her (Tilsley, "*Emma*"). Neither of the early BBC adaptations takes any serious liberties with the storyline or characters of the novel. The studio sets cited in the screenplay indicate the range of settings: drawing rooms at Hartfield and Randalls, Harriet's bedroom at Hartfield, the Post Office, Fords' shop, a ballroom, a balcony, Knightley's study, and the Donwell gardens.

Since 1960, *Emma* has been made into four cinematic versions, all of which are currently available on tape, laserdisc, or DVD. The first, entitled *Emma*, appeared on BBC-2 TV in six parts during July and August 1972. It was dramatized by Denis Constanduros and directed by John Glenister. Paramount released the second, entitled *Clueless*, to theatres in 1995. *Clueless* was written and directed by Amy Heckerling. Of the third and fourth, both entitled *Emma*, Miramax released one to theatres in the United States in July 1996 and in Great Britain in September 1996. The other was produced by Meridian Broadcasting for ITV and presented in Great Britain in November 1996 and in the United States on the A&E Television Network in February 1997. The A&E mini-series was produced by Sue Birtwistle and based on a screenplay by Andrew Davies, the same team which had created A&E's *Pride and Prejudice* the previous year. It won two Emmy Awards for 1997—for its production design team and for Jenny Beavan's costumes. The Miramax film was written and directed by Douglas McGrath, in his directorial debut. He had previously co-written, with Woody Allen, the Oscar-nominated screenplay for *Bullets Over Broadway*. He shot the film in England in forty-one days during the summer of 1995. Rachel Portman's musical score won the Academy Award for the Best Original Score for a Musical or Comedy in 1995; Ruth Myers' costumes were nominated for the award for Best Costume Design.

With the exception of *Clueless*, which is set in the late 1990s, these cinematic versions of the novel retain the period setting of the novel. *Clueless* not only updates the time of the novel, but it moves Emma, called Cher (Alicia Silverstone) in the film, to Hollywood, California, and makes her a student at Bronson Alcott High School. She lives in a palatial mansion in Beverly Hills, her father is an irascible corporate litigator, and her mother is dead. She spends much of her time shopping at the mall and doing make-overs on her friends. Silverstone is wonderful as Cher—cocky and manipulative, but warm and vulnerable as well. Cher's stepbrother, Josh (Paul Rudd), is the son of one of her father's previous wives. Cher's initial attitude toward Josh, who is the Mr. Knightley of the film, is scorn. He may be an older college man, but he is, like, *boring* with his interest in current events and in literature. He calls her "a superficial space-cadet." The antagonism which exists between these two bears little similarity to the relationship which existed between Emma and Mr. George Knightley, but it is very much part of conventional Hollywood romantic comedy, in which the male and female leads customarily start out disliking each other. The film certainly owes as much to Hollywood film tradition as it does to Jane Austen's *Emma*. As one might expect from a film with a Hollywood setting, it abounds in references to films. Cher points to a large painting of her mother and refers to her as a "Betty," meaning as beautiful as Betty Grable; an attractive man is a "Baldwin," (William Baldwin). Cher and her best friend, Dionne, are both named for famous singers (Cher and Dionne Warwick).

One of the most interesting and effective aspects of the film is Cher's voiceover narration. Nora Nachumi astutely points out that this voiceover narration closely approximates Austen's ironic third-person narrator. She further maintains that *Clueless* is the film that is most true to Austen's "spirit of pop-cultural critique" (130). Cher's voiceover commentary usually explains or expands upon something which we have already seen. Early in the film she speaks with great confidence and authority, conveying much of the same kind of certainty that we associate with Emma. For example, while at a party in the Valley, Cher observes Tai dancing with Elton and she congratulates herself on her success in matchmaking. She says, "I had to give myself snaps for all the good deeds I was doing. It was so great. Love was everywhere. Even though I was alone, I was really happy for Tai. It's like that book I read in ninth grade that said, 'Tis a far, far better thing doing stuff for other people.'" However, the viewer soon realizes that her assessment of situations is often warped by her own very materialistic and wrong-headed notions.

One should ask oneself, as Heckerling apparently did, "What would Emma be like if she lived today?" Certainly she would be rich, as Cher is, thanks to her father's law practice. She would circulate among other rich persons, as Cher mainly does. Her best friend is an African American girl, Dionne (Stacey Dash), who obviously has money. Cher lives in a big house, is learning how to drive her own jeep, has a computer program to select her costume for the day, buys designer clothes, and talks on her cell phone constantly. She gives instructions to the housekeeper and, like Emma, "manages" her father (Dan Hedaya). In an interesting twist, she is the one who tries to get her father to eat healthy food, whereas Mr. Woodhouse cautions Emma and everyone else against eating rich foods. She also attempts to manipulate people. We see her successfully making a match between her grouchy speech teacher, Mr. Hall (Wallace Shawn) and a frowsy French teacher, Miss Geist (Twink Caplan). Then we see her abject failure as she attempts to match her plebian protégé, Tai (Brittany Murphy), with an upscale big man on campus, Elton (Jeremy Sisto). In the novel Mr. Elton shocks Emma by proposing to her. In *Clueless* Elton, who is driving Cher home after a party, makes a pass at her. Cher gets out of the car, Elton drives off, and Cher, left alone, is robbed and forced to lie on the ground in her designer dress. She has to call her stepbrother to come to pick her up.

Clueless (Paramount 1995). Cher (Alicia Silverstone) asks Josh (Paul Rudd) to take a break from his Nietzsche. (MOMA)

Cher, who is generally disdainful of high school boys, finds herself attracted to Christian (Justin Walker) and sets out to seduce him, not realizing that he is gay. Christian is as close as the film comes to Frank Churchill, and, as in the novel, Cher/Emma is mistaken about the male object's love interest. At a dance, Cher is so preoccupied with Tai's having no one to dance with, that she fails to notice Christian's obvious interest in the other men. Rather, she thinks that he may be falling in love with her because he doesn't look at the other girls. Cher is pleased when her stepbrother comes to Tai's rescue. Josh, however, has come to the dance to "look after" Cher, because he is jealous of Christian. He has apparently experienced a kind of epiphany as he watched Cher come down the stairs in her home, to the strains of "Gigi," in her skin-tight white Calvin Klein dress. Josh's rescue of Tai, of course, parallels Mr. Knightley's rescue of Harriet at the dance and precipitates Tai's falling in love with Josh. There is even a situation parallel to the gypsy attack on Harriet. In *Clueless*, Tai is talking to some boys at the mall, while Christian and Cher stand nearby. When the boys are about to push Tai over a railing so that she is in danger of falling to the next level, Christian comes

Clueless (Paramount 1995). Cher and friends: front l–r, Christian (Justin Walker), Dionne (Stacey Dash), Cher (Alicia Silverstone), Tai (Brittany Murphy), Travis (Breckin Meyer); back l–r, Amber (Elisa Donovan), Elton (Jeremy Sisto), Murray (Donald Faison), Josh (Paul Rudd). (MOMA)

to her rescue. This incident does not cause Cher to think Tai is in love with Christian, but it does give Tai status among their friends so that she begins to assume social ascendancy over Cher. Depressed by Tai's transformation and by her own lack of a boyfriend, Cher cannot concentrate on her driving test and fails it.

When Cher returns home on foot after failing her driving test, she finds Tai talking with Josh. Tai then tells Cher that she is getting rid of certain little souvenirs she associated with Elton (a tape of "Rollin' with the Homies" and the towel that Elton had used to apply ice to her head at the Valley party) and that she now cares for Josh. A low point for Cher's self-esteem comes as Tai, miffed at Cher's suggestion that Josh and Tai don't "mesh" well, says to Cher, "It is, like, why am I even listening to you to begin with. You're a virgin who can't drive." Stinging from this put-down and mulling in voiceover this new development, Cher realizes that she is in love with Josh. This revelation comes as a fountain behind Cher begins to spray water and a fuchsia light illuminates the spray. She decides to give her soul "a complete make-over" so that she might be the kind of girl Josh could like. She gets involved in charitable activities and watches the news, instead of the cartoons, on television. She also makes up with Tai, who has returned to being romantically interested in Travis (Breckin Meyer), a reformed druggie skateboarder. However, Cher is "clueless" about how to go about attracting Josh's interest. She feels that she cannot use her usual flirting techniques on him—sending herself candy, prancing around in her cutest outfits. During this period of uncertainty, Cher forsakes her designer outfits and mini skirts to wear blue jeans and simple tops. She even wears her hair uncurled and pulled back from her face. One evening when one of Cher's father's associates accuses her of sabotaging her father's law case, Josh comes to her defense. The two of them end up kissing on the winding staircase. The last scene of the film is a wedding set in a garden, and the viewer's first impression is that it is Cher's and Josh's wedding. But, as Cher says in voiceover, "As if! I am only sixteen, and this is California, not Kentucky." It is the wedding of the teachers Miss Geist and Mr. Hall. Cher and her girlfriends, their boyfriends, and Josh are all present, the boys wagering on who will catch the wedding bouquet. Cher ends up with the bouquet, and Cher and Josh kiss.

It is clear from the preceding summary that the film retains many elements of the novel, including the same emphasis on Cher/Emma's realization that she has endangered her own happiness by meddling in the lives of others. The plot, however, is simpler than the plot of *Emma*. It has dropped the subplot of the subterfuge of Jane Fairfax and Frank Churchill; it has dropped the Bateses. It has transmuted the Westons into Miss Geist and Mr. Hall. And, it has added a community of high school students. Within this community, social stratification is apparent. Elton considers himself superior to Tai because of who his father is; he looks upon Cher as being on his level. Dionne refers to Elton as "way popular" and says that, "He's, like, the social director of the crew." Cher tells Tai that she will be accepted in the upper social strata at school because she is being seen associating with Cher and Dionne. Travis is obviously on a lower level. He's a skateboarder and comes to school stoned. Cher scorns skateboarding as passé, and says of drug use, "It is one thing to spark up a doobie and get laced at parties, but it is quite another to be fried all day." Josh has status because of his foster father's wealth and because he is a college man.

A significant difference which Heckerling has made in updating the novel to the last decade of the twentieth century is the changing of the main character's age from twenty-one to sixteen. She probably felt that an American high school student is more likely to experience the kind of idleness that Emma experienced as an unmarried female than an American woman at any other stage of her existence. At the age of twenty-one, a young woman of the upper middle class in the United States is likely to be preparing to graduate from college and to embark on a career. Also, a college is a more egalitarian environment than a high school. Social standing, in most colleges, is more likely to be based on leadership roles or academic achievement than on parental status or popularity, and like their college teacher mentors, college students tend to wear grunge. Thus, as we compare *Clueless* to *Emma*, it is inevitable that we compare the manners of each time setting. We note the much greater freedom of movement of young women of today. We also note the greater risks which they run. It may have been played for humor, but Cher's being stranded on foot in a strange part of the city and being robbed at gunpoint would be highly possible for today's teen and not funny at all. How sheltered and safe Emma's existence looks! As for Emma's shock at Frank Churchill's irresponsibility in coming into the society of young ladies with the appearance of being unattached, consider Cher's shock at realizing that Christian is gay. However, the film attaches no blame to Christian; rather, Cher appears naive for assuming that he is heterosexual.

Another way in which the environment of the film differs from that of the novel is in the greater presence of sexual activity in the lives of the characters. Cher is called upon to defend her decision to remain a virgin until she finds someone worthy of her sexual favors. Tai, whose conversation reveals her sexual experience, expresses amazement at Cher's being a virgin. Although Dionne and Murray (Donald Faison) are in a relationship, Dionne is said to be technically a virgin. After they have a traumatic experience driving on the freeway, Dionne's virginity goes from "technical to non-existent." Thus, it appears that sex is a topic for discussion and that for high school girls to have experienced some type of sexual experience is more common than not.

Most of the music which pervades the film is popular rock music. It is loud, it is mostly fast-paced, its lyrics are inane, and the performers include Salt-n-Pepa, David Bowie, Lightning Seeds, Radio Head, Cracker, and the Muffs. Music is sung or played over the action of the

Emma (BBC 1972). Emma Woodhouse (Doran Godwin), Mr. George Knightley (John Carson), and rear, Mr. Woodhouse (Donald Eccles). (BBC Picture Archives)

film; occasionally it is integrated into the film itself, usually through a television set or a car radio, as is the case when Christian plays a tape of Billie Holiday singing "Miss Brown, to You." On this occasion, Cher reveals her ignorance when she refers to Billie Holiday as "him." "Rollin' with the Homies," performed by Coolio, becomes Tai's theme song after she dances with Elton to that song. Music is also used ironically, as when "Thus Spake Zarathustra" plays as the viewer sees, like the obelisk in *2001: A Space Odyssey*, a long black portable telephone photographed from a low position. This time Cher is waiting for a call from Christian. The use of Lerner and Loewe's "Gigi" also is referential and ironic.

Clueless uses the main characters and chief plot elements of the novel, but it has heightened the humor. In other cinematic treatments of Austen's novels, the screenwriters are able to use some of Austen's witty dialogue. In this film, however, the dialogue is all the invention of Amy Heckerling. Its style is informal and slangy. The only lengthy speeches are those spoken in voiceover. To appreciate the successful combination of the visual and the auditory in this film, one only has to watch one time the really insipid television spin-off, also entitled *Clueless*. Although the roles of several of the minor characters, such as Amber, Dionne, and Murray, are played by the actors in the film, and although Heckerling was involved in the production, the wit and style are conspicuously missing. Since Cher is played by another comely blonde—Rachel Blanchard—Alicia Silverstone, a primary reason why *Clueless* is such a good film, is also missing.

Among the cinematic versions of the novel which retain the early nineteenth century setting, the ways in which the filmmakers differ in their uses of their source reflect not only the time constraints dictated by the format, but differences in the actors, uses of setting, and choice and staging of scenes. Intended for theatrical release, the Miramax *Emma* runs 121 minutes; the Meridian/A&E Emma runs 100 minutes and was presented on television on two consecutive nights. The 1972 BBC version (257 minutes) is a true mini-series, designed to run on six consecutive nights on television. This version is the closest to the novel in its inclusiveness of the scenes and characters described in the novel. If what the viewer wants is a literal translation, unencumbered by superior acting, imaginative staging, or on-location shooting, the 1972 BBC version is the way to go.

The actors and actresses in the lead roles inevitably create the ambiance of a film. One critic commented that he found the Meridian/A&E version "less romanticized" than the Miramax version because the actors in the major roles are "plainer"; Kate Beckinsale (*Pearl Harbor*, 2001) is not as beautiful as Gwyneth Paltrow (*Shakespeare in Love*, 1998) (Greenfield 33). No one would maintain that Doran Godwin, Emma in the BBC version, is as beautiful as either Beckinsale or Paltrow. The difference between Paltrow and Beckinsale, however, may not be just a matter of beauty. Since Emma is a character who is easy to dislike, having an appealing actress like Paltrow play the role is an advantage. She makes Emma a sympathetic figure, even when she is at her most wrongheaded, and she is easy to forgive when she admits that she has been wrong. McGrath commented on his first look at the actress in *Flesh and Bone*: "She was completely mesmerizing; you can't keep your eyes off her, and her voice has the same intoxicating mix of honey and whiskey as that of her mother […]" (74). Regarding the way Paltrow appears in the film— her hair swept up and away from her face, her long neck unadorned, in clothing with simple lines—Nora Nachumi says, "[…] [T]his Emma, the film tells us, *deserves* to be on a pedestal because she truly is a young goddess" (136). Troost and Greenfield have pointed out that McGrath has reduced the roles of Frank Churchill and Jane Fairfax and has given Emma 41 percent of the dialogue, as compared to Kate Beckinsale's 33 percent in the Meridian/A&E *Emma*. Emma, and thus Paltrow, is more the center of attention in the Miramax film (4–5).

Emma (A&E 1996). Mr. George Knightley (Mark Strong) and Emma (Kate Beckinsale). (Photofest)

Beckinsale, on the other hand, seems querulous and cold; Godwin, stiff and superior. Monica Lauritzen, who interviewed John Glenister, reports that from his study of the novel and of several critiques, he concluded that Emma "seemed to fit the classic case of the psychoneurotic." Thus, he was looking for "somebody who would appear highly strung" (117). He felt that Godwin was just right for the part. Janey Fothergill, the casting director for the Meridian/A&E version, felt that Beckinsale possesses many of Emma's personality traits: "She has a great confidence, is very intelligent and is aware of the fact that she's good-looking, and well spoken" (Birtwistle, *Emma* 15). This concept of Emma is the more traditional one. These same qualities could be stated of Gwyneth Paltrow. The big difference is a matter of charisma, and Paltrow has it.

Other casting choices are important in shaping the overall impression. The choice of the paunchy and graying John Carson for the role of Mr. Knightley in the BBC version emphasizes the age difference between Emma and Mr. Knightley. He exudes solidity and complacency. John Carson is a good choice for Mr. Knightley only if the viewer particularly wants the dramatization of the novel to be non-romantic. For sex appeal, however, Mark Strong (*Anna Karenina*, 2000) in this role in the Meridian/A&E version is better. He looks mature, but vigorous. He is particularly convincing when seen observing the harvest on horseback. Neither of the other actors playing the role could have carried off this scene. Director Diarmuid Lawrence wanted an actor who had energy and authority, but he didn't want a "stuffed shirt." Lawrence said, "[...] [W]hat's quite delightful about Mark Strong's interpretation is that he is also able to get quietly into a juvenile rage about Frank Churchill[...]" (Birtwistle, *Emma* 6). Mark Strong is certainly the most intense of the actors playing this role. Although Jeremy Northam (*The Golden Bowl*, 2000), Mr. Knightley in the Miramax film, is a smaller man than the other two and does not exude the authority of the others, he seems more sensitive and vulnerable. He could not have carried off the scene in the Meridian/A&E film in which Mr. Knightley addresses his friends and tenants at the harvest banquet. His acting style is understated, and he is good at sly irony. There are more witty lines for Mr. Knightley in the Miramax film than in the other versions. For instance, in the scene in which he and Emma compete at shooting arrows at a target, when Emma's aim deteriorates so that she misses the target entirely, he quips, "Please don't kill my dogs." In another scene, in which he is standing with the massive Donwell Abbey behind him, he tells Emma he would rather not go to the ball but would prefer to stay home, "Where it's cozy." Of the three actors, he comes across as the most tender in the proposal scene.

Another important role is that of Harriet Smith. For there to be a clear distinction between her and Emma's qualities of character and social positions, the actress chosen should contrast with the actress playing Emma in both physical appearance and manner. However, it is also desirable that during the course of the film she show a growing assurance. For the 1972 version, Glenister wanted a blonde "Shirley Temple type," "someone who loved her food," "a slightly round and puppy fattish girl" (Lauritzen 118). He chose Debbie Bowen to play this role and had her dressed in frilly caps and pastel colors. Bowen compares well to the other two actresses who play the role. She is perpetually smiling, except when showing distress or fear. This version emphasizes her vacillating nature. She not only has trouble deciding on the colors of ribbons and where to have the ribbons delivered but is also capable of being in love with three different men in one year.

Samantha Morton delivers the best portrayal of Harriet Smith, largely because she is such a good actress. After the making of *Emma*, Morton excelled as Jane Eyre in the 1997 BBC/A&E version of Bronte's novel. She is better at conveying the nuances of Harriet's developing character than Bowen. We see Harriet progress from fearful worshiper of Emma, to confident companion, to assured recipient of Mr. Knightley's attentions. Her Harriet never appears stupid, as does Bowen's Harriet. One significant omission from the Meridian/A&E version is Mr. Elton's riddle. This incident, in which Harriet is unable to puzzle out the meaning of the riddle without Emma's assistance, is one of the chief evidences of Harriet's lack of intelligence. Although Morton's Harriet is unable to decipher an anagram in the Box Hill scene, she doesn't appear completely stupid, only slightly dense. In the Miramax film, Toni Collette is good at looking and acting stupid, but she is so very unprepossessing that it is difficult to imagine that Emma would be interested in her as a friend. The term "bovine" may even creep into the viewer's mind. Having seen Collette in modern dress in *The Sixth Sense*, which appeared after *Emma* and for which she received an Academy Award nomination, I realize that she is not so lumpy as the high-waisted dresses she wore in *Emma* made her appear. The director also apparently instructed her to look as foolish as possible. As if to emphasize her bad qualities, she is shown posing for a picture in classical draperies holding a lyre in one hand, with her other arm curving over her head. Her portrayal of Harriet reveals few gradations of development or nuances of feeling. She holds nothing back. She gushes with happiness—over puppies, Mr. Elton's pencil, Mr. Martin's letter—or weeps copiously at disappointments. In her tendency to excess, Collette is, perhaps, a more pathetic figure than the other Harriets.

The role of Frank Churchill would appear to require little except that the actor be young and charming and able to convince the audience that everyone will like this character, even after it becomes apparent that he has deceived a great many people. However, Sue Birtwistle, producer of the Meridian/A&E film, calls Frank Churchill "a particularly complex character to play" (16). She characterizes him as "charming, energetic and handsome, but ... also cruel and potentially dangerous" (16). Frank is often compared to Austen's other unscrupulous charmers—John Willoughby, Henry Crawford, and George Wickham. This comparison is somewhat unfair, since Frank Churchill does not seduce anyone. Screenwriter Andrew Davies psychoanalyzed Frank as a "dangerous misogynistic charmer," who treats Jane badly because he fears her power over him (Birtwistle, *Emma* 11). However, if Frank is so dangerous, let us remember that Emma said that had she been in Frank's situation, she too might have found amusement in a little deception. Mr. Knightley, the moral center of the film, does not roundly condemn him, hoping that the love of a good woman may lead him in the right path.

All three of the actors who portray Frank Churchill are effective. If any conveys the dangerous aspect of Frank, it is Raymond Coulthard, in the Meridian/A&E version. At least once we see him out of temper, after Jane quarrels with him at Donwell Abbey. Robert East of the BBC version and Ewan McGregor of the Miramax film emphasize the charm of the young man. In the Miramax film it is Frank who suggests that Mr.

Dixon is the one who sent the pianoforte to Jane. In the other versions, Frank merely goes along with Emma's suggestion. McGregor's Frank is mischievous and teasing. He is also romantically appealing. Emma is not the only one who is bowled over when Frank begins singing with her as she plays the pianoforte at the Coles' party. Some members of the audience felt the same way. In a bit of casting against type, Ewan McGregor only shortly before played the modern anti-hero in *Trainspotting* (1996), but he is a romantic hero in *Moulin Rouge* (2001). Coulthard also sings at the pianoforte with Emma, but the song and the delivery have less romantic suggestiveness. It is directed at Jane and alludes to Mr. Dixon since it concerns Ireland. McGregor's song emphasizes the choice of a maiden with "golden hair," which in this film is Emma.

Jane Fairfax, another important character in the novel, is described as beautiful and accomplished. Emma knows that Jane is the more accomplished pianist and singer of the two, and she does not like being second-best. When Emma attempts to find out from Jane her impressions of Frank Churchill, she meets with evasion. This response gives Emma a reason to dislike Jane—her reserved temper. She is pleased to hear Knightley praise women with open tempers—among whom she naturally includes herself.

In the BBC *Emma*, Jane Fairfax is played by Ania Marson. A beautiful, slender young woman, with dark hair and eyes, she furnishes a good physical contrast to Doran Godwin. She is, however, stiff in her movements and halting in her speech. She appears to be speaking through clenched teeth. These qualities make her convincing since they suggest that she is holding something back. Olivia Williams plays Jane in the Meridian/A&E film. She also is beautiful. The director frequently shows Williams' face in closeup, enabling the viewer to see her expressive eyes. Although she rarely smiles and has little dialogue, Williams conveys a wide range of feelings with her eyes. For example, when Frank asks Emma to reserve the first two dances at the ball for him, Jane, who has been playing the piano and showing pleasure, now shows her unhappiness. When she is dancing at the ball at the Crown Inn, we see a close-up of her face as she watches Frank move around her in the dance. She looks in love. At the harvest banquet, after her engagement to Frank has become known, she gleams with happiness. It is no wonder that Kevin Costner selected her to be the heroine of his movie *The Postman* (1997), but unfortunate that this film's failure did not advance her career. Jane Fairfax of the Miramax film (Polly Walker) is also a beautiful woman, this time of the buxom physical type with dark hair and eyes. It is difficult to think of this robust Jane as being physically weak and susceptible to colds. Although Ms.

Walker makes a striking appearance, she is little to be seen in this version and has little dialogue.

There are outstanding performances in the minor roles in all three films. Donald Eccles, who plays Mr. Woodhouse in the BBC version, is particularly effective. The director said that he chose him because he was so slender and fragile looking, in contrast to the rotund Miss Bates (Lauritzen 118). One can well believe that this Mr. Woodhouse generally dines on gruel. He also appears to be oblivious to much of what is going on around him, but can be querulous when opposed. The other two Mr. Woodhouses appear to be better nourished and more physically able. Denys Hawthorne, in the Miramax film, conveys a sense of humor and is not so fearful of every draft. Bernard Hepton, in the Meridian/A&E film, is the most irascible of the trio. However, he has some funny lines taken from the novel, and a few that are added. For instance, at the beginning of the film Mr. Woodhouse, Emma, and Miss Taylor are on their way to the church for Miss Taylor's wedding. Mr. Woodhouse seriously recommends that Miss Taylor reconsider her intention of getting married and starts to give the signal to the coachman to turn the carriage around. When Miss Taylor declines this suggestion, Mr. Woodhouse says: "But it's all very disturbing, Emma. Six good hens and now Miss Taylor. It's a sad business." His mention of the loss of six hens refers to the chicken house raid of the night before, and his associating the loss of the chickens with the loss of Miss Taylor is indeed ironic.

Of the actors who play Mr. Elton, Alan Cumming (Miramax) gives the most nuanced performance, credibly balancing the comic with the serious. Since making *Emma*, Cumming has shown up in a great variety of roles in a variety of films: as Rooster Hannigan in *Annie* (1999), Saturnius in *Titus* (1999), and Fegan Floop in *Spy Kids* (2001). In light of his performances in these roles, it is easy to understand how Cumming moves so effortlessly from obsequious suppliant, to outraged rejected suitor, to spiteful enemy, to compliant husband. Timothy Peters of the BBC version is perhaps the most simpering of the Mr. Eltons. Dominic Rowan plays the role in the Meridian/A&E film.

It is more difficult to decide which actress of those who play Mr. Elton's wife comes across as the most obnoxious. Fiona Walker plays the role in the BBC version. Her role is the largest, since that of Augusta Elton is much cut in the other two versions. We get to see her in a succession of gaudy costumes. She conveys well how loud and vulgar Augusta is with her "caro sposo" and her intrusive familiarity with Emma. In the Meridian/A&E film, Lucy Robinson is also effective. Her role as one of the Bingley sisters in the A&E *Pride and Prejudice* is not greatly different from that of the vulgar Mrs. Elton. One of the most striking differences in the three actresses' rendering of the role of Mrs. Elton lies in that of Juliet Stevenson in the Miramax film. Her Mrs. Elton consistently interrupts Mr. Elton as he attempts to speak. He can never complete a sentence without Augusta's overwhelming it with her own spin on the subject. Although this habit is not mentioned in the novel, it is certainly in keeping with the character. She also talks with food in her mouth.

Among the other actors, Greta Scacchi is probably the most appealing. This beautiful mature actress appears in the Miramax film, where she is Mrs. Weston, the tolerant confidante to whom Emma tells her secrets. Although she has an air of knowing everything, she is quite wrong to conclude that Mr. Knightley is romantically interested in Jane Fairfax. Samantha Bond, who plays this role in the Meridian/A&E version, has a history with Austen films. She also played Maria Bertram in the BBC *Mansfield Park* (1983).

The actresses who play the important role of Miss Bates are interesting in part because of their different physical types and/or ages. The scene in which Emma insults her at the Box Hill excursion in the novel is a turning point in all of the cinematic versions. The Miss Bates of the

Emma (Miramax 1996). L–r, Mrs. Bates (Phyllida Law), Jane Fairfax (Polly Walker), Frank Churchill (Ewan McGregor), Miss Bates (Sophie Thompson). (MOMA)

BBC film is the oldest and plumpest of the three. Glenister chose Constance Chapman for this role, he said, because of her "marvellous, sad, comic quality" (Lauritzen 118). Prunella Scales, who plays Miss Bates in the Meridian/A&E version, was familiar with the role because she had recorded the novel for audio cassette and for radio. Scales was eager to play Miss Bates, but disappointed to find that the part had been cut to about a tenth of what it was in the novel. She was also distressed to find that her voice was to be more in evidence than her person (Birtwistle, *Emma* 22). In order to make the character appear older, Scales wore a wig and stained the edges of her front teeth (Birtwistle, *Emma* 53). Her Miss Bates looks thin and undernourished; she moves quickly and talks quickly.

By far the most entertaining Miss Bates is that portrayed by Sophie Thompson in the Miramax film. She is a "young old maid"; she plays Miss Bates as a woman in her thirties, her own age. She wears little round glasses, through which she peers at the world. She smiles constantly and chatters good naturedly all of the time she is on screen. In fact, one often hears her voice before seeing her. She also affects a kind of hysterical giggle. The first scene in which she appears is typical of her behavior. She has come to a party at Hartfield, and as she and her mother enter, she can be heard thanking her host for inviting them. She then launches into thanks to Emma for the pork loin which the Woodhouses had sent to them. *Giggle.* "What a happy porker it must have come from." *Giggle.* She compliments Emma on her appearance. Then she praises Mr. Elton for his sermon on Daniel in the lion's den. She says that it left them "speechless" and that they "have not stopped talking about it since." After dropping a few more observations, she makes a beeline off screen right to talk to someone else.

Mrs. Bates has no speaking part in any of the three cinematic versions. In the BBC version this character (Mary Holder) is often in the background of scenes in which Miss Bates is a central figure. At home she is to be seen sitting close to the fire, knitting. She is also present, but silent, at a party at Hartfield and at the Coles'. In both of the other films, she is used primarily for humor. She becomes the "straight woman" for Miss Bates. Much emphasis is placed on her being hard of hearing, so that sometimes she is vaguely aware that she is being spoken to but cannot understand what is said. It is ironic that the person closest to the talkative Miss Bates cannot hear what she is saying. In an amusing scene at the beginning of the Meridian/A&E film, Mr. Woodhouse and Miss Bates discuss the virtues of an egg softly boiled while they pass the egg between them. According to the stage directions, "Mrs. Bates is dying to get stuck into her egg, but it keeps coming closer and going back—now

Miss Bates seems about to help her to it, but she gets sidetracked" (83). Finally Mr. Elton peels it for her. At other times, Mrs. Bates (Sylvia Barter) appears to be dozing in her chair, paying no heed to anyone. On one occasion, with Miss Bates absent, Frank and Jane have apparently been renewing their acquaintance, when Emma and Harriet arrive. Frank pretends to have been leveling the pianoforte, but he and Jane both rise from the piano bench looking flustered. The biggest reaction—and a silent one—that Mrs. Bates ever makes is a look of horror as the new pianoforte is hoisted up to the window.

Mrs. Bates in the Miramax film is played by Phyllida Law, the mother of Sophie and Emma Thompson. The humor derived from Mrs. Bates is even more pronounced in this version. In the scene at Hartfield described above, after Miss and Mrs. Bates arrive at the party and as Miss Bates thanks Emma for the pork loin, Miss Bates screeches "PORK" at her mother. Then, after telling Emma she looks like an angel, she screeches "ANGEL" at her mother. At the same party, Miss Bates is reading a letter which Frank Churchill had sent to his father. Mr. Knightley is seated on a bench between Miss Bates and Mrs. Bates. Miss Bates speaks across him to her mother as if she would show her the letter. Mrs. Bates looks up in response. But when Miss Bates shifts her attention to Mr. Knightley, Mrs. Bates turns away and reaches for a grape. Director Douglas McGrath said of his casting of Phyllida Law, "She will play Mrs. Bates like Jack Benny," with "weary resignation" (77). It is evident from this remark, as well as from other examples previously given of the way so many of the minor characters are used in comic ways, that McGrath, like Emma Thompson in *Sense and Sensibility*, mined the novel in order to extract humor. Like Thompson, his background is comedy—specifically, writing for *Saturday Night Live*.

The only other role of particular interest is that of Robert Martin, and the only actor who plays this small role in a distinctive manner is Alistair Petrie, in the Meridian/A&E film. Perhaps to be expected in this the most socially revisionist of the three films, this Mr. Martin is obviously critical of the queen of Highbury. After Harriet has refused him, Mr. Martin is no more than coldly courteous to Emma. When at the harvest banquet, Emma approaches Harriet and him, he is defensive but not subservient. It is obvious that he blames her for Harriet's earlier rejection of his suit. Emma puts out her hand to him, and he slowly and unsmilingly accepts it. We see much more of Petrie than we see of the Robert Martins in the other films, and we have more of a sense of his character. We also see him dressed like a working man, whereas the dress of the other Robert Martins is not greatly different from that of a country gentleman.

Since I have called the Meridian/A&E film "socially revisionist," it may be appropriate to define what I mean by this term. Whereas the other films appear to accept the social environment of the early nineteenth century, the Meridian/A&E *Emma* contains fairly explicit critiques of it. The "uppity" attitude of Robert Martin is one of these. Another comes as Harriet and Emma are on their way in an open carriage to visit the Martins. The carriage pauses on a hill, from which they can see Donwell Abbey and the woods and fields around it. Emma informs Harriet that all of these farms on the Donwell estate belong to Mr. Knightley and that everyone living on the estate is a tenant or servant of Mr. Knightley. Harriet says, "I should never have thought one man could own so much." She quips, "The sparrows and the skylarks don't belong to Mr. Knightley, do they?" Emma responds, "Perhaps not, but the woodcock and the pheasant certainly do." This exchange reflects a twentieth-century way of looking back at a time when the privileged few had more than their fair share of the wealth. Jane Austen's Mr. Knightley may express his respect for the intelligent and hard-working farmer who is his tenant, but he does not express any sense of guilt about owning such a grand house and so much land.

Yet another illustration of a modern perspective exists in the harvest banquet which concludes the film. The coming together of Mr. Knightley, his social equals, and his tenants is nowhere in Austen's novel or in either of the other two films. In Jane Austen's England, although the squire might have provided a feast for his tenants and servants outdoors or in another public setting, and even have dined with them, his friends and family would have dined separately. Augusta Elton is rightly astonished at the idea of sitting down with "hobbledehoys." Andrew Davies, in his efforts to find a way to bring all the characters together at the end of the film, hit on the idea of showing Mr. Knightley observing the harvest and then presiding over a harvest supper in Donwell Abbey. He says that he wanted to "show Knightley as an ideal old-fashioned landowner who wanted to share and celebrate with his tenants" (Birtwistle, *Emma* 57–58). He goes on to say, "I think that in a historical period like the one we're living through there's a nostalgia—an 'angry' nostalgia even—for any time when you had some sense of fairness—where you might not have had much money but you could believe that you would be treated fairly" (58). In other words, he created an idealized situation which would be appealing to people who are ignorant of the reality of the early nineteenth century but who would like for it to have been that way. It is closer to reality to show Emma visiting a poor family, as she does in the Miramax film, even feeding an old woman soup, than it is to show her inviting them to dinner at Hartfield, inside or out. In the BBC film, we also see Emma visiting the poor, but not dining with them.

Carol Dole maintains that, while the Meridian/A&E version is the most obviously revisionist, both of the American film versions—*Clueless* and the Miramax *Emma*—undermine the notion of class while subscribing to it. She points out that, in spite of the apparent social hierarchy in *Clueless*, we see Cher and Tai apparently functioning as equals at the end of the film. This demonstrates an "American faith in class mobility" not apparent in Jane Austen's novels (75). The Miramax *Emma* also tends to downplay class difference, for example, by having Mr. Knightley call Robert Martin "a good friend," and by having Emma refer to the object of her charity as a "poor lady." We see few servants in this version—the tea that Mr. Knightley and Emma take after their archery has just appeared on a table nearby. However, both films "aestheticize the upper-class lifestyle," by showing beautiful people living in beautiful houses enjoying luxuries (Dole 75). The Meridian/A&E adaptation shows the luxurious life-style of the gentry, but it attempts to show at what cost it is maintained (Dole 72).

The openings of the three period versions reflect the directors' and screenwriters' different ideas about opening scenes. The novel, after some exposition concerning the Woodhouses and Highbury, begins with Emma enduring the laments of her father on the evening after Miss Taylor has been married. The BBC version begins in a similarly leisurely fashion with Emma arriving home after the marriage. The makers of this film were obviously not much concerned with immediately catching the attention of the viewer. We see a shot of an elegant mansion surrounded by blooming hydrangeas and of a carriage pulling up to it. The scene shifts to the interior where Emma enters, pauses at the bottom of some stairs, then starts upstairs. There she finds Mr. Knightley and Mr. Woodhouse discussing the loss of "poor" Miss Taylor through her marriage to Mr. Weston. Emma claims to have made the match and plans to make another for Mr. Elton. Mr. Knightley opposes her plan for Mr. Elton. Mr. Woodhouse laments the serving of cake at the wedding.

In contrast, the Meridian/A&E version has a dramatic opening. It is night, sounds of tumult come from the chicken house, and the gardener fires a shotgun. Emma, in nightclothes, looks out of her bedroom window as if to discover the source of the noise. The credits play during these first scenes. The suggestion that thieves are stealing chickens recurs at the end of the film, where thieves are at work among the Donwell chickens even as music from the harvest banquet can be heard. This recurrence of the mention of chicken thieves not only brings the film full circle but reminds the viewer that Mr. Woodhouse has been persuaded that Mr. Knightley should be his son in-law so that he might live at Hartfield and protect them from chicken thieves. The next morning Mr. Woodhouse, Emma, and Miss Taylor are in a carriage on their way to Miss Taylor's wedding. To the sounds of wedding music, Mr. and Mrs. Weston come out of the church, say their farewells and then depart in a carriage. Next we see Mr. Woodhouse and Emma at opposite ends of a long table, obviously missing Miss Taylor. Mr. Knightley, who has been in London, enters and discusses the wedding with them.

The opening of the Miramax film, although not so sensational, nevertheless intrigues and invites the viewer. It opens with a close-up of a spinning ball, reminiscent of a globe of the world in a starry sky, but when it slows down, we perceive it to be a painted ball which Emma has created as a gift to the Westons and which she is holding up for Mrs. Weston to examine. It suggests the little world of Highbury of which Emma is the queen, and also prepares the viewer to focus on this world. The film ends with another look at such a ball, with the names and faces of the characters on it. Among Emma's first words is the statement: "The most beautiful thing in the world is a match well made." Thus she prepares us for her matchmaking career. Other elements present at the beginning of this film include Mr. Woodhouse expressing horror at the spectacle of cake being consumed and Mr. Elton complimenting Emma. Unlike the other films, this one has Mr. Knightley saying that he can give Emma advice because he is practically a brother to her.

The scenes in which Harriet is introduced also make for interesting comparison. In the novel, Mrs. Goddard, the schoolmistress, has asked for permission to bring Harriet Smith to an evening card party at Hartfield. Although Emma knows Harriet only by sight, she welcomes the prospect of a young person to talk to. In the BBC version, Mrs. Goddard brings Harriet to call on Emma in the afternoon. At this time Emma invites both of them to an evening party at Hartfield. Harriet is much concerned about her appearance, checking her bonnet while looking in a mirror. In the Miramax version, Mrs. Goddard has brought Harriet Smith with her to a party at Hartfield, and introduces her to Emma at that time. These two scenes are rather similar, but the Meridian/A&E film introduces a new element. Here, following a cut in which Emma has just said that it would be a shame for Mr. Elton to be single any longer, Emma is in church, watching Mr. Elton as he leads the singing from the pulpit. Then a beam of sunlight falls on Harriet. This visual device makes the point that Harriet is the chosen one. Outside the church Emma asks Mrs. Goddard to bring Harriet to her father's whist party.

The ways in which the three cinematic versions handle the attack of the gypsies also exhibit significant differences. In the novel Emma is told that half a dozen children, including a "great boy" and a "stout woman," assailed Harriet and Betsy Bickerton (*E* 332). Harriet gave them a shilling, but they pursued her clamoring for more money. Frank Churchill arrived on foot just in time to rescue her. The BBC version is close to the incident reported in the novel. As Harriet and her friend Betsy walk along a country road, some gypsy women see them and send children to beg from and harry the pair. Betsy runs away, but Harriet runs and falls over a log. Then Frank Churchill appears on horseback and frightens away the gypsies. In the Meridian/A&E version, children and women surround Harriet and Miss Otway, pulling at their clothes and putting their hands in Harriet's purse. The children ask for a penny and say that they are starving. Miss Otway runs away, and Harriet falls. Frank Churchill rides to the rescue. The addition of possibly starving children is another aspect of the heightened social consciousness of the Meridian/A&E film. The Miramax film differs from the others in two important ways. Here Emma is walking with Harriet in a wooded area when they are attacked by adult male and female gypsies. One calls to another to get the purse. Harriet falls and Emma tries to fend off the gypsies. Then Frank appears on horseback. This latter treatment involves Emma in the adventure, and it involves more threatening adult gypsies.

The Meridian/A&E version is distinctive in its use of scenes which represent Emma's fantasies or dreams. For instance, in the Meridian/A&E version, Emma fantasizes that Mr. Elton and Harriet have just been married. The screenplay states: "All the girls from Mrs. Goddard's school are throwing apple blossoms in a very sugary soft-focus scene. Mendelssohn, everything." Mr. Elton says: "How can I ever thank you enough, Miss Woodhouse, for showing me where true joy was to be found! Mrs. Elton and I are eternally indebted to you!" Harriet says: "And to think that I should turn out to be the daughter of a baronet!" (Birtwistle, *Emma* 84). Another time, Emma, after hearing of Mr. Dixon's rescue of Jane Fairfax during a storm at Weymouth, visualizes a storm-tossed boat, and sees Jane almost swept overboard, when Mr. Dixon pulls her back. They look passionately into each other's eyes. Another fantasy occurs at the Christmas party at Randalls. As Emma looks at Frank Churchill's portrait, it comes to life, speaks, and kisses her hand. Showing Emma's fantasies effectively places emphasis on an important aspect of Emma's personality—her over-active imagination.

The strawberry picking is handled a little differently in all three versions. In the novel the strawberry picking occurs at Donwell Abbey, followed the next day by a carriage trip to Box Hill. Mr. Knightley has invited the whole party, including Mr. Woodhouse, to come to Donwell Abbey. The Westons, Emma, her father, Miss Bates, Mrs. Elton, Harriet, and Jane attend. Mr. Woodhouse, of course, is ensconced in a comfortable room in front of a fire with Mrs. Weston for company. Two significant things occur. Mrs. Elton informs Jane that she has found her a situation and urges her to write an acceptance immediately. Jane excuses herself and sets out to walk home. Frank writes later that he met Jane as she was walking home and they quarreled. When he arrives at Donwell, he is in a bad humor. The BBC version has compressed the strawberry picking and the trip to Box Hill into the same day. A large group of men and women gather at Donwell for the strawberry picking. Mrs. Elton attempts to organize the group and takes it upon herself to announce that a cold collation is set up in the dining room. Later a smaller group, consisting of Emma, Mr. Weston, Miss Bates, Mrs. Elton, Mr. Knightley, and Frank Churchill, set out in two carriages for Box Hill. Mrs. Weston and Mr. Elton are not in attendance. Jane has been at Donwell, but she left to walk home after Mrs. Elton pressured her to accept the governess position Mrs. Elton had found for her. Frank Churchill arrives shortly after Jane has left.

The Meridian/A&E film's handling of the strawberry picking is the most distinctive, since much more emphasis is placed on the actual picking of the berries and the incongruities involved. Mrs. Elton is wearing a huge hat and carrying a beribboned basket over her arm. She tells Miss Bates that she feels like a simple shepherdess and wishes she could have come on a donkey. Miss Bates asks innocently whether she likes sheep. Mrs. Elton does not respond but continues to praise everything "simple and natural," and then to complain of the heat. In spite of Mrs. Elton's praise of the simple and natural, Mr. Knightley's servants in full livery are moving kneeling pads from place to place so that the ladies do not have to kneel on the ground. The Meridian/A&E version also shows Mr. Woodhouse by the fire inside the house. This version makes clear that, after Mrs. Elton urges Jane to take the position, Jane talks to Frank. We see Jane speaking angrily to Frank as Jane is leaving. Then Frank is in a bad humor as he talks to Emma, complaining about how warm he is. He promises to be in better humor the next day for the Box Hill outing.

The Miramax film compresses the events of the strawberry picking and the visit to Box Hill even more than the BBC version. Here the strawberry picking occurs at Box Hill. The party is seen meandering up a hill, pausing occasionally to pick berries. Harriet and Emma are together; Harriet tells Emma that she is in love with a gentleman far superior to Mr.

Elton. Emma assumes that she is talking about Frank and encourages her. We see in the background Frank with Miss Bates and Jane, and Mr. Knightley with the Westons.

The staging of the Box Hill scene differs considerably in the three cinematic versions, but in each version the dialogue of the insult is similar to that in the novel. In the novel the party consists of the Eltons, Mr. Weston, Mr. Knightley, Miss Bates, Jane, Harriet, Emma and Frank. The Eltons take Miss Bates and Jane in their carriage; Emma and Harriet go in another; the men go on horseback. The BBC version shows the group on its way in two open carriages. Once on the hill, the party spreads out— Mr. Weston snores, Miss Bates reads, Mrs. Elton complains to Mr. Knightley about a bug on her neck, Harriet sits alone, and Frank is chatting with Emma. Since the party have eaten earlier that day at Donwell, there is no picnic lunch in this version. Frank complains about the dullness of the party and, as in the novel, commands that they tell Miss Woodhouse what they are thinking. Mrs. Elton is indignant at the thought of Miss Woodhouse commanding her. Frank then says that Miss Woodhouse commands from each of them "one thing very clever" or "two things moderately clever—or three things very dull indeed...." Miss Bates says, "'Three things very dull indeed.' That will just do for me, you know. I shall be sure to say three dull things as soon as ever I open my mouth, shan't I" (370). Emma says, "Ah, ma'am, but there may be a difficulty. Pardon me—but you will be limited as to number—only three at once" (370).

While the insults are basically the same in the three adaptations, the reactions of the party to the insult vary somewhat. In the BBC version, Mr. Knightley looks grim as Miss Bates, who is seated next to him, looks hurt. (Jane and Mrs. Weston are not present in this version.) Apparently oblivious to Emma's having committed an impropriety, Mr. Weston laughs and poses a conundrum in praise of Emma. Emma appears unaware that her quip has been unseemly until Mr. Knightley tells her after the others have gone to the carriages, "It was badly done!" She is shown in tears riding in the carriage.

The Meridian/A&E film differs from the others particularly in the way it emphasizes the trouble which a picnic on Box Hill causes the servants. There are two carriages, three men on horseback, and a wagon filled with tables, chairs, and boxes. I counted twelve servants, including the grooms. Davies, in the screenplay, refers to the "idle rich" as waiting until the servants set up the lunch (Birtwistle, *Emma* 135). The emphasis on the servants is much in keeping with the whole film's social commentary.

It is also at Box Hill that Frank asks about the plans of Mr. Perry, the apothecary, to set up a carriage. Mr. Perry's plans are mentioned in the novel and in both the BBC and Meridian/A&E films, and constitute an important clue to Frank's attachment to Jane. McGrath, however, chose to eliminate this clue entirely from the Miramax film. In the Meridian/A&E version, Frank's father says that he does not know of such a plan and did not write to Frank about it. Frank looks at Jane slyly and says that he must have dreamed it. Later, as he, Emma, Jane, Harriet, and Mr. Knightley sit under a tree and play anagrams, Frank gives Jane letters which form the word "blunder." When he gives her letters which spell "Dixon," she reacts angrily and gets up. After the others go to where the tables are set up, Mr. Knightley asks Emma, "Do you understand the relationship between those two?" Emma says that there certainly is no attachment on Frank's side. Later, Miss Bates says that since only she and Jane know of Perry's plan, it is odd that Frank had dreamed it. Frank is overly attentive to Emma, saying that he has been under her influence since he met her in February. It is at this point that he makes the commands which lead to Emma's insulting Miss Bates. Following the insult, both Mr. and Mrs. Weston and Mr. Knightley register disapproval at Emma's cruelty to Miss Bates. This film also focuses more on Miss Bates's unhappiness, and on Emma's awareness of the disapproval of her friends. After the insult, the Eltons ostentatiously get up and walk off. Frank comments on how much they are alike. He says, "Very lucky, marrying as they did on such a short acquaintance formed in a public place! How many a man has committed himself on a short acquaintance and regretted it the rest of his life." Jane, sensing that this statement alludes to his engagement to her, says, "Such things do occur, undoubtedly. But only the weakest characters will allow such an unfortunate acquaintance to be an oppression for ever. Excuse me." This reaction is a surprise to everyone but Frank.

The Miramax film omits both the reference to Perry's plans and the game of anagrams, and in this version Emma appears to be drawn into the insult because of Frank's efforts to shift attention from Jane. As the party is seated on the ground in a circle around a cold picnic lunch, Mrs. Elton tells Jane that she has found her a position. Jane protests that she is not ready to take a position, but Mrs. Elton insists that she take it. Frank, overhearing this conversation, interjects his "commands" chiefly as a way to stop Mrs. Elton from persisting in her torment of Jane. The Eltons, rather than yield to Emma's commands, announce that they plan to pick more berries. Then Emma insults Miss Bates. In this film Mrs. Weston and Mr. Knightley both look disapproving, but although Emma appears to be aware of their disapproval, she is later surprised at the heat of Mr. Knightley' reproof. In fact, Mr. Knightley actually seizes Emma's arm. Some viewers, mindful of the serious breach of good manners which

Knightley commits by this rough treatment, may feel that this action is not only inappropriate but unlikely for this character.

The scenes leading up to and including Mr. Knightley's proposal to Emma also make for interesting comparison. The BBC and the Meridian/A&E films are similar to each other and to the events described in the novel, except for there being less dialogue, up to the point where Emma is called upon to respond to his proposal. In the novel, it has been raining, but when the rain ceases, Emma goes out for a walk. After a few turns in the shrubberies she sees Mr. Knightley, apparently just returned from London. He walks with her, commiserating with her over Frank's supposed betrayal of her. He is so delighted at her confession that she does not care for Frank that he is inspired to go further. He says that he envies Frank Churchill, but when she declines to ask him the cause of this envy, he persists. Because she thinks that he is about to speak of his feelings for Harriet, she asks him not to commit himself now. Then he looks so dejected that she relents and says that as his friend she will hear anything he wants to say. At this point he says, "Tell me, then, have I no chance of ever succeeding?" (430). Then we have about a page detailing Emma's reflections as her lover urges her to respond. However, rather than tell us what Emma said, Jane Austen indulges in one of what Sid Gottlieb calls her "characteristic anti-climactic dedramatizations" (Conf. Paper, July 1, 1999). "What did she say? Just what she ought, of course. A lady always does" (*E* 431). Shortly after the proposal, Mrs. Weston gives Emma the letter which Frank wrote explaining and defending himself. After Emma shows Mr. Knightley the letter, they come to an understanding about their living arrangements. Mr. Knightley is willing to come to live at Hartfield.

In the BBC version, the proposal itself occurs in a gazebo, where Emma and Mr. Knightley have taken refuge from the dampness. They are sitting as Mr. Knightley tells her that he cares for her. She is silent. The film then cuts to Mr. Woodhouse, who is in the house worrying about his daughter's health and who has actually sent for Mr. Perry. Back in the gazebo, apparently Emma has given Mr. Knightley a positive response, so that they now decide to keep their plans secret until Emma can prepare her father. There is no embrace. In its discretion in the handling of the proposal, certainly this version is closest to the treatment in the novel, but it is not dramatically satisfying. As in the Meridian/A&E version, the winning argument with Mr. Woodhouse for the marriage is that Mr. Knightley will be a defense against chicken thieves. In the Meridian/A&E version, the proposal itself takes place in the garden and it is followed by a close-up of a very innocent looking kiss.

The Miramax version plays up the comic elements of Emma's uncertainty as she tries to decide whether Mr. Knightley loves Harriet. The director has used a series of mini-scenes to show the wavering processes of her thoughts. When she talks to Mrs. Weston, she tries to prepare herself for how he will look if his brother has approved his match with Harriet; as she prepares the menu, the cook asks whether Mr. Knightley will be there for dinner, since Emma has ordered his favorite dish; she gets up in the middle of the night to take down Harriet's picture; and she is seen in the church praying in voiceover that Mr. Knightley not marry anyone except herself. She walks out of the church and almost runs into Mr. Knightley. The proposal itself takes place under the branches of a giant oak tree. He asks her to tell him whether there is any hope for him. She says that if she is silent it is that she does not want to awake from this wonderful dream. He says, "Marry me, my wonderful, darling friend." They kiss. Almost immediately she says that she cannot abandon her father. He says that he will come to live at Hartfield, and they embrace again. At this point the camera backs into a long shot of the pair embracing under the tree.

The conclusions of the cinematic versions also differ. In the novel, Emma writes to Harriet telling her of her engagement to Mr. Knightley, and Harriet's letter to her shows some resentment. However, Emma gets her sister to invite Harriet to London. Mr. Knightley reports to Emma that Robert Martin had gone to London on business, had seen Harriet at the John Knightleys' house, and when he had proposed to her again, she had accepted. When Emma tells her father of her intention to marry Mr. Knightley, he is distressed, but after the Westons are robbed of their turkeys, he decides that he would like to have Mr. Knightley in the house. The wedding is summarized in the last paragraph. Hearing the details from her husband, Mrs. Elton thought it shabby: "Very little white satin, very few lace veils; a most pitiful business!" (*E* 484).

The BBC rendering of these final pages is faithful except that Emma writes to Harriet for a meeting, not telling her about the engagement. Thus, Emma is spared Harriet's ill will, since Harriet accepts Mr. Martin's proposal before she knows about Emma's engagement. This film ends with a gathering at Hartfield of Jane and Frank, the Westons, and Mr. Knightley, during which the couples congratulate each other and admire the Westons' baby. True to his character, Mr. Woodhouse tries to keep Mrs. Weston (Ellen Dryden), a new mother, from drinking wine. Mr. Woodhouse was right, this time, to try to prevent a nursing mother from drinking alcoholic beverages. The BBC version is the only one in which Mrs. Weston goes through a pregnancy and produces a baby. Ellen Dryden is so large that it is never readily apparent that she is pregnant, but Mr. Woodhouse frequently refers to "poor Miss Taylor's" unfortunate condition.

The Meridian/A&E version ends, as has been indicated, with a harvest and a harvest dinner. Before these, however, Harriet comes to tell Emma that she has accepted Robert Martin. Harriet breaks her news before Emma has a chance to tell her of her own engagement. Again, Emma is spared recriminations. Then in one short scene, Emma tells Mr. Woodhouse of her wish to marry Mr. Knightley. He protests, but when Emma mentions the theft of poultry, he relents.

The Miramax version squeezes in a great deal with some quick cutting. With the camera shooting from outside of Hartfield through a window at a middle distance, we first see Mr. Woodhouse elated at the news which Emma and Mr. Knightley give him. Next we see the Westons congratulating them. Then we see Frank, Jane, and Miss Bates rejoicing at the news. Next there's a cut to Emma giving Harriet the news in the same room, again from a perspective outside of the window. Harriet rushes away in tears. No dialogue accompanies these scenes. In the next scene, obviously after a lapse of time, Harriet comes into the solarium to tell Emma that she is going to marry Robert Martin. The final scene shows Emma and Mr. Knightley coming out of a church down a path toward the camera. Their friends line the path on both sides. At the end of the path they pause and kiss. In close-up we see Mrs. Elton, who says in an aside that there is "a shocking lack of satin." We then return to the painted globe with which the film began. One item of interest on the painted globe is a picture of the Westons with a baby, the only reference to a baby in the film.

Some elements unique to the Miramax film include Emma's puppies. On two occasions Emma invites Harriet to the stables to visit the puppies, both times apparently to distract her from her disappointment over Mr. Elton's preference for others. Apparently the scene's only purpose is to add some humor and variety of scene. One time Harriet cries because a puppy's eyes remind her of Mr. Elton's eyes. Another, more significant element is Emma's driving a gig, once when she goes to visit Harriet and another time when she gets stuck in the stream and has to be rescued by Frank Churchill. In another scene, Emma appears to be competent with bow and arrow. Both her control of her horse and her mastery of the bow function symbolically to show her will to control situations. However, her control is threatened when her gig becomes stuck and when her aim goes awry. In this latter situation, Mr. Knightley is telling her how wrong she is to interfere between Harriet and Mr. Martin.

Emma (Miramax 1996). Both Emma Woodhouse (Gwyneth Paltrow) and Mr. Knightley (Jeremy Northam) are armed and dangerous. (Photofest)

Emma starts out by shooting better than Mr. Knightley, but after he berates her, she ends up missing the target entirely. Both the driving a one-horse vehicle and shooting arrows at a target would have been acceptable activities for a young woman in Jane Austen's time, but it is unlikely that the old fussbudget Mr. Woodhouse would ever have condoned her driving a gig.

The settings of the three cinematic versions differ in a variety of ways. The BBC mini-series was shot primarily on sets created at the BBC either for this film or recycled from sets made for others. I counted about fourteen different interiors. Very few scenes appear to have been filmed outdoors, and at least two of these could have been sets. Only four scenes have obviously been filmed outdoors. Filming outside the studio takes more time than filming in the studio and thus costs more. Economy was the driving force behind the reluctance to go on location, and economy was the byword for production of the BBC Classic Serials in the sixties and seventies (Lauritzen 30–32). The Meridian/A&E production had the luxury of on-location shooting. The filmmakers sought out country houses, countryside, gardens, ruins, and a real village to use as their settings. They used Trafalgar Park in Wiltshire for the exterior of Hartfield, its gardens, and several of the main rooms. Sudeley Castle, in Glouces-

tershire, became the exterior of Donwell Abbey, and Dorney Court, in
Berkshire, became Randalls. The great hall at Broughton Castle, near
Banbury, served as the location for the harvest banquet. Thame Park, in
Oxfordshire, supplied the Hartfield dining room, bedroom, painting studio, the Martins' farm and house, the gypsy camp, and the cottages of the
poor (Birtwistle, *Emma* 34–38). Lacock Village, a National Trust village
in Wiltshire and often used as a set for period films, was Highbury
(Birtwistle, *Emma* 27). Since the shooting of the film occurred during the
summer, it was necessary to change the appearance of some exteriors in
order to show the proper season—for example, snow on the ground on
the night of the Christmas party. The novel runs from the early fall of
one year to the following fall. The filmmakers apparently made no effort
to avoid scenes set outdoors, and even added a few outdoor scenes that
are not in the novel at all. I mention, for example, the scene in which
Robert Martin observes Jane Fairfax walking in an obviously agitated
frame of mind through the fields. Another example is the scene in which
Mr. Knightley on horseback watches the harvesters in the fields.

The Meridian/A&E film makes a nice contrast to the Miramax
Emma in the uses of setting and costume to reflect the seasons. In the
Miramax film the viewer has no consistently clear sense of season. Certainly the fall setting early in the film is apparent when Emma and Harriet are walking through the arbor made of the branches of apple trees;
there are apples on the ground and on the branches (obviously stuck in
place). Also, one scene takes place in a room which is being decorated with
apples and fall flowers. There is snow during the Christmas Eve party.
However, when Frank Churchill arrives in Highbury in February, Emma
is riding in a gig wearing a short-sleeved yellow and white summer dress.
This is neither seasonal nor sensible. The scene in which Harriet poses
for a picture, a scene set in late autumn (and indoors in the novel and in
both of the other two films), is set outdoors, with Emma and Harriet
both lightly clad. The scene in which Emma shoots arrows with Mr.
Knightley is also set in the autumn, but again Emma is lightly dressed in
a short-sleeved orange-colored dress. Contrary to the custom of the times,
Emma often does not wear a hat while she is outdoors, as in the archery
scene and when driving the gig.

Paltrow may not be dressed for the season, but she looks really beautiful. Hilary Alexander points out that she looks as if she had just "stepped
off a John Galliano catwalk" and adds that her dresses exude "a modern,
sexy allure" (2). Kali Pappas says that the costume designer combined elements of various styles of the period from 1805 to 1815. She adds that the
sleeveless chemise dress, worn under a sheer white blouse, which Emma

wears as she confides to Mrs. Weston that she loves Mr. Knightley, doesn't match anything that she has seen from the era, but falls into the "fantasy category." She postulates that Myers was trying to achieve an "airy, fairy-tale quality" to go with the Rachel Portman score and the beauty of the settings ("*Emma* Two" 3).

Jenny Beavan, who designed the costumes for *Sense and Sensibility*, also designed the costumes for the Meridian/A&E version. Beavan apparently chose to mix styles from the first two decades of the nineteenth century. Pappas points out that she also dressed each of the women in distinctive styles to suggest their different personalities. For example, for Emma she chose a gown with "a short, tucked hem, puffed oversleeves, long undersleeves, and a gathered bodice." She made several similar gowns from the same pattern. She also chose tall, big hats for Emma to suggest her domineering character (3). Mrs. Elton is the most "trendy" of the women. She wears frills at her hem, lots of trim and braid, and bold colors. The clothing for all of the women is in keeping with the season. Both Emma and Harriet wear fitted long-sleeved pelisses of a heavy fabric during the winter, and Mrs. Weston wears some beautiful Indian shawls.

The costumes of the Miramax film contrast not only with those of the Meridian/A&E film but with Joan Ellacot's costumes in the 1972 BBC version, since in the BBC version we see much variation in the dress of the ladies as appropriate to their characters and in keeping with the season of the year. Harriet wears soft colors and simple bonnets; Emma wears more sophisticated styles. Through the winter months, in the outdoor scenes Emma can be seen wearing an ermine-lined cape and a maroon long-sleeved spencer.

John Glenister tried to use the weather and time of year to reinforce psychological states of his characters and also to indicate the progression of their relationships (Lauritzen 123). Glenister said in a letter that he consciously began and ended his film showing hydrangeas in bloom, flowers which he says bloom in early autumn. He adopted Austen's idea to show Emma, just before Mr. Knightley returns from London, first housebound by the rain and then able to go out for a walk. He shows her from a perspective outside a window, looking out into the rain as she waits for the rain to stop. The time is one of loneliness and doubt for her, since she is unsure of Mr. Knightley's feelings. Her mood of gloom is well expressed by the weather. Glenister says that when she meets Mr. Knightley she is "a bedraggled, sad creature," no longer crisp and sparkling (Lauritzen 122).

In contrast to the Meridian/A&E film, which succeeds in using landscape effectively, not only to show the season but to provide appropriate backdrops for the action and characters, the director of the Miramax film has selected merely beautiful settings as backdrops for his heroine. Unlike the novels *Sense and Sensibility* and *Pride and Prejudice*, *Emma* gives few cues to the filmmaker as to the kinds of landscape to use. The novel's omniscient narrator comments on the view of the countryside around Donwell Abbey: "It was a sweet view—sweet to the eye and the mind. English verdure, English culture, English comfort, seen under a sun bright, without being oppressive" (*E* 360). I believe that the Meridian/A&E film fulfills our expectation of fields under cultivation, gardens one might expect to find in Surrey, and nothing really wild or spectacular. However, in the Miramax film, we do not see characteristic British landscapes. Rather, we see a green lawn with a beautiful (modern) tent set up where Emma and Harriet may sew and gossip. We see a great house, a lake, and a spreading green lawn on which Emma and Mr. Knightley shoot arrows and take tea. We see a giant tree with wide-spreading limbs under which Mr. Knightley proposes to Emma. We also see Mr. Knightley with Emma and Mrs. Weston in the gardens behind Hartfield (filmed at Mapperton House). In the episode of the gypsies, we see a trail through a wooded area, and prior to the proposal we see Mr. Knightley and Emma walking down a path between woods and a stream. However, we get little sense any particular English countryside. It was made on location in England, and used the village of Evershot, in Dorset, and three great houses—Stratford Saye, Croydon House, and Mapperton. Caroline Evans says that many of the locations are "very unauthentic," and that "This Highbury looks like a patchwork of villages from all over Dorsetshire, which is exactly what it is!" (www.pemberley.com/kip/emma/chron.html).

The soundtrack of the BBC film relies heavily upon the pianoforte, which both Emma and Jane play during the film and which is appropriate music for the period. Each of the six episodes in the BBC serial begins with a signature tune, a period dance tune called "The 29th May." Glenister saw this tune as desirable to get the viewer into the appropriate mood for the serial (Lauritzen 124). This lively tune is also played as dance music at the Coles' party and at the Crown Inn (Lauritzen 124). Jane plays on the pianoforte a piece by Schumann and a piece from Schubert's *Rosamunde* ballet. We hear Emma practicing the same piece from the *Rosamunde* ballet and hear it in the background while Emma walks despondently in the wet garden. There is no other "mood" music in the film (Lauritzen 125).

By contrast the background music in the Meridian/A&E version is orchestral, relying mainly on the piano. One theme, which is associated with Donwell Abbey, relies heavily on horns and is reminiscent of the theme tune associated with Darcy and Pemberley in the BBC/A&E *Pride and Prejudice*. Music is heard most often in transitions from one scene to another, but occasionally it is used to intensify the incident being shown, as in the case of the rather overwrought music in the background of the storm at sea which Emma imagines after hearing of Mr. Dixon's rescue of Jane. As in the other adaptations, Emma plays and sings a simple tune, this time an Irish song "To Love and Ireland," with Frank joining in the singing. Afterwards, Jane Fairfax plays and sings an Italian song, and Frank joins in singing when she acquiesces to his request that she play an Irish song.

The music of the Miramax *Emma* was composed and orchestrated by Rachel Portman and features solos by the harp, clarinet, and flute. Unlike John Glenister, Douglas McGrath made copious use of music to reflect and to set the mood. In this film both Emma and Jane sing and play the pianoforte.* Their contrasting types of songs indicate both the nature of the singer and the singer's expertise in singing and playing. Emma begins, singing an English translation of an Italian aria. Its simplicity suits both her talent and character. It might be noted here that Emma is shown playing the pianoforte wearing gloves. Jane Fairfax sings and plays (without gloves) a piece from John Gay's *The Beggar's Opera*, called "Virgins Are Like the Fair Flower," a piece both melancholy in tone and difficult of execution (www.pemberley.com/kip/emma/2music).

In all three films, dancing plays an important part, just as it does in the BBC/A&E *Pride and Prejudice*. George Bluestone has written about the way dancing in the 1940 version of *Pride and Prejudice* reflects relationships (130–131). In the novel *Emma* dancing occurs in two places. One of these is the party at the Coles' and the other the Crown Inn. In the BBC film, these are the locations of the dancing, but the Meridian/A&E film has three instances of dancing—at Randalls, at the Crown Inn, and at the harvest banquet. Surprisingly the Miramax film has only one instance of dancing—at the Crown Inn.

The importance of the dancing at the Crown Inn is shown by its inclusion in the novel and in all three film versions. In the novel, Mr. Elton slights Harriet, causing Mr. Knightley to "rescue" her, a good deed which inspires Harriet to turn her affections to Mr. Knightley. Ironically, this is also the scene in which Mr. Knightley shows most clearly his attachment for Emma. When he asks with whom she plans to dance the last set, she

---

Kathryn Libin points out that although the pianofortes in Emma, Sense and Sensibility, *and* Pride and Prejudice *are authentic period instruments, they emit a modern sound (189).*

responds, "With you, if you will ask me." She goes on to say that it is not improper since they are not brother and sister. He says, "Brother and sister! no, indeed" (*E* 331). The dialogue in the films in the dance scenes mirrors closely that in the novel.

In the novel Jane Austen makes no effort to describe dancing, rather than to tell who danced with whom. In the various film adaptations of *Emma*, the viewer may see not only who danced with whom, but how they looked at their partners and at others in the room and how the music sounded. The filmmakers also convey ideas through the choreography and the type of music chosen. In the Miramax film, the dancing is used in a particularly effective manner. As Emma is dancing with Frank, she keeps looking at Harriet and is obviously fretting about her being left alone. Emma is visibly pleased when Mr. Knightley approaches Harriet and then leads her into the dance. He and Harriet dance rapidly and triumphantly from the back of the double line of dancers to the front. In the final dance of the evening, Mr. Knightley and Emma dance to a much slower tempo. This dance is a variation on "Mr. Beveridge's Maggot," the dance which Elizabeth and Darcy dance at the Netherfield Ball in the BBC/A&E *Pride and Prejudice* ("*Emma* 2 Non-soundtrack Music"). It is emotionally charged in *Pride and Prejudice*, and it conveys much of the same charge in the Miramax *Emma*.

Jane Gibson, in charge of the choreography in the Meridian/A&E film, used the dancing in the final scenes to create a visual image of the harmony which exists among the three couples and thus to conclude this story about matchmaking. Gibson choreographed a variation on "Mr. Isaac's Maggot" and "Step Stately." First Mr. Knightley leads Emma down the length of the room, followed by Frank Churchill and Jane Fairfax, followed by Robert Martin and Harriet. The whole company form into pairs behind them. The three men and three women in lines move towards each other; then, holding the hands of their partners, they turn away to form a circle of six. Gibson called this forming of a circle "an enduring symbol of harmony" (Birtwistle, *Emma* 70).

In sum, *Emma* has inspired four creditable adaptations. Even the 1972 BBC adaptation, which suffers from a certain claustrophobia, has its appealing qualities. Davies' sociological approach makes the Meridian/A&E adaptation particularly interesting, and the McGrath film is illuminated by the presence of Gwyneth Paltrow. The most imaginative of the four, however, is Amy Heckerling's tour de force, *Clueless*, which reminds us that there will always be Emmas among us.

VI

Persuasion

Jane Austen wrote *Persuasion*, her last completed novel, between August 8, 1815, and August 6, 1816. During the summer of 1816, she began to feel ill of the disease of which she ultimately died, at the age of 42, on July 18, 1817. Many have speculated that the emphasis on the autumnal setting and on the aging twenty-seven-year-old heroine reflects the mood of Austen at that time and her awareness of her own unmarried situation. The novel portrays a woman who has been slighted and neglected within her family. When she has a second chance at love, she rejects the values of her family and follows her own best instincts. When she was nineteen, Anne Elliot, daughter of a baronet, Sir Walter Elliot, had wanted to marry Frederick Wentworth, a naval officer just beginning his career, but her father and a family friend, Lady Russell, convinced her to reject him. Eight years later, she meets her former lover again, and when he reiterates his proposal, she follows her own inclinations in choosing to marry him. The story resembles that of *Mansfield Park* to the extent that it is a kind of "ugly duckling" tale. Anne goes from being perceived as a plain, unloved old maid, called upon to play as others dance, to being seen as attractive and sought as a wife by two eligible gentlemen.

The story begins with Sir Walter Elliot, who has been living beyond his means, reluctantly deciding to go to live in Bath while renting his mansion, Kellynch Hall. With him go Elizabeth, his eldest daughter, and her good friend, Mrs. Clay, the daughter of Mr. Shepherd, a lawyer. His daughter Anne goes to Uppercross to spend some time with her sister Mary, intending to join her father in Bath after two months. While she is at Uppercross, Admiral Croft and his wife rent Kellynch Hall, and shortly afterwards Captain Frederick Wentworth, Mrs. Croft's brother, comes to visit them. Wentworth is the man who had asked Anne Elliot to marry him eight years before. When he comes to pay his respects to the Musgroves, the two unmarried Musgrove girls, Louisa and Henrietta, vie for his attention. Anne still loves Wentworth and is distressed to find him so seemingly indifferent to her and so receptive to Louisa's blandishments. When Wentworth announces his plan to visit a friend in Lyme, Charles Musgrove, his sisters, his wife, and Anne decide to go with him for an overnight outing. At Lyme, they find Wentworth's friend Captain Harville and his family and Captain Benwick, another friend, whose fiancée has recently died. Anne finds herself discussing poetry with Benwick, whose interest in Anne inspires jealousy in Wentworth. By his attentions to Louisa, however, Wentworth appears to have committed himself to her. Anne also notices a young man at the inn who shows some interest in her. This turns out to be William Elliot, her cousin, who will inherit the Kellynch estate after Sir Walter's death. On the morning that they plan to return to Uppercross, Louisa foolishly jumps off the steps leading down from the Cobb and injures her head. Wentworth returns to Uppercross to inform Louisa's parents of the accident, taking Anne and Henrietta with him. Then he returns to Lyme.

At the end of December, Anne goes to Bath with Lady Russell. Here she meets William Elliot, who has renewed his acquaintance with Sir Walter. Although Elizabeth is interested in Mr. Elliot as a possible spouse, he seems more interested in Anne. Anne also visits her old school friend, Mrs. Smith, who is ill and poor. Soon, Wentworth and the Crofts come to Bath. Anne is delighted to hear that Wentworth is free of his entanglement with Louisa Musgrove, since Louisa, while recuperating from her injury, has fallen in love with Benwick. Anne also realizes that Wentworth must be still in love with her because he is jealous of William Elliot's attentions to her. Lady Russell urges her to marry William Elliot and thus claim her rightful position as the lady of Kellynch Hall. Mrs. Smith, however, reveals to her the base character of Mr. Elliot so that she is not tempted to marry him. One of his motives is the desire to be close to Sir Walter to keep him from marrying Mrs. Clay. At this point, Anne's main problem is to get Wentworth to overcome his pride and renew his suit to her. When the Musgroves come to Bath to buy wedding clothes for Henrietta and Louisa, Anne visits them at their inn. Wentworth is also there. After he overhears a conversation she has with Captain Harville, in which she says that women love longer than men when there is no hope, he decides to take a chance that she still loves him. He writes her a note asking that she meet him outside to let him know her feelings. They meet, they are reconciled, and they plan to marry. When Mr. Elliot finds out, he leaves for London, where Mrs. Clay joins him. Wentworth

Persuasion (BBC 1960). Anne Elliot (Daphne Slater) and William Elliot (Derek Blomfield). (BBC Picture Archives)

resigns himself to being happier than he deserves and Anne enjoys being a sailor's wife.

The history of the dramatization of *Persuasion* is shorter and less varied than that of *Sense and Sensibility, Emma,* and *Pride and Prejudice.* During four consecutive weeks from December 30, 1960, to January 20, 1961, BBC TV presented the first television adaptation of the novel. It was based on a screenplay by Michael Voysey and Barbara Burnham and was presented in black and white in four parts (Wright 450). Daphne Slater, who had played Elizabeth Bennet in the 1952 *Pride and Prejudice,* played Anne Elliot, and Paul Daneman (*Zulu,* 1964, "A Perfect Spy," 1987) played Captain Frederick Wentworth. Two more recent cinematic adaptations are available for viewing, both carrying the title of the novel and both set in the nineteenth century. One was dramatized by Julian Mitchell, produced and directed by Howard Baker, and presented on ITV in five parts from April 18 to May 16, 1971. It runs 225 minutes on videotape. The BBC presented the other on BBC-2 in April 1995 and subsequently released it in theatres. Its first appearance in the United States was at the Telluride Film Festival on September 3, 1995. It opened throughout the country in October to good reviews. This adaptation was based on Nick Dear's first screenplay for a feature film and was directed by Roger Michell. It runs 104 minutes and is available on videotape, laserdisc, and DVD.

As might be expected, the 1971 version tells more of the story of the novel and takes fewer liberties with the plot. However, the 1995 film captures far better the spirit of the times and is more sophisticated in its visual style. Unlike most other cinematic versions of Austen's novels, this film presents a world in which the heroine is not beautiful, the hero is roughhewn, men often go about in worn and dirty clothes, and some of the characters live in grubby-looking houses. This film could hardly be disparaged, as others have been, as a pretty piece of "heritage" promotion (Sales, *Representations* 14–25).

The role of Anne Elliot was played by Ann Firbank (*A Passage to India*, 1984; *Anna and the King*, 1999) in the 1971 television production and by Amanda Root in the 1995 film. This character is presented very differently in the two versions. In the 1971 version, the character looks much the same throughout. She is slender, she is well-dressed as appropriate to the occasion, and she is always elaborately coiffed. The film-makers made no effort to show Anne as dowdy and as having lost her "bloom." Early in the film, Lady Russell (Marian Spencer) indicates to the viewer that Anne has declined in appearance when she tells Anne that she should have married Charles Musgrove (William Kendall). "You were very attractive then," she says. Anne is dressed more elaborately and more colorfully while in Bath, but otherwise no change is apparent. When she arrives in Bath, Sir Walter (Basil Dignam) compliments Anne on her looks and says that she must have gained weight. Even more problematic, however,

Persuasion (BBC 1995). Anne Elliot (Amanda Root) listens to the complaints of her sister, Mary Musgrove (Sophie Thompson). (MOMA)

is Firbank's lack of success in conveying that the character has intense but hidden feelings. The actress is consistently placid in her demeanor.

In the 1995 film, a conscious effort was made to show Anne undergoing a change of appearance. Amanda Root (*Forsyte Saga*, 2001; *Anna Karenina*, 2000), with her thin lips and mousy brown hair, is not a beautiful woman. Michell said that he wanted an actress "who could blush," and he commented on Root's "innocent quality" (BBC Press Release). In Nick Dear's printed screenplay, the stage directions indicate that in Anne's first appearance in the film she is less well dressed than her sister, Elizabeth, and that she looks the older of the two (5). Throughout the first part of the film, Anne is plainly dressed, rarely smiles, and wears her hair pulled back in a simple knot, with strands straggling loose. The combination of her appearance and the fact that everyone takes advantage of her renders her exactly the way she seems to her family, to the Musgroves, and even to Wentworth—a plain old maid on the fringes of life. As we first see her at Kellynch Hall, she enters the room quietly and sits away from the fireplace, near which her father stands and Elizabeth lounges, eating candy. Later, at Uppercross, we observe how Anne plays the pianoforte while everyone else dances. Roger Sales has emphasized the similarity of Anne's function in the family to that of a servant ("In the Face" 191). She has charge of the keys at Kellynch Hall, as a housekeeper would, she follows her sister's order to catalogue the pictures and clean the store room, and at Uppercross she picks up toys and tends to Mary's sick child.

Sid Gottlieb has observed that Michell uses close-ups and shots of Anne positioned off center, "with her head tilted downward, a posture of worry, weight, and perhaps even submissiveness" (3). He adds that she is often seen looking out of windows or staring at nothing, creating a picture of a woman "who is distracted, uneasy, preoccupied, uncomfortable ... and desirous of relief, escape" (3). Anne's position as an outsider is also suggested by her often being shown alone. After she hears that Wentworth has said that she has changed so much that he would not have recognized her, Anne is seen alone in her room at Uppercross Cottage looking at herself in the mirror. The camera is behind Anne, and we see her pensive face only in the mirror. Later, as she prepares to meet Wentworth for the first time in eight years, she sits before her mirror evaluating her appearance. The candlelight in this scene reveals little besides Anne's face and helps to emphasize her isolation and her desperation as she believes that Wentworth no longer loves her.

When Anne goes to Lyme and experiences the stimulation of William Elliot's and Captain Benwick's admiration (and of sea air on her pale cheeks), she begins to look better. When we see her in Bath, she has almost been transformed. She is wearing pretty clothes, her hair is stylishly dressed, and, as in the novel, her father even compliments her on her complexion and suggests that she is not so thin as she was. Anne looks particularly good in a long pink pelisse and a little pinkish-brown bonnet. Nick Dear's stage directions state: "Anne is looking better and better: her hair is lustrous, and she spends more time on it; her cheeks are rosy; she has put on a little weight" (62). Indeed, this weight gain is not obvious to the viewer, and although the modern viewer will tolerate straggly hair and pallor, most will not gladly see a heroine show the addition of weight. The director has perhaps attempted to convey this weight gain by having Anne in several scenes wear clothing more closely fitted to her body than she had worn before she went to Bath. In two scenes set in Bath she wears a pale blue form-fitting spencer with little pleats in the back. Early in the film, she wears mostly loose dresses and voluminous capes.

At Uppercross, as well as at Bath, Anne is buffeted by strong emotions. The director stated that he was drawn to the story because of its "psychological intensity" and the "realism in the way people behave." He also commented on "a kind of 'held in' quality to the two main characters," and asserted that "they don't always express their feelings" (disc cover). He has had to convey these feelings without benefit of the novel's omniscient narrator or a person in whom Anne could confide, as Elizabeth Bennet confides to her sister Jane. In the Miramax *Emma* director McGrath used voiceover to convey Emma's emotions as she dwells on her newfound love for Knightley, and in the Miramax *Mansfield Park*, director Rozema used voiceover to present what Fanny writes in her journal. Gottlieb emphasizes the way Michell used the camera to convey these strong emotions (3–4). For example, in the first meeting of Anne and Wentworth at Uppercross Cottage, Anne says only two words, "Captain Wentworth," when Mary introduces her as a former acquaintance of Wentworth. Dear's stage directions state that Anne grips the back of her chair tightly. Michell first shows a close-up of Anne's face registering shock, then zooms in to show Anne's fingers gripping the chair.

During the long walk in the country, during which Anne must witness Louisa's flirtations with Wentworth and his attentiveness to her, Anne suffers in silence. We see her haggard face as she listens to Wentworth praise Louisa for her determination always to stick to her purpose and listens to Louisa tell Wentworth that Lady Russell persuaded Anne not to marry Charles Musgrove. On their way back, Wentworth notices how tired Anne looks. When the Crofts ride up in their gig, he asks them to take Anne the rest of the way. A close-up of Wentworth's hands on Anne's waist as he assists her into the gig, followed by mid-range shots of both Anne and Wentworth, communicates well the suppressed feelings of the pair at this proximity. Anne registers only mute wonder at this physical contact and at this evidence of his concern for her. As Nick Dear says in his stage directions, "She has felt his touch, smelt his smell [...]" (42). After Anne is seated, she looks toward Wentworth, who turns away as if to avoid eye contact with her.

During Anne's ride in the gig, Mrs. Croft comments on Wentworth's marital prospects. She says that "anybody between fifteen and thirty may have him for the asking. A little beauty, a few smiles, and a few compliments to the Navy, and he's a lost man." Mrs. Croft is speaking in fun, unaware that Anne is in love with Frederick, but aware that he is likely to marry one of the Musgrove sisters. In the novel, Wentworth makes this speech about himself to his sister (*PN* 62). He appears to suggest that it doesn't matter whom he marries, but he knows even as he says it that it does matter. At that time he has no desire to see Anne Elliot again, but his idea of a wife has been shaped by his familiarity with Anne's good qualities. After he has a chance to compare the Musgrove girls to Anne, he realizes that no one is equal to Anne.

The turning point in Wentworth's attitude toward Anne comes at Lyme, where he sees her admired by two men. In the 1995 adaptation, on the evening of the party's arrival in Lyme, we see Benwick and Anne *tête à tête* before the fire reciting poetry to each other. A close-up of Wentworth's face shows him looking speculatively at the pair. Later, as Anne and the others are ascending the steps from the beach, Mr. Elliot steps back to allow them to pass. He lifts his hat and looks admiringly at Anne. Anne is aware of his admiration and of Wentworth watching this silent exchange.

Another scene which emphasizes visually the intensity of Anne's and of Wentworth's unverbalized feelings is the concert in the Assembly Rooms at Bath. By this time, Anne is sure that Wentworth cares for her, but she does not know how to overcome his doubts about her feelings. Here, when Anne observes that Wentworth is leaving the concert, she gets up from her seat and hastens toward the rear of the room to intercept him. We observe that many concert goers watch her haste in amazement. Their expressions indicate the impropriety of her haste and of her calling out to Wentworth. Her uncharacteristic impropriety and his brusqueness in response to her question about why he is leaving convey their mutual strong feelings, without either actually stating these feelings. The circling mobile camera emphasizes the chaotic nature of their emotions.

Persuasion (BBC 1995). Captain Frederick Wentworth (Ciarán Hinds) precedes his admirers on the beach at Lyme, followed by, l–r, Louisa Musgrove (Emma Roberts) and Henrietta Musgrove (Victoria Hamilton). (MOMA)

Captain Wentworth is portrayed by Bryan Marshall in the 1971 film and by Ciarán Hinds in the later version. Bryan Marshall has had a long career, mostly on British television, playing in such classics as *Vanity Fair* (1971) and *The Merry Wives of Windsor (1982)*. One striking difference in the ways these two actors are presented is that whereas Marshall wears Regency civilian apparel throughout, Hinds is usually dressed in a naval uniform. Hinds' tall stature and rugged face are entirely appropriate for this self-made man of action, and his uniform is a constant reminder of his difference from most of the other male characters. Since the more recognizable actors bring with them a baggage of association with the other roles they have played, some viewers may recall Hinds as Rochester in the 1997 BBC production of *Jane Eyre*. He glowers and sulks almost as well as Colin Firth or Laurence Olivier. In fact, he is a far more romantic figure than mousy Amanda Root. Hinds commented on how well Jane Austen "understands a man's heart and how delicate it can be sometimes" (Webster). He also liked the irony that Wentworth, a competent leader of men in his profession, is "socially inept" in the presence of Anne

("Hindsite"). While at Uppercross, and even in Lyme, he is noticeably cool to Anne, thinking that he no longer loves her and wishing to show his displeasure with her for having rejected him. On the other hand, he is open and charming to Henrietta and Louisa, who salve his ego with their adulation. In Bath, however, he is particularly stiff and uneasy around Anne, because by this time he has admitted to himself that he still loves her, but he doubts his success with her. He has heard the rumors that she plans to marry Mr. Elliot. Indeed, he encounters her often in the presence of her attentive cousin. His pride and uncertainty make him speak roughly to Anne, in spite of her overtures toward him. He also fears that she is still under the influence of Lady Russell.

A chief function of the minor characters in the novel is to furnish contrasts to either Anne or Wentworth, or occasionally to other characters. Austen describes the appearances of her minor characters in *Persuasion* more than in any of her other novels, so that the character contrasts there are often differences of both appearance and personality. Thus we are informed that Mrs. Musgrove was of "substantial size" (*PN* 68), and Mrs. Croft, "though neither tall nor fat, had a squareness, uprightness and vigour of form." She also had "bright dark eyes, good teeth [...] [and a] reddened and weather-beaten complexion" (*PN* 48). "Mrs. Clay had freckles, and a projecting tooth, and a clumsy wrist [...]" (*PN* 34). Mr. and Mrs. Musgrove are like their home, not elegant or refined, but comfortable and friendly. In their lack of pretentiousness and their generosity toward their children, however, they are very unlike the Elliot family. In her adventurous spirit, Mrs. Croft contrasts with both Mrs. Musgrove and Lady Russell. She is confident in who she is, does not worry about her complexion, and is happy as long as she can be with her husband. Anne admires Mrs. Croft and listens with interest to her stories of life at sea with her husband. Anne follows her lead when she chooses to marry a sailor. Mrs. Croft also has an "openness" which Anne looks for in her friends. Both she and Mrs. Smith are without pretense or secretiveness, unlike her snobbish sisters and the deceitful Mrs. Clay. Mrs. Clay's physical defects cause Elizabeth to be lulled into thinking that her father could never marry such a woman, but Anne sees Mrs. Clay's "assiduous pleasing manners" (*PN* 34) and her youth as likely to appeal to Sir Walter. The other young women in the novel—Mary, Elizabeth, Henrietta, and Louisa—are not described but furnish striking personality contrasts to Anne.

In the selection of the actors for the minor roles and in the presentation of the minor characters, the two films continue to illustrate very different looks. The 1971 film tends to present all of the Elliots, the Musgroves, the Harvilles, and Captain Benwick (Paul Chapman) as well dressed in the style of the Regency. The men wear cut-away coats and tight long trousers, even when walking outdoors or hunting. In the 1995 adaptation, Captain Harville (Robert Glenister) and Captain Benwick (Richard McCabe) wear naval uniforms which show signs of wear and are not very clean. Both Harville and Benwick are unattractive men—Harville with a plain face and crooked teeth, and Benwick with a round, bearded face and a pudgy body.

In the 1971 adaptation, Sir Walter (Basil Dignam) and Elizabeth (Valerie Gearon) are, of course, more elaborately dressed than anyone else, especially in the scenes set in Bath, when they are going out into society. In the 1995 film, Sir Walter's hair is obviously dyed. His cutaway coats and knee breeches are immaculate and made of rich fabrics. He wears low, slipper-like shoes, and never appears in riding boots. His clothing varies from the elaborate, when he is at home, to the more elaborate, as when he is presented to Lady Dalrymple and her daughter. In the interests of "naturalness," the director has chosen not to have the men wear wigs, as one might have expected Sir Walter to do when in society (BBC press release). As in the novel, Sir Walter is shown to be fond of admiring himself in the mirror or in any shiny surface, and no matter how extreme the flattery of Mrs. Clay (Charlotte Mitchell), to Sir Walter it appears justified. The actors in both films present Sir Walter in such a way that he is too obviously ridiculous for the viewer to hate him. In the 1995 film, Sir Walter (Corin Redgrave) even appears pathetic as he frets about how to address Lady Dalrymple (Beatrix Mackey) and later as he leads his family in bowing before Lady Dalrymple and her daughter, Miss Carteret (Angela Galbraith). At the concert in the Assembly Rooms, Miss Carteret looks at the dozing Sir Walter with amusement. He is the last in a long line of Austen's foolish or absent parents, who, through neglect or misbehavior, cause their children grief. The reader of the novel and the viewer of the films may rejoice that, although Anne had given up Wentworth because of her father's negative view of him and because of Lady Russell's persuasion, Anne prevails in the end and Sir Walter is frustrated at every turn. Sir Walter learns that his heir has run off with Mrs. Clay, and he must be resigned to the fact that Mr. Elliot has rejected his favorite daughter, Elizabeth.

Both Frederick Wentworth and Admiral Croft appear in striking contrast to Sir Walter both in appearance and in manner. We never see Sir Walter in a natural setting, whereas we see both Wentworth and Croft walking and riding, or, in the 1995 film, on board ship. Admiral Croft comes across as intelligent and down to earth. He is even witty as he jokes to Anne about how well Wentworth has recovered from Louisa's engagement to Captain Benwick. When he visits at Charles and Mary Mus-grove's home, he wins over her two rowdy sons by rocking them on his knees and then by making and sailing a paper boat with them. It is inter-esting to observe, however, that in the novel, although Admiral Croft (John Woodvine) is presented as a capable leader of men at sea, Mrs. Croft is indispensable for keeping him out of ditches while he is driving his gig (*PN* 92). In the 1995 version, Wentworth wonders aloud to Louisa where the Crofts' gig has overturned that day. The Crofts' marriage appears to be both a love-match and a partnership of equals, a marital relationship which perhaps anticipates that of Anne and Wentworth. In both films, Anne listens attentively as Mrs. Croft (Fiona Shaw) describes her travels with her husband on his ships, and at the end of the 1995 ver-sion, we actually see Anne on board Wentworth's ship.

The Musgrove parents in both films provide the contrast which they furnish in the novel. They dote on their children, dealing generously with their eldest son, Charles, and indulgently with their daughters, Louisa and Henrietta. The novel and the films also emphasize that when the two daughters wish to marry, their parents do not make objections but assist them to marry the men they love—again in contrast to Sir Walter's behav-ior to Anne. In the 1995 version, both Mrs. Musgrove (Judy Cornwell) and Mr. Musgrove (Roger Hammond) are fat and jolly. When Anne vis-its them, she enters a home, not a sterile showplace like Kellynch Hall. Sheldon Manor near Chippenham in Wiltshire served as the Musgrove great house. The exterior is impressively large and ancient, but the inte-rior looks comfortable and lived in. This setting contrasts with the aus-tere grandeur of Kellynch. Dear's stage directions on Anne's first visit to the great house call for a drawing room "decorated in the old style," "roar-ing log fires in two huge old farmhouse grates" (16). The walls are pan-eled in a dark wood, the furniture looks comfortable, and there's a bright carpet on the floor. Few servants are in sight, and these few are dressed in ordinary rough clothes. When Mr. Musgrove and Charles enter, Dear's directions call them "ruddy, hearty, jovial countryfolk." He says further, "Their boots are caked in mud, but nobody cares" (17). In keeping with Dear's portrayal of the Musgroves as plain "countryfolk," Sir Walter later refers to Louisa as "the farmer's daughter."

In the 1971 version, however, the Musgrove house appears to be more grand in size and much more orderly within doors—no mud, no dogs. This Mr. Musgrove (William Kendall) is fat and jolly, but his wife (Noel Dyson) is lean. On Anne's first visit, Charles (Rowland Davies) and Mary bring their two little boys, who begin to fight and scream and have to be carried away by Charles and the maid. This provides an occasion for Mrs.

Musgrove to complain to Anne that Mary spoils her children. We have already heard Mary confide to Anne, as they were on their way to the big house, that Charles is to blame for the boys' bad behavior and that Mrs. Musgrove gives them too many sweets when they visit her.

One rather ambiguous situation involving Mrs. Musgrove, which is treated in the 1971 adaptation but is omitted from the 1995 adaptation, has to do with Dick Musgrove, a good for nothing who had died while serving in the navy. Mrs. Musgrove is overcome with sadness when she realizes that her dead son had once served under Captain Wentworth. Wentworth finds it hard to be sympathetic, but he composes himself and enters into serious conversation with her. In the novel Austen's narrator says something remarkable for its coldness: "Captain Wentworth should be allowed some credit for the self-command with which he attended to her large fat sighings over the destiny of a son, whom alive nobody had cared for" (*PN* 68). Apparently Austen had little understanding of or sympathy for a mother's love for a scapegrace child. Indeed, she had little interest in small children and is never sentimental about children in her novels. Mary's two little boys spread mayhem wherever they are. At one point Wentworth rescues Anne from little Walter as he climbs on her back. In the novel, Anne finds the "domestic hurricane" (*PN* 134) created at Uppercross Hall by the Musgrove children and the visiting Harville children less than soothing to the nerves, and Lady Russell resolves not to visit the Musgroves again at Christmas because of the children's noise.

Mary Musgrove, Anne's snobbish and hypochondriacal sister, is very different from the capable and sensible Anne. In the 1971 version, Mary (Morag Hood) is slender, pretty and well dressed. Her manner is consistently peevish. She complains about her health and about her husband's inattentiveness; she is much concerned about her status and is forever finding reason to fear that she is being slighted. In Lyme, after Louisa has fallen, she even insists that as a member of the Musgrove family she has a better right than Anne to stay in Lyme, refusing to yield to Wentworth's and her husband's opinion that Anne would be the more capable attendant on Louisa. In the 1995 version, she is played by Sophie Thompson (Miss Bates in the Miramax *Emma*), who is not pretty at all. She is unattractive and thoroughly dowdy. In the first scene in which she appears, we see her looking out the window, watching for the arrival of Anne. As soon as Mary sees Anne, she lies down on the window seat and pretends to be ill. After Anne has been with her for a short time, Mary apparently forgets about her illness and gets up to arrange some flowers. When Anne reminds her of her illness, she lies down again. In the next scene, Mary is in the dining room preparing to attack a huge ham and talking about taking a walk after luncheon. The point that Mary is disgustingly healthy is reiterated as we see her eating a big breakfast on the morning that Captain Wentworth comes to call. In contrast, Anne seems to eat very little. The lack of pretentiousness of Mary's husband, Charles (Simon Russell Beale), contrasts well with Mary's concern with appearances. He is customarily clad in corduroy pants and clothing suitable for hunting. Even when he is in Bath, his clothing is undistinguished and comfortable looking.

Charles Musgrove's sisters are nicely differentiated in both adaptations. Henrietta is much less sure of herself than her outspoken sister, Louisa. The 1971 adaptation emphasizes the way Henrietta (Mel Martin) fluctuates between her cousin, Charles Hayter, and Wentworth. It includes a scene in which Charles (Paul Alexander) is discussing his prospects with Henrietta on a couch, while Louisa (Zhivila Roche) looks out the window expectantly. When Louisa reports sighting Wentworth, Henrietta jumps up and runs to the window, leaving Charles talking to himself. The 1995 adaptation shows Charles (called Henry in this version) Hayter (Isaac Maxwell-Hunt) arriving on horseback at the Musgroves' house at night. He enters the room as Wentworth is swinging Henrietta (Victoria Hamilton) around in the dance. Obviously jealous, Henry leaves immediately in a huff. Both versions show Louisa urging Henrietta to go to the Hayter farm to make up with Henry/Charles. (Although Victoria Hamilton plays the diffident sister in this film, she plays the role of Maria Bertram, the more impetuous sister, in the 1999 version of *Mansfield Park*.)

Both adaptations indicate how Louisa, encouraged by Wentworth's praise of her decisiveness, progresses to her fateful leap off the steps of the Cobb. The 1971 version gives a much fuller version of the walk in the country, during which Anne overhears Wentworth telling Louisa that she should always keep to her purpose. He obviously is thinking of Anne's lack of resolution when she allowed Lady Russell to talk her out of marrying him. Later, he sees Louisa's willful and reckless behavior as foolish, greatly different from the careful, reasonable behavior of Anne. In the 1995 version, while in the chaise traveling back to Uppercross from Lyme with Anne and Henrietta, Wentworth sputters, "Damned foolish!" as he thinks about Louisa's fall, and perhaps about his own share of the responsibility for her actions.

In the 1995 adaptation, Phoebe Nicholls plays the role of Elizabeth Elliot, Anne's older sister. As Nick Dear portrays her and as Nicholls plays her, Elizabeth is unladylike in the way she sprawls on her chair with her legs stretched out in front of her, laughs loudly, talks while she has food in her mouth, and licks her fingers. Rebecca Dickson points out that this interpretation of the character misrepresents the role as Austen drew it and misrepresents the way the eldest daughter of such a family would have behaved (46). In the novel, the narrator tells us of Elizabeth's slights against Anne and shows Lady Russell's indignation over Elizabeth's preference for Mrs. Clay as her "most important and valuable assistant" (*PN* 34). In the film, Elizabeth says to Anne, "[…] since no one will want you in Bath, I am sure you had better stay here." In the novel, Elizabeth makes such a statement, but she does not make it directly to Anne. Mary has said that she wants Anne to stay with her, and in response, Elizabeth says, "Then I am sure that Anne had better stay, for nobody will want her at Bath" (*PN* 33). In this case, as in others, Dear has changed the context of the statement to place the speaker in the worst possible light. At other times he has characters state baldly what is only implied in the novel. An example is Sir Walter's response to Wentworth's request for permission to marry Anne. He says, "You want to marry Anne? Whatever for?" The effect is to coarsen characters such as Elizabeth, Sir Walter, and Mary by making them bad-mannered as well as mean-spirited.

In the scene in which Sir Walter puts pressure on Anne to go with the family to Lady Dalrymple's, Sir Walter chides her for preferring a nobody named Mrs. Smith to members of the nobility. Anne refuses to go. She says, angrily, "No, Sir, I will not. I have a prior engagement, with Mrs. Smith—who is not the only widow in Bath, with little to live on, and no surname of dignity." This scene is far more dramatic than the scene described in the novel, and it is good theatre. A modern audience may be pleased to see Anne finally stand up for herself. However, the scene requires Anne to show disrespect to her father by defying him and by slighting his guest, Mrs. Clay. In the novel, the omniscient narrator says, "[…] Anne could have said much and did long to say a little, in defence of *her* friend's not very dissimilar claims to theirs, but her sense of personal respect to her father prevented her. She made no reply. She left it to himself to recollect, that Mrs. Smith was not the only widow in Bath between thirty and forty, with little to live on, and no sirname (sic) of dignity" (*PN* 158). Thus, with her usual self-control and her sense of decorum, she avoids an ugly scene. Anne may be ready to resist the efforts of her father or Lady Russell to persuade her to courses of action which she considers wrong, but she is not confrontational. In the interest of creating dramatic tension, Dear has to a certain extent sacrificed consistency of characterization.

In keeping with the tendency of the 1995 version to emphasize that the Musgroves are country people, we see that Mary and Charles live in what Dear refers to as a "farmhouse" (13). Its rooms are small, and its furniture is old and battered. Since Mary is a poor manager, its rooms are also messy. When Anne comes in, she immediately begins picking up toys which are scattered about. By contrast, in the 1971 version, the room in which Mary greets Anne is large and its furniture is elegant. This is obviously no simple farmhouse. The novel states that the Musgroves had renovated a farmhouse for Charles and his bride, so that now Uppercross cottage has French windows, a "viranda" (sic) and "other prettinesses" (*PN* 36). It is likely, however, that such a cottage would not be any more elegant than the unpretentious Chawton Cottage, which belonged to the Chawton estate and was where Jane Austen lived during her last years. Anyone who has visited Chawton Cottage knows that it could never have been elegant or beautiful.

The 1995 adaptation consistently deglamorizes the life-styles of the characters. When Anne goes to Uppercross from Kellynch, she rides in a farmer's cart, with a pig and a goose as companions. In contrast, in the 1971 version, Anne arrives at Uppercross riding in Lady Russell's elegant carriage. In the 1995 film, when the Musgroves, Wentworth, and Anne take their long walk in the country, they become disheveled and get mud on their clothing. Michell said that he "wanted them to have hair over their faces when it's windy and wet [...] [and] wanted them to get muddy when they go for a walk in a ploughed field" (BBC press release). Similarly, in the 1995 version, the Harville's house in Lyme is small and cluttered. One can see by Mary's reaction that it does not meet her standards of elegance. The others show no disapproval; rather they are pleased with the camaraderie of the sailors. In the 1971 version, Mary is even more disapproving, yet the rooms are larger and better furnished.

William Elliot, played by David Savile in the 1971 version and by Samuel West in the 1995 film, provides a striking contrast to Frederick Wentworth. Both actors present a character who has manners, assurance, and conventional good looks. In the novel Anne arrives at the conclusion that Mr. Elliot is not "open" (*PN* 161). Although she has known him for a month, she "could not be satisfied that she really knew his character" (*PN* 160). In the 1995 film, Anne says to Lady Russell, "Why do I feel that I know him so little?" In the novel, when Anne is said to prize "the frank, the open-hearted, the eager character beyond all others" (*PN* 161), she is contrasting Wentworth with Mr. Elliot. Frank Churchill and Jane Fairfax in *Emma* are also found guilty of not being "open," and they, like Mr. Elliot, have something to hide.

In the 1995 adaptation, the character of William Elliot has been darkened to make him more of a villain than he is in the novel. Apparently Nick Dear felt that merely to have led Mrs. Smith's husband into living beyond his means and then to have neglected to assist the widow are not bad enough. This Mr. Elliot has squandered his money and wants to marry Anne to insure that he will inherit the estate. He has also apparently become involved with Mrs. Clay, so that she readily goes with him to London after Anne has rejected him. Certainly, this way he can prevent Mrs. Clay from marrying Sir. Walter. At several points in the film, Mrs. Clay shows more than a casual interest in Mr. Elliot. For instance, when she, Anne, and Elizabeth are in the confectioner's shop, she indicates that, rather than ride in the Dalrymple's carriage, she would prefer to walk home with Mr. Elliot. Another time, Anne sees Mr. Elliot talking with Mrs. Clay in the street; he is touching her hand as the two part. We are never told, however, that Mr. Elliot and Mrs. Clay go off to London together. The 1971 version indicates that Mr. Elliot wants to marry Anne to prevent Mrs. Clay from marrying Sir Walter. Mrs. Smith (Helen Schlesinger) says that he has plenty of money, but he wants the title. She also says that Mr. Elliot refused to assist her with her business affairs. We are less prepared in the novel and in this adaptation for Mr. Elliot's and Mrs. Clay's interest in each other. Anne sees the pair together and later questions Mrs. Clay, but Mrs. Clay is evasive in her answers. Only after Wentworth and Anne become engaged, do we know that a connection exists between Mr. Elliot and Mrs. Clay. At that time in the television serial we see Mr. Elliot assisting Mrs. Clay into a coach, telling her that she can buy clothes in London. The novel merely states that Mr. Elliot left Bath for London; shortly after, Mrs. Clay appeared in London, under Mr. Elliot's "protection" (*PN* 250).

The screenwriters for these adaptations did not have to stray far from the novel to contrive effective conclusions. Nick Dear's film uses pieces of both of Austen's two conclusions. However, instead of Wentworth's declaring his love for Anne at the Admiral's house, as he does in Austen's first conclusion of the novel, Wentworth asks to speak with Anne in the Pump Room. Here he claims to be inquiring on behalf of the Admiral whether Anne and Mr. Elliot would like to move into Kellynch Hall when they are married. Lady Russell (Susan Fleetwood) interrupts them before Anne can respond. Later, at the White Hart Inn, Wentworth is busy writing at a small table while listening to Captain Harville and Anne talking about the relative strength of male and female attachments. He leaves a letter for Anne in which he declares his love for her and asks her to give him a sign if she returns his love. Shortly afterwards they meet outside. The scene in which Wentworth and Anne are finally brought together in understanding is largely without dialogue. After Charles leaves the pair, Wentworth takes Anne's hand and says, "I tried to forget you. I thought I had." The film shows a close-up of their two hands coming together. Anne says nothing but looks up at him. Then he bends over to kiss her. Meanwhile, all other eyes are watching the circus troupe wending its way noisily down the street. The point of view expands to show the circus troupe and the crowd going one way, as Wentworth and Anne go the other way, toward Camden Place, arm in arm. Although some critics have lamented the too public nature of this intimate moment (e.g. Sutcliffe 12), ironically, the effect of the crowd and the loud circus music is to isolate the lovers.

The 1971 adaptation does not show Wentworth inquiring on behalf of the Admiral. The scene at the inn, where Wentworth overhears Anne's conversation with Harville, is handled similarly to that in the 1995 film. When Anne meets Wentworth outside the inn, he asks her, "Where shall we go?" She responds, "Anywhere you like, so long as it's not to my father's." She takes his arm and he places his hand on hers. As they walk, they converse — he lamenting the loss of eight and a half years, she telling of her frustration at the pressures of Mr. Elliot and Lady Russell at the concert. She tells him that he should not have been jealous. He tells her, "I've never loved anyone but you, Anne." She tells him, "No one will ever persuade me to do anything again except you." The scene ends with a long shot from a low position showing the pair as they walk across a lawn.

This adaptation ends with a series of brief scenes tying up loose ends of the plot. Anne tells Lady Russell that she loves Frederick. We see Mr. Elliott hurriedly putting Mrs. Clay into a coach and getting in himself. At the party, Elizabeth looks for Mrs. Clay, and Colonel Wallis reports that Mrs. Clay and Mr. Elliott have gone off to London. During the party, we also see Lady Russell speaking with Wentworth, the Crofts offering their congratulations to Anne, and Wentworth telling Anne that in time he will try to forgive Lady Russell. Wentworth asks Anne whether she would have accepted him sooner if he had asked her. When she says that she would have, he blames himself for his pride. They kiss slowly, twice. Unlike the 1995 version, however, the pair are indoors and alone when they kiss. As we see them together in this final scene, Wentworth's last speech is: "I shall have to put up with being far happier than I deserve." This speech is only a slight variation of the speech which ends Chapter XI in the novel (*PN* 247).

The penultimate scene in the 1995 adaptation shows the card party at Sir Walter's apartments. It is evening, and the room glows with candlelight. As Anne circulates among the tables, Elizabeth warns her not to monopolize Wentworth. Only in this adaptation do we have any indication that Elizabeth is making a play for Wentworth. As Anne pauses at Lady Russell's table, Lady Russell takes her arm and tells her to make a decision and stick to it. It is not clear whether she means that Anne should choose William Elliot or just be firm in whatever decision she makes. Anne assures her that she intends to decide for herself. Of course, she has already decided to marry Wentworth. Then William Elliot takes her aside to ask her whether she accepts his proposal, made at the concert, to "adore" her for the rest of her life. She puts him off as Wentworth and Harville enter. Wentworth immediately informs Sir Walter that Anne has accepted his proposal of marriage, and he asks Sir Walter for permission to set the date. It should be observed that Wentworth does not ask Sir Walter for the hand of his daughter, but only for permission to set the date. The novel does not describe this meeting or whether Sir Walter's consent was requested. We are merely told, "Sir Walter made no objection, and Elizabeth did nothing worse than look cold and unconcerned" (*PN* 248). In the film we see that Sir Walter is amazed. Elizabeth is angry. William Elliot and Mrs. Clay exchange glances and rise from their seats as if to go.

The opening of the final series of scenes in the 1995 adaptation is deceptive. We see Anne sitting in a small room, writing, and we hear the sounds of birds. When she gets up from the desk, we realize that she is on a ship. She goes out of the cabin and onto the deck, then climbs up to the quarterdeck to stand beside Wentworth. (These scenes were filmed on the HMS *Victory* at Portsmouth.) We see them in a medium shot; then in a long shot we see the ship outlined against a brilliant sunset. This latter, very beautiful shot was taken from the film *The Bounty* (1984). Here, as throughout the film, the viewer is made aware that Wentworth's proper milieu is not the drawing room, but the sea, and Anne takes her rightful place beside her sailor husband. The film opens with scenes of ships and men at sea, and it ends the same way.

Like all of the films of the 1990s based on Austen's novels, *Persuasion* benefits from the larger expenditure of money than the BBC put forth during the 1970s and 1980s. This advantage shows particularly in the way the film moved out of the studio and into the great houses, the city of Bath, Lyme, and the countryside of southwest England. This on-location shooting brings a greater realism to the later adaptation. It also enabled the filmmakers to make fuller use of setting for symbolism and for creation of mood. It is particularly important in an adaptation of *Persuasion* that the viewer be aware of autumnal nature and weather during the early scenes. In the novel, on the long walk in the country, Anne tries to get her mind off Wentworth and Louisa by thinking about the beauty of autumn. In the 1971 adaptation, as Wentworth walks arm in arm with Louisa, Anne recites to Henrietta some lines from James Thomson's *The Seasons: Autumn*: "Soothe the throbbing passion into peace/ And woo love quiet in the silent walks." This quotation is particularly appropriate since Anne is trying to subdue her passion for Wentworth and endure the sight of his courtship of Louisa. Anne, at the age of twenty-seven, is apprehensive about the onset of the winter of spinsterhood. Both the 1971 version and the 1995 version show fallen leaves and other signs of autumn. The 1995 version gives the more beautiful presentation of nature. The opening scenes at Kellynch Hall showing men raking and burning leaves and showing a herd of sheep against the green field are particularly beautiful, but later, when Anne is leaving Kellynch and seeing these same signs of autumn, there's a sense of her sadness at leaving her home. The scenes at Lyme are also beautifully filmed. As in the scenes at Kellynch, at Lyme we see common people at work. While the Musgrove party, Harville, Wentworth, and Benwick are sightseeing, women cut up fish, and men work around boats on the shingled beach. At this time of year, the beach and the Cobb are deserted except for those who live there, or like the Harvilles, have chosen to winter there.

The Georgian mansion, called Kellynch in the film, is both visually pleasing and appropriate as Sir Walter's family home. Roger Sales points out that Sir Walter's title is probably little more ancient than the house. The house was almost certainly built during the eighteenth century, and the title may have been bought, since according to the novel it was awarded after Charles II came to the throne, a time when titles were bought and sold ("In the Face" 172).

The opening scenes of the 1995 film are far the more imaginative than those of the 1971 adaptation, in that they establish both the historical context of the film and the problems facing the Elliot family. As the titles appear, first we see the underside of a boat in the water, then a close-up of oars, then shots of men rowing the boat, and finally the admiral seated in the bow. We realize that the boat is heading toward a ship. Then we cut to a gig carrying a man and a woman toward a great house. When the gig stops in front of the house, a herd of creditors besiege the pair (Mr. Shepherd and Mrs. Clay), who hurry into the house. A circling camera brings a chaotic quality to the scene. Then the scene shifts back to the boat as it reaches the ship. From the perspective of those on the ship, we see Admiral Croft climb aboard and begin to inspect the men. A cut returns us to Kellynch Hall, where Lady Russell dismounts from a carriage and enters the house. Another cut takes us back to the ship, where below decks the Admiral tells the officers that the war is over and they are going home. Bonaparte has been confined to Elba. This statement makes clear to the viewer that the date is 1814. In the penultimate scene of the film, at the Elliots' party, the Admiral announces that Bonaparte has left Elba and that there will be another war. More than in the novel or in the 1971 adaptation, we have a sense of the historical context, and we realize the importance of the naval officers to England in this time. The intercutting which opens the film also immediately establishes the contrast between the plight of the Elliot family, suffering only the inconvenience of having overspent their income, and the life and death issues which face those who serve in the Royal Navy.

Another emphasis more apparent in the 1995 film than in the 1971 adaptation is the superfluity of liveried servants at Kellynch Hall. To avoid the continued expense of keeping up the appearance that Sir Walter considers necessary if he were to stay at Kellynch, the family removes to Bath, where their smaller dwelling will enable them to reduce the numbers of servants as well as other costs. I counted ten servants in livery lined up at Kellynch Hall to watch Sir Walter depart, and three more on the carriage. This number does not include the many others who would cook, clean, and work outdoors. We see close-ups of several of the liveried servants as well as others attached to the estate. Their expressions range from disdain to curiosity. As Elizabeth leaves she tells Anne that Anne ought to visit every house in the parish—"It is the Elliot way." This observation is ironic, since this duty is being dumped on the family member with the least status.

The novel makes clear that Admiral Croft, the new tenant of Kellynch Hall, is more deserving of honor and respect than Sir Walter or Sir Walter's heir. If Sir Walter is selfish, improvident, and vain, William Elliot is no better. Anne appears to be tempted briefly at the thought of assuming the role of her mother at Kellynch, as the bride of William Elliot. Certainly, she would be the most worthy mistress of the place. Since this will not occur, and since the next mistress of Kellynch Hall may be Mrs. Clay, if she is able to cajole William Elliot into marrying her, the reader is left with the feeling that the true men of quality in England are her naval officers.

The cinematic versions of *Persuasion* clearly show the suitability of this novel for adaptation. The narrative is simple. It moves its main character from Kellynch Hall, to Uppercross, to Lyme and to Bath within the course of nine or ten months. For a film of theatrical length—in this case 107 minutes—Nick Dear's screenplay manages to include all of the important actions of the novel, to include most of the characters (omitting only Colonel Wallis), and to develop the main themes of the novel. The chief problem for the filmmaker is to convey the transformation of Anne Elliot from plain and passive to pretty and sought after. The most significant deviation from the novel is the darkening of William Elliot's character. Some viewers were disappointed that Anne Elliot was not played by a more beautiful actress than Amanda Root, but this kind of quibble is to be expected of readers whose imaginations have conjured up their own pictures of Austen heroines and who can accept no substitutes. Although the film had only limited theatrical release, it was well received by both film critics and Janeites. Having watched it many times, I can testify that it wears well. I consider it one of the best cinematic adaptations of Austen's novels.

VII

Northanger Abbey

Northanger Abbey was published, with *Persuasion,* in December 1818, after the author's death in July. According to Cassandra Austen the novel was written between 1798 and 1799 (Austen *MW,* facing 242); it was apparently completed and sold in 1803 to Crosby & Co., but never published. Austen regained the rights to the novel in 1816. She may have revised the novel after 1803, even before she purchased the copyright (Austen *MW,* xi–xii). In many respects the slightest of Austen's completed novels, *Northanger Abbey* is also the least typical. It is heavy-handed in its satire—on the gothic novel, on the picturesque, on hypocrisy—and very little happens in the course of the novel. Its seventeen-year-old heroine is the least complicated of Austen's protagonists, and its minor characters are not memorable. It is no wonder that in 1803 it did not inspire its prospective publisher with confidence that it would appeal to the novel-reading audience of the time. Nor has it been a popular choice for modern readers, or for television and theatrical adaptation.

In the first chapter the narrator tells us that Catherine Morland as a child did not appear to be heroine material. Up to the age of fourteen she preferred horseback riding, cricket and base ball to reading books of information. We find that at fifteen she was "almost pretty" (*NA* 14). From fifteen to seventeen she was "in training for a heroine" (*NA* 15), yet her accomplishments were few. When the reader meets her, she is, according to the omniscient third-person narrator, "about as ignorant and uninformed as the female [...] at seventeen usually is" (*NA* 18). Longing for adventure, she gladly accepts the invitation of the wealthy and childless Mr. and Mrs. Allen when they invite her to accompany them to Bath. Here, she meets Henry Tilney, a young clergyman of about twenty-four years of age. After a few days in Bath, Mrs. Allen renews her friendship with an old school friend, Mrs. Thorpe. It turns out that Catherine's eldest brother, James, is interested in Isabella Thorpe, who soon becomes Catherine's bosom friend. Isabella and Catherine read gothic novels together, walk together, and confide in each other. After a short absence, Henry returns to Bath, with his father and his sister, Eleanor, and Catherine cultivates Eleanor's friendship. She has made an appointment to walk with Eleanor and Henry, but James Morland and John Thorpe, Isabella's brother, talk her into going on a trip to Blaize Castle. They turn back before they reach the castle, so that Catherine misses both her walk with the Tilneys and a visit to the castle. After she has apologized to the Tilneys, she makes another date to walk with them. Again Isabella, James and John attempt to cajole her into going with them, but she resists their entreaties and walks with the Tilneys to Beechen Cliff. Isabella and James become engaged and receive Mr. Morland's sanction, but Isabella appears to be displeased with the amount of money James will receive. When Henry's elder brother, Captain Frederick Tilney, arrives in Bath, Isabella accepts his attentions, in spite of her promises to James. General Tilney invites Catherine to accompany Eleanor, Henry and him back to Northanger Abbey for a visit.

Catherine is delighted at the opportunity to be with Henry, to develop her friendship with Eleanor, and particularly to visit a real abbey. She is disappointed to find the abbey has been modernized, but still manages to let her imagination run wild. After a minor disappointment in finding that a document found in an old cabinet is only a laundry list, she fantasizes that the General has either murdered his wife or has locked her up in the abbey. She is greatly embarrassed when Henry finds her exploring outside his dead mother's room and realizes what she was expecting to find.

Catherine begins to wonder why she has not heard from Isabella. Eventually a letter arrives from James telling her that his engagement is off and that Isabella has rejected him in favor of Captain Tilney. Then a letter from Isabella comes begging Catherine to intercede with James on her behalf. Apparently Captain Tilney was only flirting with her and has now left Bath. Catherine finally realizes the shallowness and mercenary nature of her bosom friend.

After Catherine has been at Northanger Abbey for four weeks, Eleanor asks her to extend her visit. Catherine sees no reason not to accept if her parents are willing for her to stay. Throughout her visit at the abbey, the General has been very attentive to Catherine. She is puzzled at this attentiveness and even uncomfortable at his solicitude. However, when General Tilney returns after a short visit to London, he tells Catherine that she must leave the next morning. She is astonished and angry that she has not even been given time to notify her family and to have them make arrangements for her travel. She does not understand why the General has turned against her.

When Catherine gets home, she is unhappy at having thus been separated from Eleanor and Henry. She has begun to feel that Henry wants to marry her. In a few days, Henry rides up, explains that the General sent her away because he had found out that she was not wealthy, and proposes marriage to her. Catherine's father gives his permission, and eventually the General also blesses the marriage.

Unfortunately, there have been no television or film adaptations of *Northanger Abbey* during the 1990s. However, in July 1998, the *Sunday Independent* reported that Andrew Davies had written a screenplay for a two-hour adaptation to be shown on ITV the following spring (Thorpe 13). Then, in May 1999, an internet report said that Miramax was co-producing a nine-million dollar feature production of *Northanger Abbey* based on Davies' screenplay. Shooting was, according to this source to begin in Bath in the fall of 1999 (Crabb 1). It now appears that the project is on hold. Davies says that Miramax bought his screenplay but that his version will "almost certainly never appear." He speculates that the poor critical and popular reception of Miramax's latest Austen adaptation, *Mansfield Park*, is responsible for the studio's reluctance to invest in another one at this time (e-mail 1/11/01). It may strike some people as illogical for a studio to decide that, because *Mansfield Park* was a relative failure at the box office, another adaptation of an Austen novel would not succeed. *Mansfield Park* was hampered by a lack of star power, by its limited release, and by its radical reinterpretation of the story of the novel. It would have been a more viable product if Gwyneth Paltrow, Winona Ryder, or even Reese Witherspoon had played the role of Fanny Price. Davies said that Rachael Lee Cook, from *She's All That* (1999) was being discussed for the role of Catherine Morland (e-mail 1/11/01). However, for an adaptation of *Northanger Abbey* to find an audience at the theatre, not only a charismatic actress but considerable tinkering with the story may be needed.

Davies' unpublished screenplay illustrates the kind of tinkering that might be required. It heightens the rivalry between Henry Tilney and John Thorpe, makes clear that Isabella is sexually involved with Captain Frederick Tilney, and permits Catherine to see Henry Tilney naked. Like the 1987 adaptation, Davies' screenplay introduces erotic fantasy scenes and dreams. Davies develops the notion, which Austen introduced early in the novel, that Catherine had been a tomboy. He shows her racing her horse against Henry Tilney, shooting arrows, and (in a fantasy) hitting a

Northanger Abbey (BBC 1986). Catherine Morland (Katharine Schlesinger) and Henry Tilney (Peter Firth). (BBC Picture Archives)

villain with a bat. This Catherine would be more like Davies' Elizabeth Bennet in her physicality, and she would be quicker to catch on to Henry's irony. Austen's Catherine frequently seems unbelievably slow on the uptake. The success of the A&E *Emma* and the 1995 *Pride and Prejudice,* for which Davies wrote the screenplays, indicates that he has a good feel for what appeals to the modern audience.

The sole cinematic adaptation of *Northanger Abbey* was produced by BBC/A&E and first shown on BBC-2 in February 1987.* The screenplay was written by Maggie Wadey, who later wrote the screenplay for the 1994 adaptation of Edith Wharton's *The Buccaneers.* Giles Foster, who wrote and directed the 1985 adaptation of George Eliot's *Silas Marner,* directed the ninety-minute adaptation of *Northanger Abbey.*

The BBC *Northanger Abbey* represents an interesting anomaly among Austen adaptations of the seventies and eighties. The adaptations of the 1970s were made on the cheap, hardly ever went outdoors, were boringly faithful to the novels, and were meticulous in their attention to period detail. By comparison, the adaptations of the 1990s were lavish in their expenditures of money and time, went out of their way to introduce modern attitudes, made effective use of appropriate and gorgeous on-location

---

Contrary to the opinion of some critics ("Adaptations," Berardinelli) I cannot accept Ruby in Paradise *(1992) as an adaptation. It may have been inspired by Jane Austen, but its connection to* Northanger Abbey *is remote. Ruby (Ashley Judd) reads Austen novels and empathizes with their heroines, but other than that, her experiences are too different from Catherine's for the film to be considered either a commentary or an analogy.*

settings, and often took considerable liberties with the novel. Of the three adaptations made in the 1980s, *Sense and Sensibility* and *Mansfield Park*, are hold-overs from the seventies. *Northanger Abbey*, on the other hand, anticipates the adaptations of the nineties. It takes irreverent liberties with the novel and with historical accuracy, it introduces a modern psychological approach to the heroine, and it uses its on-location settings effectively.

The most striking element of the adaptation is the connection which it makes between Catherine Morland's sexual awakening and her reading of a Gothic novel—Ann Radcliffe's *The Mysteries of Udolpho*. Whereas the novel *Northanger Abbey* opens with a brief history of Catherine's life and brings us up to the point when she is invited to accompany the Allens to Bath, the film opens with a long shot of a church, then with the sight of a basket of plums, white high-topped shoes, and a white skirt partially covering a leg clad in soiled white stockings. Then we see the owner of the leg, Catherine (Katharine Schlesinger), reclining on a tree limb reading. In voiceover we hear a woman's voice telling someone that they must escape from the castle, and in particular from "the horrors of that evil chamber." Suddenly we see what looks like an engraving which shows a huge male figure outlined against a Gothic arched window and carrying the supine body of a woman. In the background, up a short flight of stairs, a sprawling dead body can be seen. These shots and the following ones are accompanied by discordant music, the sound of bells, and choral chanting. The film suggests that this engraving is an illustration in *The Mysteries of Udolpho* and that such a scene occurs in the novel. Yet nowhere in Radcliffe's novel does this scene occur. In *The Mysteries of Udolpho*, Emily fears Montoni and may even be attracted to his strength, but he never carries her anywhere. Count Morano's ruffians pick her up after she faints upon discovering a body behind a curtain, but that is not what is depicted in the engraving. The image of male domination, which figures in this illustration, is, however, central to Catherine's imaginings throughout the film.

Next we see Catherine, no longer reading, but with her head back against the tree limb, smiling with her lips parted, apparently in a kind of sexual ecstasy. The subsequent shot shows Catherine, wrapped in a sheet up to her armpits, being carried by a large man framed by a Gothic window as in the engraving. The viewer does not realize at this point that the man is General Tilney (Robert Hardy), whom Catherine has not met, but who figures as the chief villain in all of her fantasies and whose face can be seen and recognized more clearly in later dreams and fantasies. (This is the same Robert Hardy who is so genial and funny in the 1995

Sense and Sensibility.) We see a close-up of Catherine's face, wearing heavy makeup, eyes and lips agape. The man places Catherine on a bed and lays a sword across one of her arms. And, at this point Catherine hears her brother calling her back to her mundane world. She jumps down from the tree and chides her brother for disturbing her. She tells him that "[...] literature and solitude are as necessary to a young woman's development as sunshine is to ripe fruit." The fantasy now completely dissolved, she bites into a plum, and they run through a graveyard toward home. Catherine revisits this fantasy later in the film, and she has other waking and sleeping dreams.

In another recurring fantasy, Catherine, wrapped in a sheet, is being dragged along by two men—one the same man in the previous fantasy, but the other, a man with red hair, apparently an assistant. She first has this waking fantasy when she and the Allens are in a carriage on their way to Bath. In the first appearance of the red-haired man, we do not see his face clearly. In a later fantasy, he seems to be John Thorpe (Jonathan Coy), who also has red hair. Catherine has this fantasy again while visiting Northanger Abbey. On the first occasion, no hero comes to rescue her. On the second, Henry Tilney (Peter Firth) rides up on a white horse; she breaks away and runs to him. He lifts her up behind him and they ride off. Thus, as time passes, Catherine puts recognizable faces on her villains and eventually conjures up a hero.

Contemporary reviewers and later critics have suggested that the adaptation indulges in sensationalism for its own sake. Gethyn Thomas in a review in the *Western Mail* (1987) found the "Gothic visions" "too like the modern school of Ken Russell" (*Women in Love, Valentino*) (12), and Bruce Stovel in an article in *Persuasions* (1998) calls the film a "Ken Russell–style romp" (236). In its fast cutting and its striking visual images, the adaptation may indeed show Russell's influence. However, if one is looking for influences, one might plausibly mention Fellini (*8½*), particularly in the uses of extreme costumes and grotesques. It has been pointed out that the bathing scene in particular shows Fellini's influence (M. Roberts 135, Nokes 186). In this scene, Catherine, Mrs. Allen (Googie Withers), Isabella (Cassie Stuart), John Thorpe and others are bathing, the women clad in orange bathing dresses and elaborate feathered hats, each with a small plate hanging from a ribbon around her neck.*

This scene may appear bizarre, but it reflects to a certain extent the custom. Women wore canvas gowns and petticoats, with pieces of lead attached to the bottom of the gowns to keep them from floating. Women might have bowls, tied to their arms with ribbons, to hold handkerchiefs, perfumes, smelling salts. However, they wore caps, not the elaborate feathered hats shown in the film. An engraving "The Old Cross Bath" shows men and women in the same bathing area. Like John Thorpe, men wore broad brimmed hats to keep the waer out of their eyes. (Crathorne 31–32)

Besides showing the influence of contemporary filmmakers, Ms. Wadey probably also drew on modern critics' analyses of the appeal of the gothic novel. These critics leave no doubt that a primary appeal of gothic novels has been and continues to be sexual. Lionel Stevenson said that Radcliffe "[...] had a knack of stimulating the reader's own dream-making function, which then took over and supplied the private horrors of each individual imagination. Probably, too, her central theme—a pure, pale maiden persecuted by a vicious but dominating sadist—became a powerful sex symbol for both male and female readers" (165). Steven Bruhm, in his book *Gothic Bodies,* cites authorities as diverse as Edmund Burke and the Marquis de Sade for their association of observed or empathized pain as a source of pleasure (1ff). In discussing the film, Marilyn Roberts associates the violence of the male abductor and his phallic sword with the "repressed attraction to the father Freud maintains is the source of the beating fantasies often reported by neurotic patients [...]" (133). Whether the damsel is being threatened by sexual predators or whether the hero is carrying her off, the appeal is still sexual. It makes very good sense for a modern cinematic adaptation of this novel about a young girl who is looking for love and adventure to show her indulging in erotic fantasies. Although Roberts asserts that the "garish sensationalism" of the fantasies do not "mesh" with the modest, naive Catherine of the novel (133), one should notice that the fantasies show only male domination and nothing specifically sexual. Catherine's limited sexual experience allows her to imagine nothing more graphic.

The interesting thing about Catherine's imaginings is that her imagined villains are real villains—John Thorpe is actually in league with the General in that he is supplying him information (false, as it turns out), and Henry at the end of the film implies that his father is almost as bad as Catherine had imagined. He is not a murderer or a sexual predator, but he has preyed upon Catherine for her supposed large dowry. When he is disappointed, he casts her out to fend for herself. He is ultimately even more like Radcliffe's Montoni than Catherine's fantasies portray him, because both Montoni and General Tilney are motivated by lust for money, not for sex, and both are cruel and unfeeling in their treatment of women.

Jane Austen's attitude toward the Gothic novel as expressed in the novel is ambiguous. On the one hand, Henry Tilney—who represents both good sense and good taste—claims to be an avid novel reader. He says (and perhaps exaggerates) that he has read hundreds of gothic novels and that he has read all of Ann Radcliffe's novels. (His sister, Eleanor, also is fond of Radcliffe's novels.) He further states, "The person, be it

gentleman or lady, who has not pleasure in a good novel, must be intol-
erably stupid" (*NA* 106). John Thorpe, on the other hand, who is Henry's
polar opposite, says that he read *Tom Jones* and *The Monk*, but thinks that
all others are "the stupidest things in creation" (*NA* 48). By making these
judgments, he reveals that he prefers masculine adventure and a more
coarse-grained gothicism. Catherine might have learned restraint and have
rejected her suspicions of the General's having done away with his wife
if she had really understood the lessons to be learned in *The Mysteries of
Udolpho*. In this novel, Emily's father urges her to use reason and to exercise self-control. At the end of the novel, Radcliffe reveals all of Emily's
fantasies to be ill-founded. Catherine, however, does not learn these
lessons. She has so much enjoyed the vicarious pleasures of fright that
she seeks to find them for herself. Rather than criticizing Radcliffe or her
novels, Austen is more likely criticizing the unsophisticated reader of
Radcliffe's novels.

Katharine Schlesinger is effective as Catherine Morland. She is
young, pretty, but not beautiful, and was relatively unknown at the time.
After *Northanger Abbey* she played the lead in the BBC's *The Diary of Anne
Frank* (1987) and has recently appeared in the television mini-series "In
the Beginning" (2000). She brings a great deal of credibility to the role
of a naive young woman who experiences her first exposure to the great
world. She is young enough to be taken for seventeen, and her responses
seem fresh. This character is much like Marianne, in *Sense and Sensibility*, in her fantasies and her enthusiasm, but one can hardly imagine Kate
Winslet in the role of Catherine. Winslet always brings an air of rebel-
lion to every role she plays, and the Catherine of the novel has nothing
of the rebel in her makeup.

In the novel, one of the main qualities which Henry Tilney admires
about Catherine is her naiveté. A young man of twenty-four, he is used
to sophisticated society and tired of its artifice. Thus, when he first dances
with Catherine, he is aware of how fresh and unspoiled she is. In the film,
as Henry rows a boat containing Catherine and Eleanor, he says that he
will hate to see her lose her naturalness. The clear implication is that this
loss of naturalness is inevitable. He says that unlike most women she says
what she means. Catherine's naturalness derives from her goodness and
her inexperience with the world. However, her reading of gothic novels
prepares her to see the world in extremes—innocence and evil—without
the shades of reality. Henry tells her at one point, "[…] [A]rt is as different
from reality as water is from air." At this time Catherine is not ready to
learn this truth, because she wants to live the fantasy life of a heroine, but
she learns finally that life is considerably more complicated than that.

Catherine might have developed a better knowledge of the world sooner had she had better guidance while in Bath. The Allens, when they give advice, often give it too late to be helpful to Catherine. Mrs. Allen is interested only in dressing herself and Catherine in fashionable clothing and in finding acquaintances with whom to associate. She apparently has no inkling that the Thorpes are less than desirable acquaintances. In the film, Mr. Allen tells her that riding alone in a carriage with a young man is improper. He tells her this only after she has ridden with John Thorpe in his curricle. Mrs. Allen is concerned about how dirty Catherine would get her clothing in an open carriage, not about impropriety. Catherine's brother, her friend Isabella, and Thorpe had urged her to go. She tells the Allens that she wishes they had advised her earlier. In both the novel and the film she shows a great deal of independence when she resists her friends' urging that she break her appointment with Eleanor Tilney and ride with them again. In the film, she says to the Thorpes, "If I cannot be persuaded into doing wrong, I cannot be tricked into it." Catherine's friendship with Eleanor enables her to become acquainted with a woman who is superior to Isabella in both character and conduct. In both novel and film, Eleanor appears to be intelligent, cultivated, and moral—very different from Isabella.

Wadey develops the idea, mentioned only in the last chapter of the novel, that Eleanor has long been attached to a young man and that when he acquired a title and a fortune, her father permitted her to marry him. In the novel, Eleanor does not tell Catherine of her feelings for a young man. In the film, we see that Eleanor (Ingrid Lacey) is reluctant to attend the cotillion ball, but her father asserts forcefully that the family will attend it. He apparently wants her to mix in society and perhaps find a rich husband. Eleanor obviously feels constrained by her father's demands. On Catherine's first night at Northanger Abbey, she overhears Eleanor say to Henry, "How long must I go on living in this house?" Following Catherine's receiving the letter from James, Eleanor tells Catherine that she has been in love with Thomas, a young officer in Frederick Tilney's regiment, since she was fourteen. When his family was ruined, her father forbade her seeing him, but they meet secretly. At this point Catherine realizes the meaning of the note which she found in the chest in her room; it was a note arranging a meeting between Eleanor and Thomas.

When Eleanor reveals her forced estrangement from her lover, she tells Catherine that she will do nothing foolish. She values "good sense" above everything. Catherine says, "Even in love?" Eleanor responds, "Especially in love." Marilyn Roberts feels that the film's showing Eleanor to be meeting her lover secretly and expressing anger to Henry about the

General's high-handed treatment of her makes her too modern and erodes the difference between Eleanor and Isabella (136). However, when Eleanor states that she will "do nothing foolish," she highlights that distinction. Unlike Isabella, Eleanor will not behave dishonorably. In defense of the filling out of Eleanor's character, one could maintain that the viewer needs to see her as something more than a contrast to Isabella—a person with a life of her own.

Catherine's great charm is that she acts and speaks spontaneously. After she returns from her first ride, she runs through the streets to the Tilneys' apartment to speak to Eleanor. In the novel, she is denied admittance, but is able to explain the situation to Henry at the theatre that night. She blurts out that she would have preferred to walk with Henry and Eleanor. On the next day when she plans to walk with Eleanor, she finds that John Thorpe has told Eleanor that Catherine has changed her plans. She runs to the Tilneys' apartment and bursts into their presence. "Whatever might have been felt before her arrival, her eager declarations immediately made every look and sentence as friendly as she could desire" (*NA* 102). The film merges the two visits and omits her attendance at the theatre. In the adaptation, after John Thorpe tells her that he has made her excuses to Eleanor, she runs through the streets to the Tilneys' residence, brushes past the servant at the door, and bursts in upon Eleanor, Henry, and their father. She rapidly explains what has happened. Eleanor and Henry appear amused at her impetuosity and willing to forgive her. At this time, Eleanor introduces her to their father, who is cordial to Catherine but who makes her uncomfortable by speaking admiringly of the "elasticity" of her walk. Henry, Eleanor, and Catherine then set out on their walk.

Peter Firth, who plays the role of Henry Tilney, although less well known than big brother Colin, has had a busy career in both television and theatrical films. He played in BBC's *Joseph Andrews (1977)* and *Tess* (1979), and in the Hollywood films *Hunt for Red October* (1990), *Amistad* (1997), and *Pearl Harbor* (2001). Henry Tilney is in many ways the most interesting character in the novel. He sees in Catherine a blank slate on which he may write, if he chooses. He comments at one point that "a teachableness of disposition in a young lady is a great blessing" (*NA* 174). The narrator also tells us that "a persuasion of her partiality for him had been the only cause of giving her a serious thought" (*NA* 243). Thus, Catherine is pretty, she is present, she is willing to be taught, and she admires him. What more could an eligible bachelor want? (Let only a cynic answer, "Money.") In the film Henry takes every opportunity to encourage her admiration and to shape her mind. He shows off his appreciation of nature, his familiarity with Gothic novels, and his knowledge of the world.

In the novel the narrator tells us that Henry speaks "with fluency and spirit," and with "archness and pleasantry in his manner" (*NA* 25). Catherine does not grasp the meaning of all of his wit but she is astute enough to think that "[...] he indulged himself a little too much with the foibles of others" (*NA* 29). In the exercise of his wit he is more like one of the male characters in one of Congreve's comedies of manners than like a romantic hero. He is probably the wittiest of Jane Austen's male characters. Ironically, in his manner he is more like Frank Churchill and Henry Crawford than like the other good guys of Austen's novels, who tend to be serious and stodgy.

Catherine is all the more ready to admire Henry after being exposed to John Thorpe. This young man is ostensibly interested in Catherine, but he is even more interested in himself. He rattles on about his gig and his prowess in buying and selling horses. He also curses frequently and is disrespectful to his mother and sisters. Catherine grows tired of "the effusions of his endless conceit" (*NA* 66), and seeks to avoid him whenever possible. In the film Thorpe makes a convincingly coarse and sensual contrast with the handsome and refined Henry Tilney. Ironically, Thorpe is partly responsible for Catherine's success with Henry. Had he not misled General Tilney as to Catherine's pecuniary prospects, the General would never have encouraged Henry's interest her. I have no doubt that he would have suggested that Henry go home to Woodston while Catherine was at the Abbey, if indeed he had invited her to the Abbey at all.

Henry Tilney is one of Austen's most likeable clergymen. Like Edward Ferrars and Edmund Bertram, Tilney is a gentleman who happens to be a clergyman. Jane Austen, who had a clergyman father and brothers, knew that not all clergymen are officious toadies. Catherine's father is a clergyman and her brother James is a clergyman in training. She is perfectly ready to accept the attentions of this witty, attractive gentleman. Even Isabella would have been happy to marry a clergyman if he had enough money. Only the worldly Mary Crawford and giddy Lydia Bennet disdain to consider marrying clergymen. In the film, Catherine tells Eleanor that she thinks it important that "a clergyman should be amusing." The fact that Henry does not dress in any distinctive way to indicate his vocation would not have been unusual in the eighteenth century. In the novel, however, there are many references to Henry's duties and to his possession of the living at Woodston; Catherine, Eleanor and her father visit Henry there. Viewers of the film would not necessarily pick up on Henry's being a clergyman. One critic has even said, erroneously, that his vocation is not mentioned at all (Collins 159). The fact that Henry's vocation is mentioned only once suggests that the filmmakers chose not to emphasize it, presumably on the theory that a modern audience might not think a clergyman suitably romantic for a girl of Catherine's temperament. Henry Tilney, however, is no Mr. Collins.

Henry Tilney's relationship to his elder brother, Captain Frederick Tilney (Greg Hicks), is more clearly delineated in the adaptation than in the novel. Frederick is obviously a rake in both. He has no intention of marrying a girl with no money, and he is merely playing with Isabella. In both novel and film, Catherine urges Henry to tell Frederick that Isabella is engaged. Henry responds that Frederick "knows what he is about" (*NA* 149). In the film, she and Henry have this exchange while at the ball. She says that Frederick probably thought Isabella wanted to dance. As they have this conversation, the viewer sees Isabella and Frederick dancing and flirting. Henry says that Catherine gives other people her own motives, and he adds that Frederick "knows what he is about." After the dance, Frederick and Henry take snuff, and Frederick claims to have been teaching Henry how to behave. It is apparent, however, that although Henry is too worldly to criticize his elder brother, he has not taken Frederick as his mentor.

In the BBC adaptation, Catherine sees Henry at the first dance she goes to, but he does not dance with her. She and Mrs. Allen have come on their first visit to the Assembly Rooms, but both are disappointed at not seeing anyone they know. The room is crowded and they have to push their way through the crowd. As they go upstairs to escape the press of people, Henry is walking behind them. Mrs. Allen complains about having torn her gown, and Henry tells her that she has only lost a ribbon. He then looks admiringly at Catherine, who returns his look. He engages Mrs. Allen in a learned discussion of the cost of muslin—a discussion taken directly from the novel. In the film, however, it appears that he pursues the topic to prolong his contact with Catherine. He leaves them when a porter summons him to meet a lady. Catherine looks over the balcony to observe him taking the arm of a beautiful young woman. That she wondered about the relationship between Henry and the young woman is made clear later when she is obviously relieved to hear that Henry has a sister. Ms. Wadey has combined elements of two different evenings in the novel, the first when Mrs. Allen and Catherine go on their first visit to the Upper Rooms and a few nights later when they visit the Lower Rooms.

A casual viewer might not have noticed in these early scenes in Bath that General Tilney and his friend the Marchioness (Elaine Ives-Cameron) appear twice. As the Allens' carriage stops in front of the Upper Rooms on their first arriving in town, Catherine looks out the window at the people going into the building. On his third or fourth look at the point of view shot, the viewer, may notice General Tilney and the Marchioness standing in front of a window of the second story. Several days later, when Catherine and Mrs. Allen visit the Upper Rooms, Catherine notices General Tilney and the Marchioness across the ballroom talking. The viewer has thus been exposed to the General and his hideous friend well before Catherine meets him. This is not the case in the novel, where the General is not mentioned until Catherine sees him with Eleanor, after Catherine's ride with John Thorpe.

In the novel, Catherine meets Isabella Thorpe at the Pump-Room. Isabella's mother sees Mrs. Allen and recognizes her as an old school friend. When Catherine is introduced, it is revealed that the Thorpes know her brother James. Isabella at once claims Catherine as her bosom friend, and the pair are much together—walking, shopping, reading novels. In the novel, it is Isabella who introduces Gothic novels to Catherine. In the film, however, it is clear that Catherine has discovered *The Mysteries of Udolpho* before she ever met Isabella (Cassie Stuart). Thus, in the film Isabella is not to blame for Catherine's fantasizing.

Novelist Fay Weldon, who wrote the screenplay for the 1980 *Pride and Prejudice*, has commented that a possible weakness in the novel *Northanger Abbey* is its lack of "Bath colour" (101). Certainly the author's use of the Bath setting is different from its use in *Persuasion*. In *Northanger Abbey*, Austen showed Bath as the seventeen-year-old heroine experienced it. She emphasized the unending social occasions—the visits to the Pump Room, the assemblies, the plays, the concerts, shopping in Millsom Street, rural excursions to Beechen Cliff, and Sunday walks in the Royal Crescent. *Persuasion* shows the city from the perspective of Anne's socially conscious father, who is much impressed by the Dalyrymples' Laura Place address, pleased with his own house in Camden Place, and disdainful that Anne would deign to visit anyone living in the Westgate Buildings. Weldon approves of Wadey's attempts to give the viewer a sense of the way Bath looked in the late eighteenth century. Thus she praises the scene in which the ladies immerse themselves in the Bath waters (101). The film does less than the 1995 *Persuasion* to reveal the look of the city, but we do see Catherine walking, running or driving through various city streets, and we see her visiting the Pump Room and assembly rooms. Judith Wilt finds that the treatment of Bath in the novel emphasizes the strange and unexpected so that it prepares the way for the

Gothic elements introduced later (138). This statement is completely applicable to the treatment of Bath in the film. Catherine and the Allens arrive at night, so that their (and our) first look at Bath is confused by darkness and crowds of people. In the scenes of the dancing, we also have crowds and a kind of chaos. One of the more evocative and haunting scenes occurs just after Henry, Eleanor, and Catherine have been boating. When they arrive at the dock it is raining. The General and Captain Frederick Tilney are waiting outside the carriage in the rain as the others approach them. In the background is a Grecian-style temple. The General is both threatening and cajoling as he tells Catherine that he looks forward to seeing her dance. Catherine reverts to her fantasy involving the General, and the fantasy dissolves into a scene of Catherine reading aloud from *The Mysteries of Udolpho* to Isabella.

The costumes of the women in *Northanger Abbey* function primarily to suggest character and only secondarily to reflect the fashions of the times. Only Catherine and Eleanor appear to represent the admirable norm. They both dress in pale colors and wear simple hats. The apparel of the other women in Bath, particularly their hats, tends to the extreme. Mrs. Allen, Mrs. Thorpe (Elvi Hale) and Isabella are overdressed and over-hatted. When Catherine first meets Isabella, she is wearing heavy makeup, a bright red dress and a large red hat with red feathers, hardly an appropriate costume for a young unmarried woman. Her costumes throughout are over the top. At the cotillion ball, she wears a white dress with a frilly lavender overdress and a lavender headdress with feathers. Isabella not only dresses garishly, but her eyes wander about flirtatiously as she talks with Catherine. Although an engaged woman, she attends the cotillion ball and invites the attentions of Captain Tilney. Mrs. Thorpe wears heavy makeup as well as being overdressed. The Marchioness de Thierry (Elaine Ives-Cameron), the General's confidante, wears stark white makeup with beauty patches and dresses entirely in black. This character is not in the novel and supplies an air of mystery and even depravity to the film. Henry informs Catherine that at the age of sixteen the Marchioness had run off with a French count, who married her twenty years later. Only a year before the time of the novel, he was guillotined.

This latter detail helps to set the date of the events of the film around 1794, if one speculates that he may have been guillotined during the Reign of Terror. Another indicator of historical time is an item which Mr. Allen comments on as he is reading a newspaper. He says indignantly, "That little shoemaker has been charged with high treason for leading a harmless reform movement." This is probably a reference to the arrest of shoemaker Thomas Hardy on May 12, 1794, on a charge of high treason. Hardy had organized the London Corresponding Society in March 1792, a chief aim of which was to bring about representation for working men in Parliament. Hardy's arrest was the beginning of the government's systematic repression of reformers (E. P. Thompson 17–19). Mrs. Radcliffe's *The Mysteries of Udolpho* was also published in 1794. *The Monk*, however, which John Thorpe claims to have read, was not published until 1796. One may conclude that the filmmakers attempted to set the film specifically but failed to get all of their details correct.

The costumes suggest that the setting is in the mid to late 1790s. The men wear knee breeches and the older men wear plain or powdered wigs. By early in the next century, only liveried servants wore powdered hair. The male characters also wear the tricorn hats of the eighteenth century for dress, but the younger ones wear round hats during the day. The women's dresses are the high-waisted "round gowns" of the 1790s, which anticipate the simpler Regency styles of the early nineteenth century.

Northanger Abbey, the Tilneys' dwelling which Catherine visits during the novel and the film, symbolizes all of Catherine's naive gothic and romantic imaginings—her castle in air. It contains both her anticipated horrors and her lover. In the film, Catherine has seen Northanger Abbey well before she knew who lived there. She had passed the building on the way to Bath. The building used in the film is not an abbey but a castle, specifically Bodiam Castle, in East Sussex. Constructed of gray stone, with circular towers and crenellated battlements, it is surrounded by a moat and can be entered only by a causeway. As we and Catherine first see it, it exudes an air of mystery. Later, the viewer may wonder how, if the building is surrounded by water, Catherine and the Tilneys have such ready access to the gardens, which are shown to be contiguous to the building. Details, details!

In the novel, although Henry Tilney afterwards takes Catherine to task for her credulousness, he is not entirely blameless. He teases her about her expectations regarding Northanger Abbey. He asks her whether she is ready for the "horrors" of this ancient building. He mentions a "gloomy chamber," a "ponderous chest," a "violent storm," a "secret subterraneous" passage, "a large, old-fashioned cabinet" with an "inner compartment which holds sheets of paper," and a lamp which suddenly goes out (*NA* 158–160). Catherine is so intrigued that she urges him to continue. When they arrive at the Abbey, she is disappointed to find the interior modernized, her bedroom comfortably furnished, the windows clean and bright. However, she does notice a large old chest which has possibilities and which she plans to examine that evening. Later, with a storm raging outside, she does investigate the chest and finds some intriguing papers. Just then the wind blows out her candle and she hears footsteps outside. She hastily gropes her way to the bed and finally falls asleep. The next morning, in the light of day she feels foolish when she realizes that the mysterious papers are merely laundry lists.

Henry teases Catherine only a little in the film, and only after they have arrived at the Abbey. When Henry finds Catherine admiring a canary in a cage, he says to her, "Do you think you have a heart stout enough to bear the horrors of this place?" "How do your novels put it? A young girl alone in a strange dwelling full of gloomy passages. Are you not afraid?" She says, "Why should I be?" Thus Henry only alludes to possible fantasies she may have based on her novel reading. Before this conversation, Catherine has already consulted her novel. As soon as she gets to her room, she opens her traveling case and looks at the engraving showing a man carrying the helpless figure of a woman. In the film, Henry is no more to blame than Isabella for Catherine's fantasies. Catherine has been primed for gothic horrors before she met either of them.

Unlike in the novel, where emphasis is placed on how modernized the Abbey is, in the film we see narrow winding steps and mysterious corridors. In the dining room, the General is standing beneath a huge Gothic window, similar to that in the book illustration. Even Catherine's chamber and its furniture are more ancient in appearance than modern. As in the novel, Catherine's candle is extinguished, but in the film it goes out when she drops it. She also drops the papers she has found when she hears footsteps at the door and sees a glimmer of light under the door. Then the light and the footsteps go away. During the night she dreams that she is in a high-necked black dress standing on the grounds of the Abbey. A female servant tells her that the banditti are closing in and that this place is not safe. The servant promises to show her a picture of the late lady of the house. Then Catherine is running across the lawn as the General watches from a window. Next we see General Tilney standing, with bloody hands, before a large basin, while a male servant stands by with a sword. The banditti and the picture of the lady are clearly derived from *The Mysteries of Udolpho*. In the morning, the maid enters and takes most of the papers, which she calls laundry lists. One note escapes. Catherine eagerly reads, "The same day at 3:00. You and I beside the unknown woman." Although at this time Catherine does not know the meaning of this message, later she realizes that Eleanor has been meeting her lover secretly at the statue of the unknown woman in the garden. However, finding this note feeds Catherine's curiosity, which is even more whetted when the General refuses to let Eleanor show Catherine the room which had belonged to her mother.

In the film, a maid who is dressing Catherine tells her about "poor Mrs. Tilney." Her suggestion that there is a mystery surrounding Mrs. Tilney's death stimulates Catherine to investigate the room where she died. This maid is reminiscent of those in Radcliffe's novels, such as Annette in *The Mysteries of Udolpho*, who are usually responsible for spreading rumors and misinformation which frighten the heroines. When Catherine enters Mrs. Tilney's room, she is looking for some sign that Mrs. Tilney had been murdered. She is there for only moments when Henry Tilney comes in. He opens the curtains, as if to reveal to Catherine and to the viewer that this is just an ordinary room—dusty but ordinary. When he realizes what she has been expecting to find, he speaks harshly to her. He reminds her that they are living in modern times in an enlightened country, where newspapers and roads make concealment of atrocities impossible. When Austen has Henry express this reasoning in the novel, she probably is being ironic, since the horrors of the recent Reign of Terror were graphic illustrations that atrocities were still possible in the world. The French husband of Austen's cousin Eliza was guillotined in France in 1794. The anti–Jacobin frenzy in England during the middle and late 1790s indicates that Englishmen felt that a revolution was not impossible, even in England.

One scene in the film is almost as bizarre as Catherine's fantasies. At an evening party at the Abbey, Henry sings in Italian while Eleanor plays the harp and another woman plays the flute. Next, Henry and the flautist sing a duet in Italian to the accompaniment of the harp. The Marchioness is whispering gossip to General Tilney about somebody's mistress. Catherine watches appreciatively as Henry performs. The Marchioness's African page, wearing a powdered wig and a white suit takes Catherine's hand, leads her outside, and begins to turn cartwheels. This scene, which is not suggested by anything in the novel, is obviously introduced to nourish Catherine's sense of the fantastic. At this point she still believes that at the Abbey anything can happen. While watching the page turn cartwheels, Catherine adds a new element to her recurring fantasy of bondage. Henry Tilney, on a white horse, becomes her rescuer.

Janene Roberts calls the choice of theme music for the film problematic. The music, by Ilona Sekacz, combines high-pitched female vocals with harsh instrumental music to produce an eerie background, often very insistent, as in the fantasy scenes. Roberts feels that the "depressing" quality of the music is not in keeping with the mood of the novel (361). It is certainly true that the music is eerie and unsettling, but although it may be out of keeping with the mood of the novel, it is appropriate to a film which combines fantasy with gothic images.

The climactic scene in the film—which is not in the novel—shows Catherine burning her copy of *The Mysteries of Udolpho*. This is a vivid visualization of Catherine's disillusionment with the value of the novel as a guide for living. However, as a point of historical accuracy, it is unlikely that she would have burned a book which did not belong to her, and it is equally unlikely that she could have afforded to purchase the novel. The lending library would surely have been the owner of the book which Catherine so cavalierly destroyed, and the novel was published in three volumes, not the single volume which Catherine had. It is easy to forget how expensive books were in the eighteenth century compared to the cost of books today.

In the scene in which Henry Tilney confronts his father after Catherine was sent home, General Tilney is outdoors with a falcon on his wrist. John Dussinger likes this association of a predatory bird with the predatory General Tilney (166). When the General abuses Catherine for colluding with the Thorpes to "ruin" the Tilney family, Henry defends her. He tells his father that he knows that Catherine is not wealthy, but she is not a pauper. She will receive a dowry of 400 pounds a year. The General looks angry when Henry tells him that he should look to his own weakness—a reference to the General's gambling.

The final scenes, which show Catherine at home with her family and Henry's arrival to propose to her, merge into each other in an interesting way. We see Catherine in a swing listening while the Allens and her parents discuss the way General Tilney treated her. She is wearing a white dress with a gray pelisse, pearl earrings and a necklace, and her hair looks carefully dressed. Then she gets out of the swing and wanders off. With no transition, we see Catherine walking into a fog. As we look at her from behind, we see Henry Tilney ride up from in front of her. He is riding a brown horse and is clad in knee breeches, boots, vest and shirtsleeves. Catherine is dressed all in white, with no jewelry, and with her hair disheveled. The impression is that reality and fantasy are blending for Catherine in this happy ending. Henry says, "I promise not to oppress you with too much remorse or too much passion, but since you left the white rose bush has died of grief." It is difficult to believe that the cynical Henry Tilney could come up with such a romantic speech. He continues, "Does your face express all that your heart feels or may I hope that it holds a secret?" Catherine asks only whether his father knows that Henry has come to her. When he says, "Yes," they kiss. At this point we hear Catherine's little brother calling to her and we see him pause as he sees the pair together. The little brother's appearance brings us full circle in the film. We see Catherine look up at Henry with tears on her cheeks.

Northanger Abbey has always been my least favorite of Jane Austen's novels. Rereading the novel, I found myself no more pleased with it than I was before. However, I found that the adaptation grew on me as I watched and rewatched it. Ms. Wadey had a difficult task in visualizing a novel which depends primarily on language for its appeal. The satire which is such a prominent element in the novel has given way to emphasis on character and incident. The introduction of the gothic early in the film helps to tie together the two halves of the plot, which in the novel appear almost to belong to two different books. The visualizations of Catherine's fantasies and dreams effectively suggest the inner life of a rather ordinary girl, and the merging of dream and reality in the figure of General Tilney creates an interesting villain. This adaptation is not great cinematic art, but it at least attempts to break out of the confines of the novel.

Appendix: Filmography of Austen Adaptations

Sense and Sensibility
(June 4, 1950)

NBC *Philco Television Playhouse* (1 hour, live, black and white) *Directed by:* Delbert Mann; *Screenplay by:* H. R. Hays; *Produced by:* Fred Coe

CAST

Madge Evans	*Elinor Dashwood*
Cloris Leachman	*Marianne Dashwood*
John Baragrey	*Colonel Brandon*
Chester Stratton	*Edward Ferrars*
Dora Clement	*Mrs. Dashwood*
John Stephens	*John Dashwood*
Josephine Brown	*Mrs. Fenner*
Larry Hugo	*John Willoughby*
Pat Hosley	*Lucy Steele*
Cherry Hardy	*Mrs. Ferrars*

Sense and Sensibility
(1971)

BBC-2: mini-series, 4 parts (c. 200 min) *Directed by:* David Giles; *Screenplay by:* Denis Constanduros; *Produced by:* Martin Lisemore

CAST

Joanna David	*Elinor Dashwood*
Ciaran Madden	*Marianne Dashwood*
Robin Ellis	*Edward Ferrars*

Richard Owens . . . . *Colonel Brandon*
Isabel Dean . . . . *Mrs. Dashwood*
Michael Aldridge . . . . *Sir John Middleton*
Clive Francis . . . . *John Willoughby*
Patricia Routledge . . . . *Mrs. Jennings*
Milton Johns . . . . *John Dashwood*
Esme Church . . . . *Mary*
Kay Gallie . . . . *Fanny Dashwood*

Sense and Sensibility
(1981)

BBC-1: mini-series, 7 parts (174 min); *Directed by:* Rodney Bennett; *Screenplay by:* Alexander Baron and Denis Constanduros; *Produced by:* Barry Letts
Original Music: Dudley Simpson; *Film Editing:* Malcolm Banthorpe; *Production Design:* Paul Joel; *Costume Design:* Dorothea Wallace; *Graphic Designer:* Stefan Pstrowski

CAST

Irene Richards . . . . *Elinor Dashwood*
Tracey Childs . . . . *Marianne Dashwood*
Bosco Hogan . . . . *Edward Ferrars*
Robert Swann . . . . *Colonel Brandon*
Diana Fairfax . . . . *Mrs. Dashwood*
Peter Woodward . . . . *John Willoughby*
Donald Douglas . . . . *Sir John Middleton*
Annie Leon . . . . *Mrs. Jennings*
Peter Gale . . . . *John Dashwood*
Amanda Boxer . . . . *Fanny Dashwood*
Julia Chambers . . . . *Lucy Steele*
Elizabeth Benson . . . . *Mrs. Wallis*
Marjorie Bland . . . . *Lady Middleton*
Philip Bowen . . . . *Robert Ferrars*
Christopher Brown . . . . *Mr. Palmer*
Pippa Sparkes . . . . *Ann Steele*
Hetty Baynes . . . . *Charlotte Palmer*
Margot Van der Burgh . . . . *Mrs. Ferrars*
William Lawford . . . . *Clay*
Raymond Mason . . . . *Mr. Harris*
John Owens . . . . *Tom*
Gina Rowe . . . . *Susan*
John Woodnutt . . . . *Mr. Ingall*

Sense and Sensibility
(1995)

Columbia/Mirage: feature film (135 min); *Directed by:* Ang Lee; *Screenplay by:* Emma Thompson; *Produced by:* Lindsay Doran

Original Music: Patrick Doyle; *Cinematography:* Michael Coulter; *Film Editing:* Tim Squyres; *Production Design:* Luciana Arrighi; *Art Direction:* Philip Elton, Andrew Sanders; *Set Decoration:* Ian Whittaker; *Costume Design:* Jenny Beavan, John Bright

CAST

Emma Thompson	*Elinor Dashwood*
Kate Winslet	*Marianne Dashwood*
Hugh Grant	*Edward Ferrars*
Alan Rickman	*Colonel Brandon*
Greg Wise	*John Willoughby*
Gemma Jones	*Mrs. Dashwood*
Tom Wilkinson	*Mr. Dashwood*
James Fleet	*John Dashwood*
Robert Hardy	*Sir John Middleton*
Harriet Walter	*Fanny Dashwood*
Hugh Laurie	*Mr. Palmer*
Imelda Staunton	*Charlotte Palmer*
Imogen Stubbs	*Lucy Steele*
Emilie François	*Margaret Dashwood*
Ian Brimble	*Tom*
Isabelle Amyes	*Betsy*
Alexander John	*Curate*
Allan Mitchell	*Pigeon*
Josephine Gradwell	*Mrs. Jennings' maid*
Richard Lumsden	*Robert Ferrars*
Ione Vidahl	*Miss Grey*
Oliver Ford Davies	*Doctor Harris*
Eleanor McCready	*Mrs. Bunting*

Pride and Prejudice
(1940)

MGM: feature film (114 min, black and white); *Directed by:* Robert Z. Leonard; *Screenplay by:* Aldous Huxley and Jane Murfin; *Produced by:* Hunt Stromberg

Film Editing: Robert Kern; *Original Music:* Herbert Stothart; *Cinematography:* Karl Freund; *Set Decoration:* Edwin B. Willis; *Art Direction:* Cedric Gibbons and Paul Groesse; *Costume Design:* Adrian, and Gile Steele

CAST:

Greer Garson	*Elizabeth Bennet*
Laurence Olivier	*Fitzwilliam Darcy*
Maureen O'Sullivan	*Jane Bennet*
Ann Rutherford	*Lydia Bennet*
Mary Boland	*Mrs. Bennet*
Edmund Gwenn	*Mr. Bennet*
Edward Ashley	*George Wickham*
Marsha Hunt	*Mary Bennet*
Heather Angel	*Kitty Bennet*
Bruce Lester	*Charles Bingley*

Melville Cooper .... *Mr. Collins*
Edna Mae Oliver .... *Lady Catherine de Bourgh*
Gia Kent .... *Anne de Bourgh*
Karen Morley .... *Charlotte Lucas Collins*
Frieda Inescort .... *Caroline Bingley*
Marjorie Wood .... *Lady Lucas*
E. E. Clive .... *Sir William Lucas*
May Beatty .... *Mrs. Philips*
Marten Lamont .... *Mr. Denny*

Pride and Prejudice
(January 23, 1949)

NBC *Philco Television Playhouse* (1 hour, live, black and white); *Directed by:* Fred Coe; *Screenplay by:* Samuel Taylor

CAST

Madge Evans .... *Elizabeth Bennet*
John Baragrey .... *Fitzwilliam Darcy*
Viola Roache
Louis Hector

Pride and Prejudice
(Feb. 2–Mar. 8, 1952)

BBC: mini-series, 6 parts (180 min, live, black and white); *Dir/producer:* Campbell Logan; *Screenplay by:* Cedric Wallis

CAST

Daphne Slater .... *Elizabeth Bennet*
Peter Cushing .... *Fitzwilliam Darcy*
Milton Rosmer .... *Mr. Bennet*
Gillian Lind .... *Mrs. Bennet*
Helen Haye .... *Lady Catherine de Bourgh*
Ann Baskett .... *Jane Bennet*
Prunella Scales .... *Lydia Bennet*

Pride and Prejudice
(Jan. 24–Feb. 28, 1958)

BBC: mini-series, 6 parts (180 min, live, black and white); *Dir/producer:* Barbara Burnham; *Screenplay by:* Cedric Wallis (same as 1952)

CAST

Jane Downs . . . . *Elizabeth Bennet*
Alan Badel . . . . *Fitzwilliam Darcy*
Hugh Sinclair . . . . *Mr. Bennet*
Mirian Spencer . . . . *Mrs. Bennet*
Susan Lyall Grant . . . . *Jane Bennet*
Vivienne Martin . . . . *Lydia Bennet*
Phyllis Neilson-Terry . . . . *Lady Catherine de Bourgh*

Pride and Prejudice
(Sept. 10–Oct. 15, 1967)

BBC-1: mini-series, 6 parts (180 min, black and white); *Directed by:* Joan Craft; *Screenplay by:* Nemone Lethbridge; *Produced by:* Campbell Logan

CAST

Celia Bannerman . . . . *Elizabeth Bennet*
Lewis Fiander . . . . *Fitzwilliam Darcy*
Michael Gough . . . . *Mr. Bennet*
Vivian Pickles . . . . *Mrs. Bennet*
Polly Adams . . . . *Jane Bennet*
Sylvia Coleridge . . . . *Lady Catherine de Bourgh*
Julian Curry . . . . *Mr. Collins*
Lucy Fleming . . . . *Lydia Bennet*
David Savile . . . . *Mr. Bingley*
Diana King . . . . *Lady Lucas*
Stephen Grives . . . . *Edward Lucas*

Pride and Prejudice
(1980)

BBC-2: mini-series, 5 parts (226 min); *Directed by:* Cyril Coke; *Screenplay by:* Fay Weldon; *Produced by:* Jonathan Powell
   Cinematography: Paul Wheeler; *Film Editing:* Chris Wimble; *Original Music:* Wilfred Josephs; *Costume Design:* Joan Ellacott

CAST

Elizabeth Garvie . . . . *Elizabeth Bennet*
David Rintoul . . . . *Fitzwilliam Darcy*
Sabina Franklyn . . . . *Jane Bennet*
Natalie Ogle . . . . *Lydia Bennet*
Priscilla Morgan . . . . *Mrs. Bennet*
Moray Watson . . . . *Mr. Bennet*
Tessa Peake-Jones . . . . *Mary Bennet*
Clare Higgins . . . . *Kitty Bennet*
Malcolm Rennie . . . . *Mr. Collins*

Judy Parfitt .... *Lady Catherine de Bourgh*
Irene Richard .... *Charlotte Lucas Collins*
Peter Settelen .... *Mr. Wickham*
Emma Jacobs .... *Georgiana Darcy*
Marsha Fitzalan .... *Caroline Bingley*
Jennifer Granville .... *Mrs. Hurst*
Edward Arthur .... *Mr. Hurst*
Desmond Adams .... *Colonel Fitzwilliam*
Shirley Cain .... *Mrs. Philips*
Janet Davies .... *Mrs. Hill*
Peter Howell .... *Sir William Lucas*
Andrew Johns .... *Captain Denny*
Michael Lees .... *Mr. Gardiner*
Barbara Shelley .... *Mrs. Gardiner*
Elizabeth Stewart .... *Lady Lucas*
Doreen Mantle .... *Mrs. Reynolds*
Moir Leslie .... *Anne de Bourgh*

Pride and Prejudice
(1995)

BBC/A&E: mini-series, 6 parts (300 min); *Directed by:* Simon Langton; *Screenplay by:* Andrew Davies; *Produced by:* Sue Birtwistle
Original Music: Carl Davis; *Cinematography:* John Kenway; *Film Editing:* Peter Coulson; *Production Design:* Gerry Scott; *Art Direction:* John Collins, Mark Kebby; *Costume Design:* Dinah Collin, Kate Stewart

CAST

Jennifer Ehle .... *Elizabeth Bennet*
Colin Firth .... *Fitzwilliam Darcy*
Suzannah Harker .... *Jane Bennet*
Julia Sawalha .... *Lydia Bennet*
Polly Maberly .... *Kitty Bennet*
Crispin Bonham-Carter .... *Mr. Bingley*
Anna Chancellor .... *Miss Bingley*
Barbara Leigh-Hunt .... *Lady Catherine de Bourgh*
Adrian Lukis .... *Mr. Wickham*
Alison Steadman .... *Mrs. Bennet*
Benjamin Whitrow .... *Mr. Bennet*
Christopher Benjamin .... *Sir William Lucas*
Lucy Briers .... *Mary Bennet*
David Bamber .... *Mr. Collins*
David Bark-Jones .... *Lt. Denny*
Roger Barclay .... *Capt. Carter*
Anthony Calf .... *Colonel Fitzwilliam*
Jacob Casseidon .... *Robert Gardiner*
Nadia Chambers .... *Miss Anne de Bourgh*
Joanna David .... *Mrs. Gardiner*
Lucy Davis .... *Maria Lucas*

Harriet Eastcott	*Mrs. Jenkinson*
Lynn Farleigh	*Mrs. Philips*
Emilia Fox	*Georgiana Darcy*
Victoria Hamilton	*Mrs. Forster*
Tim Wylton	*Mr. Gardiner*
Bridget Turner	*Mrs. Reynolds*
Lucy Robinson	*Mrs. Hurst*
Lucy Scott	*Charlotte Lucas*
Rupert Vansittart	*Mr. Hurst*
Norma Streader	*Lady Lucas*
Marlene Sidaway	*Hill, the housekeeper*
Kate O'Malley	*Sarah, the maid*
Paul Moriarty	*Colonel Forster*

Mansfield Park
(1983)

ITV/BBC-2: mini-series (261 min); *Directed by:* David Giles; *Screenplay by:* Kenneth Taylor; *Produced by:* Betty Willingale

Original Music: Derek Bourgeois; *Cinematography:* Chris Wickham, Trevor Wimlett; *Film Editing:* Stan Pow; *Production Design:* John Bone; *Costume Design:* Ian Adley

CAST

Sylvestra Le Touzel	*Fanny Price*
Nicholas Farrell	*Edmund Bertram*
Bernard Hepton	*Sir Thomas Bertram*
Samantha Bond	*Maria Bertram Rushworth*
Liz Crowther	*Julia Bertram*
Anna Massey	*Aunt Norris*
Jackie Smith-Wood	*Mary Crawford*
Robert Burbage	*Henry Crawford*
Angela Pleasence	*Lady Bertram*
Jonathan Stephens	*Mr. Rushworth*
Christopher Villiers	*Tom Bertram*
David Buck	*Mr. Price*
Alison Fiske	*Mrs. Price*
Allan Hendrick	*William Price*
Robin Langford	*Mr. Yates*
Peter Finn	*Mr. Norris*
Susan Edmonstone	*Mrs. Grant*
Eryl Maynard	*Susan Price*
Gillian Martell	*Mrs. Rushworth, Senior*
Jonny Lee Miller	*Charles Price*
Gordon Kaye	*Dr. Grant*
Paul Davies Prowles	*Sam Price*
Katy Durham-Matthews	*Young Fanny*
Giles Ashton	*Young Tom*
Sharon Beare	*Young Julia*
Alex Lowe	*Young Edmund*

Alys Wallbank . . . . *Young Maria*
Vivienne Moore . . . . *Rebecca*
Neville Phillips . . . . *Baddely*

Mansfield Park
(1999)

BBC/Miramax: feature film (112 min); *Directed by:* Patricia Rozema
Screenplay by: Patricia Rozema; *Produced by:* Sarah Curtis
Original Music: Lesley Barber; *Cinematography:* Michael Coulter; *Film Editing:*
Martin Walsh; *Casting:* Gail Stevens; *Production Design:* Christopher Hobbs; *Art
Direction:* Andrew Munro; *Set Decoration:* Patricia Edwards; *Costume Design:* Andrea
Gale

CAST

Hannah Taylor Gordon . . . . *Young Fanny*
Frances O'Connor . . . . *Fanny Price*
Harold Pinter . . . . *Sir Thomas Bertram*
Jonny Lee Miller . . . . *Edmund Bertram*
Embeth Davidtz . . . . *Mary Crawford*
Alessandro Nivola . . . . *Henry Crawford*
Lindsay Duncan . . . . *Mrs. Price/Lady Bertram*
Victoria Hamilton . . . . *Maria Bertram*
Justine Waddell . . . . *Julia Bertram*
Sheila Gish . . . . *Mrs. Norris*
James Purefoy . . . . *Tom Bertram*
Hugh Bonneville . . . . *Mr. Rushworth*
Charles Edwards . . . . *Mr. Yates*
Sophia Myles . . . . *Susan*
Hilton McRae . . . . *Mr. Price*
Anna Popplewell . . . . *Betsey*
Talya Gordon . . . . *Young Susan*
Bruce Byron . . . . *Carriage Driver*
Elizabeth Eaton . . . . *Young Maria*
Elizabeth Earle . . . . *Young Julia*
Philip Sarson . . . . *Young Edmund*
Amelia Warner . . . . *Teenage Fanny*
Danny Worters . . . . *Boy with Bird Cart*
Gordon Reid . . . . *Dr. Winthrop*

Emma
(May 24, 1948)

BBC: television play (105 min, live, black and white); Dir/*Produced by:* Michael
Barry; *Screenplay by:* Judy Campbell

CAST

Judy Campbell . . . . *Emma Woodhouse*
Ralph Michael . . . . *Mr. George Knightley*

Gillian Lind . . . . *Miss Bates*
Richard Hurndall . . . . *Mr. Elton*
Oliver Burt . . . . *Mr. Woodhouse*
Mirian Spencer . . . . *Mrs. Elton*
McDonald Hobley . . . . *Frank Churchill*
Daphne Slater . . . . *Harriet Smith*
Joyce Heron . . . . *Jane Fairfax*

Emma

(Nov. 24, 1954)

NBC *Kraft Television Theatre* (60 min, live, black and white); *Dramatized by:* Martine Bartlett and Peter Donat

CAST

Felicia Montealegre . . . . *Emma Woodhouse*
Peter Cookson . . . . *Mr. Knightley*
Roddy McDowall . . . . *Mr. Elton*
Martine Bartlett . . . . *Mrs. Elton*
Stafford Dickens . . . . *Mr. Woodhouse*
Sarah Marshall . . . . *Harriet Smith*
Nydia Westman . . . . *Mrs. Weston*
Robinson Stone . . . . *Mr. Weston*
Nancie Hobbs . . . . *Mrs. Goddard*
Peter Donat . . . . *William Larkins*
McLean Savage . . . . *Searle*

Emma

(Feb. 26–April 6, 1960)

BBC: mini-series, 6 parts (180 min, live, black and white); Dir/*Produced by:* Campbell Logan; *Screenplay by:* Vincent Tilsley

CAST

Diana Fairfax . . . . *Emma Woodhouse*
Paul Daneman . . . . *Mr. George Knightley*
Gillian Lind . . . . *Miss Bates*
Raymond Young . . . . *Mr. Elton*
Perlita Smith . . . . *Harriet Smith*
Leslie French . . . . *Mr. Woodhouse*
Petra Davies . . . . *Jane Fairfax*
May Hallatt . . . . *Mrs. Bates*
David McCallum . . . . *Frank Churchill*
Thea Holme . . . . *Mrs. Weston*
Philip Ray . . . . *Mr. Weston*

Emma
(August 26, 1960)

CBS *Camera Three* (1 hour); *Directed by:* John Desmond; *Produced by:* John McGiffert; *Screenplay by:* Clair Roskam

CAST

Nancy Wickwire . . . . *Emma Woodhouse*

Emma
(1972)

BBC-2: mini-series, 5 parts (257 min); *Directed by:* John Glenister; *Screenplay by:* Denis Constanduros; *Produced by:* Martin Lisemore
Film Editing: Clare Douglas; *Production Design:* Tim Harvey

CAST

Doran Godwin . . . . *Emma Woodhouse*
John Carson . . . . *Mr. George Knightley*
Debbie Bowen . . . . *Harriet Smith*
Robert East . . . . *Frank Churchill*
Ania Marson . . . . *Jane Fairfax*
Raymond Adamson . . . . *Mr. Weston*
John Alkin . . . . *Robert Martin*
Constance Chapman . . . . *Miss Bates*
Ellen Dryden . . . . *Mrs. Weston*
Donald Eccles . . . . *Mr. Woodhouse*
Mary Holder . . . . *Mrs. Bates*
Timothy Peters . . . . *Mr. Elton*
Mollie Sugden . . . . *Mrs. Goddard*
Fiona Walker . . . . *Mrs. Elton*
Hilda Fenemore . . . . *Mrs. Cole*
Meg Gleed . . . . *Isabella Knightley*
John Kelland . . . . *John Knightley*
Lala Lloyd . . . . *Mrs. Ford*
Vivienne Moore . . . . *Williams*
Marian Tanner . . . . *Betty Bickerton*
Amber Thomas . . . . *Patty*

Emma
(1996)

Columbia/Miramax: feature film (120 min); *Directed by:* Douglas McGrath; *Screenplay by:* Douglas McGrath; *Produced by:* Patrick Cassavetti, Steven Haft
Original Music: Rachel Portman; *Cinematography:* Ian Wilson; *Film Editing:* Lesley

Walker; *Art Direction:* Joshua Meath-Baker, Sam Riley; *Set Decoration:* Totty Whately; *Costume Design:* Ruth Myers

CAST

Gwyneth Paltrow	*Emma Woodhouse*
Jeremy Northam	*Mr. George Knightley*
Toni Collette	*Harriet Smith*
James Cosmo	*Mr. Weston*
Greta Scacchi	*Mrs. Weston*
Alan Cumming	*Mr. Elton*
Juliet Stevenson	*Mrs. Elton*
Denys Hawthorne	*Mr. Woodhouse*
Sophie Thompson	*Miss Bates*
Phyllida Law	*Mrs. Bates*
Edward Woodall	*Mr. Martin*
Kathleen Byron	*Mrs. Goddard*
Brian Capron	*John Knightley*
Karen Westwood	*Isabella Knightley*
Polly Walker	*Jane Fairfax*
Ewan McGregor	*Frank Churchill*
Angela Down	*Mrs. Cole*
John Franklyn-Robbins	*Mr. Cole*
Rebecca Craig	*Miss Martin*
Ruth Jones	*Bates Maid*

Emma
(1996)

Meridian-ITV/A&E: television movie (107 min); *Directed by:* Diarmuid Lawrence; *Screenplay by:* Andrew Davies; *Produced by:* Sue Birtwistle
  Original Music: Dominic Muldowney; *Cinematography:* Remi Adefarasin; *Film Editing:* Don Fairservice; *Casting:* Janey Fothergill; *Production Design:* Don Taylor; *Art Direction:* Jo Graysmark; *Set Decoration:* John Bush; *Costume Design:* Jenny Beavan

CAST

Kate Beckinsale	*Emma Woodhouse*
Mark Strong	*Mr. George Knightley*
Bernard Hepton	*Mr. Woodhouse*
Samantha Bond	*Mrs. Weston*
James Hazeldine	*Mr. Weston*
Dominic Rowan	*Mr. Elton*
Samantha Morton	*Harriet Smith*
Prunella Scales	*Miss Bates*
Sylvia Barter	*Mrs. Bates*
Olivia Williams	*Jane Fairfax*
Raymond Coulthard	*Frank Churchill*
Guy Henry	*John Knightley*
Dido Miles	*Isabella Knightley*
Lucy Robinson	*Mrs. Elton*

Judith Coke .... *Mrs. Goddard*
Alistair Petrie .... *Robert Martin*
Peter Howell .... *Mr. Perry*
Phoebe Welles-Cooper .... *Elizabeth Martin*
Tabby Harris .... *Miss Otway*

Clueless
(1995)

Paramount: feature film (113 min); *Directed by:* Amy Heckerling; *Screenplay by:* Amy Heckerling; *Produced by:* Robert Lawrence, Scott Rudin
Original Music: David Kitay; *Cinematography:* Bill Pope; *Film Editing:* Debra Chiate; *Casting:* Marcia Ross; *Production Design:* Steven J. Jordan; *Art Direction:* William Hiney; *Set Decoration:* Amy Wells; *Costume Design:* Mona May

CAST

Alicia Silverstone .... *Cher Horowitz*
Stacey Dash .... *Dionne*
Brittany Murphy .... *Tai Fraiser*
Paul Rudd .... *Josh*
Donald Faison .... *Murray*
Elisa Donovan .... *Amber*
Breckin Meyer .... *Travis Birkenstock*
Jeremy Sisto .... *Elton*
Dan Hedaya .... *Mel Horowitz*
Aida Linares .... *Lucy*
Wallace Shawn .... *Mr. Hall*
Twink Caplan .... *Miss Geist*
Justin Walker .... *Christian Stovitz*
Sabastian Rashidi .... *Paroudasm*
Herb Hall .... *Principal*
Julie Brown .... *Miss Stoeger*
Susan Mohun .... *Heather*

Persuasion
(Dec. 30, 1960–Jan. 20, 1961)

BBC: mini-series, 4 parts, videotape (black and white); *Produced by:* Campbell Logan; *Screenplay by:* Michael Voysey and Barbara Burnham

CAST

Daphne Slater .... *Anne Elliot*
Paul Daneman .... *Frederick Wentworth*
Fabia Drake .... *Lady Russell*
George Curzon .... *Sir Walter Elliot*
Derek Blomfield .... *William Elliot*

Persuasion
(1971)

ITV/Granada: mini-series (225 min); *Directed by:* Howard Baker; Screenplay: Julian Mitchell; *Produced by:* Howard Baker
Film Editing by: Stan Challis; *Production Design:* Peter Phillips; *Costume Design:* Esther Dean

CAST

Anne Firbank . . . . *Anne Elliot*
Bryan Marshall . . . . *Captain Frederick Wentworth*
Basil Dignam . . . . *Sir Walter Elliot*
Valerie Gearon . . . . *Elizabeth Elliot*
Marian Spencer . . . . *Lady Russell*
Georgine Anderson . . . . *Mrs. Croft*
Richard Vernon . . . . *Admiral Croft*
Morag Hood . . . . *Mary Musgrove*
Rowland Davies . . . . *Mr. William Elliot*
Mel Martin . . . . *Henrietta Musgrove*
Zhivila Roche . . . . *Louisa Musgrove*
Noel Dyson . . . . *Mrs. Musgrove*
William Kendall . . . . *Charles Musgrove*
Charlotte Mitchell . . . . *Mrs. Clay*
Helen Ryan . . . . *Mrs. Harville*
Michael Culver . . . . *Captain Harville*
Robert Sansom . . . . *Doctor*
Paul Chapman . . . . *Captain Benwick*
Ernest Hare . . . . *Colonel Wallis*
Paul Alexander . . . . *Charles Hayter*
Gabrielle Dave . . . . *Mrs. Rooke*
Polly Murch . . . . *Mrs. Smith*
Beatrix Mackey . . . . *Lady Dalrymple*
Angela Galbraith . . . . *Miss Carteret*
Roger Williamson . . . . *Tenor*
Judith Barker . . . . *Jemima*
Edward Jewesbury . . . . *Mr. Shepherd*

Persuasion
(1995)

BBC/Sony: tv/theatrical release (104 min); *Directed by:* Roger Michell; *Screenplay by:* Nick Dear; *Produced by:* Fiona Finlay, George Faber
Original Music: Jeremy Sams; *Cinematography:* John Daly; *Film Editing:* Kate Evans; *Production Design:* William Dudley, Brian Sykes; *Art Direction:* Linda Ward; *Costume Design:* Alexandra Byrne

CAST

Amanda Root . . . . *Anne Elliot*
Ciarán Hinds . . . . *Captain Frederick Wentworth*

Susan Fleetwood .... *Lady Russell*
Corin Redgrave .... *Sir Walter Elliot*
Fiona Shaw .... *Mrs. Croft*
John Woodvine .... *Admiral Croft*
Phoebe Nicholls .... *Elizabeth Elliot*
Samuel West .... *Mr. William Elliot*
Sophie Thompson .... *Mary Musgrove*
Judy Cornwell .... *Mrs. Musgrove*
Simon Russell Beale .... *Charles Musgrove*
Felicity Dean .... *Mrs. Clay*
Roger Hammond .... *Mr. Musgrove*
Emma Roberts .... *Louisa Musgrove*
Victoria Hamilton .... *Henrietta Musgrove*
Robert Glenister .... *Captain Harville*
Richard McCabe .... *Captain Benwick*
Helen Schlesinger .... *Mrs. Smith*
Jane Wood .... *Nurse Rooke*
David Collings .... *Mr. Shepherd*
Darlene Johnson .... *Lady Dalrymple*
Cinnamon Faye .... *Miss Carteret*
Isaac Maxwell-Hunt .... *Henry Hayter*
Roger Llewellyn .... *Sir Henry Willoughby*
Sally George .... *Mrs. Harville*
Lonnie James .... *Jemima*
Tom Rigby .... *Little Charles*
Alex Wilman .... *Little Walter*
Rosa Mannion .... *Concert Singer*
Ken Shorter .... *Lady Dalrymple's Butler*

Northanger Abbey
(1986)

BBC/A&E: television movie (90 min); *Directed by:* Giles Foster; *Screenplay by:* Maggie Wadey; *Produced by:* Louis Marks
   Original Music: Ilona Sekacz; *Cinematography:* Nat Crosby; *Film Editing:* Robin Sales; *Production Design:* Cecilia Brereton; *Costume Design:* Nicholas Rocker

CAST

Katharine Schlesinger .... *Catherine Morland*
Peter Firth .... *Henry Tilney*
Robert Hardy .... *General Tilney*
Googie Withers .... *Mrs. Allen*
Geoffrey Chater .... *Mr. Allen*
Cassie Stuart .... *Isabella Thorpe*
Jonathan Coy .... *John Thorpe*
Ingrid Lacey .... *Eleanor Tilney*
Greg Hicks .... *Frederick Tilney*
Philip Bird .... *James Morland*
Elvi Hale .... *Mrs. Thorpe*

Helen Fraser . . . . *Mrs. Morland*
David Rolfe . . . . *Mr. Morland*
Elaine Ives-Cameron . . . . *Marchioness*
Angela Curran . . . . *Alice*
Tricia Morrish . . . . *Miss Digby*
Oliver Hembrough . . . . *Edward Morland*
Anne-Marie Mullane . . . . *Thorpe Sister*
Michelle Arthur . . . . *Thorpe Sister*
Sarah-Jane Holm . . . . *Jenny*
Raphael Alleyne . . . . *Page Boy*

Bibliography

"Adaptations and *Emma* Adaptations Page." *Republic of Pemberley.* 5 Jan. 2000 http://www.pemberley.com/pemb/adaptations/emma/emfaq.html>.

American Film Institute. "Harold Lloyd Master Seminar: Amy Heckerling." 14 Sept. 1995. 11 May 2001 <http://www.afionline.org/corps/haroldlloyd/heckerling/script. 1–12.html>.

Amis, Martin. "Jane's World." *New Yorker* 8 Jan. 1996: 31–35.

Austen, Jane. *Jane Austen's Letters.* Ed. Deidre LeFaye. 3rd ed. London: Oxford UP, 1995.

_____. *Emma.* Ed. R. W. Chapman. 3rd ed. London: Oxford UP, 1933. Cited as *E.*

_____. *Mansfield Park.* Ed. R. W. Chapman. 3rd ed. London: Oxford UP, 1933. Cited as *MP.*

_____. *Minor Works.* Ed. R. W. Chapman. 3rd ed. London: Oxford UP, 1933. The spelling and punctuation of this edition have not been standardized. Cited as *MW.*

_____. *Northanger Abbey* and *Persuasion.* Ed. R. W. Chapman. 3rd ed. London: Oxford UP, 1933. Cited as *NA* and *PN.*

_____. *Pride and Prejudice.* Ed. R. W. Chapman. 3rd. ed. London: Oxford UP, 1933. Cited as *PP.*

_____. *Sense and Sensibility.* 3rd ed. Oxford: Oxford UP, 1933. Cited as *SS.*

Austen-Leigh, James-Edward. *A Memoir of Jane Austen.* Ed. R. W. Chapman. Oxford UP, 1926. Rpt. 1951.

Austen-Leigh, William, and Richard A. Austen-Leigh. *Jane Austen: A Family Record.* Rev. Deidre LeFaye. New York: Barnes and Noble, 1989.

Ballaster, Ros. "Adapting Jane Austen." *English Review* 7 (Sept. 1996): 10–13.

Bannerman, Celia. Fax to the author. 24 Sept. 01.

Baron, Alexander, and Denis Constanduros. *"Sense and Sensibility."* Unpublished screenplay. BBC TV. July 1980. In the BBC Written Archives Centre. Television Drama Scripts Microfilm 460/461.

Batey, Mavis. *Jane Austen and the English Landscape.* London: Barn Elms, 1996.

Beauman, Sally. "Pride in Her Work." *Radio Times* 12 Jan. 1980:12, 15.

Beja, Morris. *Film and Literature: An Introduction.* New York: Longman, 1979.

Bentley, Hala. "The English Novel in the Twentieth Century: Televising a Classic Novel for Students." *Contemporary Review* 268 (March 1996):141–143.

Berardinelli, James. "*Ruby in Paradise*: A Film Review." 29 June 2001 <http://movie-reviews. colossus.net/movies/r/ruby.html>.

Birtwistle, Sue, and Susie Conklin. *The Making of Jane Austen's Emma*. London: Penguin, 1996.

_____. *The Making of Pride and Prejudice*. New York: Penguin Books, 1995.

Bluestone, George. *Novels into Film: The Metamorphosis of Fiction into Cinema*. Berkeley: U of California P, 1957.

Brewer, John. *The Pleasures of the Imagination: English Culture in the Eighteenth Century*. U Chicago P, 1997.

Brooks, Tim, and Earle Marsh. *The Complete Directory to Prime Time Network and Cable TV Shown 1946–Present*. 7th ed. New York: Ballantine, 1999.

Bruhm, Steven. *Gothic Bodies: The Politics of Pain in Romantic Fiction*. Philadelphia: UP of Penn, 1990.

Butler, M. *Jane Austen and the War of Ideas*. London: Oxford UP, 1987.

Campbell, Judy. "*Emma*." Unpublished screenplay. BBC TV. 1948. In the BBC Written Archives Centre. Television Drama Scripts Microfilm 31/32.

Cartmell, Deborah. Introduction. *Adaptations: From Text to Screen, Screen to Text*. Ed. Deborah Cartmell and Imelda Whelehan. London: Routledge, 1999. 23–28.

Clark, Virginia M. *Aldous Huxley and Film*. Metuchen, N.J.: Scarecrow Press, 1987.

Clueless. Dir., Screenplay by Amy Heckerling. Paramount, 1995. Laserdisc.

Collin, Dinah. "Behind the Scenes—*Pride and Prejudice*—Colin Firth." 7 July 1996 <http://www.aetv.com./specials/pride/pride/3b.html>

Collins, Irene. "The Rev. Henry Tilney, Rector of Woodston." *Persuasions* 20 (1998): 154–164.

Colon, Christine. "The Social Constructions of Douglas McGrath's *Emma*: Earning a Place on Miss Woodhouse's *Globe*." *Persuasions On-Line, Occasional Papers*, 3 (1999). 19 March 2001 <http://www.jasna.org/PolOPl/colon.html>. 1–6.

Connors, Martin, and Jim Craddock, eds. *VideoHound's Golden Movie Retriever*. Detroit: Visible Ink Press, 2000.

Constanduros, Denis. "*Sense and Sensibility*." Unpublished screenplay. BBC TV. 1971. In the BBC Written Archives Centre. Television Drama Scripts Microfilm 210/211.

Copeland, Edward, and Juliet McMaster, eds. *The Cambridge Companion to Jane Austen*. Cambridge: U of Cambridge Press, 1997.

Crabb, Michael. "Another Jane Austen Novel Heads for the Big Screen." *Info Culture* 25 May 1999. 20 July 1999 <http://www.infoculture.cbc.c...ives/bookswr/bookswr_05251999_austen.html>.

Crathorne, James. *The Royal Crescent Book of Bath*. London: Collins and Brown, 1998.

"Dances from *Pride and Prejudice*." 5 Jan. 2000 <http://www.lll.hawaii.edu/esl/bleyvroman/contra/dances/austen.html>.

Davies, Andrew. "Austen's Horrible Heroine." *Electronic Telegraph* 23 Nov. 1996. <http://www.telegraph.co.uk.html>.

_____. E-mail to the author. 11 Jan. 2001.

_____. "*Northanger Abbey*." Unpublished screenplay. c1998.

_____. "*Pride and Prejudice*." Unpublished screenplay. c1995.

_____. "Why, After 193 Years, We're Still Gripped by Jane Austen." *Daily Mail* 31 Oct. 1995.

Davies, Tristan. "Or Not to Kiss." *Daily Telegraph* 7 Jan. 1995.

Dear, Nick. *Persuasion: A Screenplay*. London: Methuen, 1996.

Devlin, D. D. *Jane Austen and Education*. London: Macmillan, 1975.

Diana, M. Casey. "Emma Thompson's *Sense and Sensibility* as Gateway to Austen's

Novel." *Jane Austen in Hollywood.* Ed. Linda Troost and Sayre Greenfield. 2nd ed. UP Kentucky, 2001.

Dickson, Rebecca. "Misrepresenting Jane Austen's Ladies: Revising Texts (and History) to Sell Films." *Jane Austen in Hollywood.* Ed. Linda Troost and Sayre Greenfield. 2nd edition. UP Kentucky, 2001. 44–57.

Doherty, Tom. "Clueless Kids." *Cineaste* 21 (Fall 1995):14–17.

Dole, Carol. "Austen, Class, and the American Market." *Jane Austen in Hollywood.* Ed. Linda Troost and Sayre Greenfield. 2nd Edition. UP Kentucky, 2001. 58–78.

Doncaster, Peter. "Jane Austen Revival Helps the National Trust." *Britannia* (1996). 28 March 2001 <http://www.britannia.com/newsbits/jausten.html>.

Duckworth, Alistair. *The Improvement of the Estate: A Study of Jane Austen's Novels.* Baltimore: Johns Hopkins UP, (1971) 1994.

_____. Rev. of *Mansfield Park,* dir. Patricia Rozema. *Eighteenth-Century Fiction* 12.4 (July 2000): 565–571.

Duffy, Joseph M., Jr. "Moral Integrity and Moral Anarchy in *Mansfield Park.*" *ELH* 23 (1956): 71–91.

Dunaway, David King. *Huxley in Hollywood.* New York: Harper and Row, 1989.

Dussinger, John A. "Parents Against Children: General Tilney as Gothic Monster." *Persuasions* 29 (1998):165–174.

Ebert, Roger. "*Sense and Sensibility.*" Chicago *Sun-Times* 13 Dec. 1995. 18 Aug. 1998 <http://www.suntimes.com/ebert/ebert_reviews/1995/12/1011206.html>. 1–3.

Eggleston, Robert. "*Emma,* the Movies, and First-year Literature Classes." *Persuasions On-Line, Occasional Papers,* 3 (1999) 11 March 2001 <http://www.jasna.org/PolOPl/ eggleston.html>. 1–6.

Emma. Dir. Diarmud Laurence. Screenplay by Andrew Davies. Meridian-ITV/A&E, 1996. Videotape.

Emma. Dir., Screenplay by Douglas McGrath. Columbia/Miramax, 1996. Laserdisc.

Emma. Dir. John Glenister. Screenplay by Denis Constanduros. BBC TV, 1972. Videotape.

"Emma." Dramatized by Martine Bartlett and Peter Donat. NBC's *Kraft Television Theatre,* Nov. 24, 1954. Library of Congress, NBC Television Collection. 1-inch Videotape.

"*Emma* 2 Locations–Mapperton House." 5 Jan. 2000 <http://www.pemberley.com./kip/emma/mapperton.html>.

"*Emma* 2 Non-soundtrack Music Notes." 2 July 1998 <http://www.pemberley.com/kip/emma/2music.html>.

"*Emma* 3 Music Notes." 5 Jan. 2000 <http://www.pemberley.com/kip/emma/3music.html>.

"*Emma 3* Dance Descriptions." 5 Jan. 2000 <http://www.pemberley.com/kip/emma/3dance.html>. 1–4.

"Emma Thompson: A Close Reading." *New Yorker* 21 Aug. 1995: 55–56.

Evans, Caroline. "Caroline Evans on Highbury in Fiction, Film, and Reality." 5 Jan. 2000 <http://www.pemberley.com/kip/emma/chron.html#top>.

Favret, Mary A. "Being True to Jane Austen." *Victorian Afterlife: Postmodern Culture Rewrites the Nineteenth Century.* Ed. John Kucich and Dianne F. Sadoff. Minneapolis, Minn.: U of Minn. P, 2000. 64–82.

Fleishman, Avrom. *A Reading of Mansfield Park: An Essay in Critical Synthesis.* Minneapolis: Minnesota UP, 1967.

Forde, John Maurice. "Janespotting." *Topic: A Journal of the Liberal Arts* 48 (1997):11–21.

Forman, Denis. Introduction. *The Making of The Jewel in the Crown.* New York: St. Martin's, 1983.

Foster, Jennifer. "Austenmania, EQ, and the End of the Millennium." *Topic: A Journal of the Liberal Arts* 48 (1997): 56–64.

Garis, Robert. "Learning Experience and Change." *Critical Essays on Jane Austen.* Ed. E. B.C. Southam. New York: Routledge, 1968.

Giddings, Robert, and Keith Selby. *The Classic Serial on Television and Radio.* New York: Palgrave, 2001.

Giddings, Robert, Keith Selby, and Chris Wensley. *Screening the Novel: The Theory and Practice of Literary Dramatization.* New York: St. Martin's Press, 1990.

Giles, Paul. "History with Holes: Channel Four Television Films of the 1980s." *Fires Were Started: British Cinema and Thatcherism.* Ed. Lester Friedman. Minneapolis: UP Minnesota, 1993. 70–91.

Gooneratne, Yasmine. "Making Sense: Jane Austen on the Screen." *Intercultural Encounters: Studies in English Literatures. Essays Presented to Rüdiger Ahrens.* Ed. Heinz Antor and Kevin L. Cope. Heidelberg: Carl Winter, 1999. 259–66.

Gottlieb, Sid. "Cinematic Approaches to *Emma* and *Persuasion.*" Millennium Film Conference. Bath, England. 2 July 1999.

Gray, Beverly. "*Sense and Sensibility*: A Script Review." *Creative Screenwriting* 4.2 (1997): 74–82.

Greenfield, John R. "Is Emma Clueless?: Fantasies of Class and Gender from England to California." *Topic: A Journal of the Liberal Arts* 48 (1997): 31–38.

Gritten, David. "A Match Made in Hollywood." *Daily Telegraph* 16 Oct. 1995: 41–42.

Hampshire County Council. "*Sense and Sensibility*—The Film." 13 Jan. 1998 <http://www.hants.gov.uk/austen/sands.html#location.html>. 1–23.

Hannon, Patrice. "Austen Novels and Austen Films: Incompatible Worlds?" *Persuasions* 18 (1996): 24–32.

Harris, Jocelyn. Rev. of *Sense and Sensibility, Persuasion, Clueless. Eighteenth-Century Fiction* 8.3 (1996): 427–30.

Harvey, James. *Romantic Comedy in Hollywood: From Lubitsch to Sturges.* New York: Knopf, 1987.

Hays, H.R. "*Sense and Sensibility.*" NBC *Philco Television Playhouse.* Unpublished screenplay. June 4, 1950. Library of Congress, NBC Television Collection. Microfilm.

Hennessy, Val. "Sense and Sensations." *Daily Mail* 2 March 1996: 59.

Higson, Andrew. "Re-presenting the National Past: Nostalgia and Pastiche in the Heritage Film." *Fires Were Started: British Cinema and Thatcherism.* Ed. Lester Friedman. Minneapolis: UP Minnesota, 1993. 109–129.

Hinds, Ciarán. "Hindsite: In His Own Words," His Official Bio for Sony. 23 Oct. 2000 <http://members.aol.com/dramaddict/ch/CHSPEAKS.html>.

Hoberg, Tom. "Her First and Her Last: Austen's *Sense and Sensibility, Persuasion,* and Their Screen Adaptations." *Nineteenth Century Women at the Movies: Adapting Classic Women's Fiction to Film.* Ed. Tepa Lupack. Bowling Green, OH: Bowling Green Ohio U Popular Press, 1999. 140–166.

_____. "The Multiplex Heroine: Screen Adaptations of *Emma.*" *Nineteenth Century Women at the Movies: Adapting Classic Women's Fiction to Film.* Ed. Tepa Lupack. Bowling Green, OH: Bowling Green U Popular Press, 1999. 106–128.

Hopkins, Lisa. "Emma and the Servants." *Persuasions On-Line, Occasional Papers,* 3 (1999) 11 March 2001 <http://www.jasna.org/PolOPl/hopkins.html>. 1–5.

_____. "Mr. Darcy's Body: Privileging the Female Gaze." *Topic: A Journal of the Liberal Arts* 48 (1997): 1–10.

Howell, Georgina. "Making Sense." *Sunday Times Magazine* 18 March 1996: 18–22.

Internet Movie Database. (Abbr. IMDb) <http://us.imdb.com.html>.

Jacobs, Laura. "Playing Jane." *Vanity Fair.* Jan. 1996: 74–76, 122–123.

Jacobson, Miriam. " A Truth Universally Acknowledged." *The College Hill Independent* 29 Feb. 1996. 18 August 1998 <http://www.netspace.org/indy/issues/o2-29-96/arts4.html>.

Jerome, Helen. *Pride and Prejudice: A Comedy in Three Acts. The Best Plays of 1935–1936.* Dodd, Mead: 1966. 356–396.

Johnson, Claudia L. "The Authentic Audacity of Patricia Rozema's *Mansfield Park*: 'Run Mad, but Do Not Faint.'" *London Times Literary Supplement,* 31 December 1999: 16–17.

._____. *Equivocal Beings: Politics, Gender, and Sentimentality in the 1790's.* Chicago UP, 1995.

_____. Introduction. *Mansfield Park.* By Jane Austen. New York: Norton, 1998. xi–xxi.

_____. *Jane Austen: Women, Politics and the Novel.* Chicago UP, 1988.

Kantrowitz, Barbara. "Making an Austen Heroine More Like Austen." *New York Times* 31 October 1999, AR: 17, 26.

Kaplan, Deborah. "Mass Marketing Jane Austen: Men, Women and Courtship in Two of the Recent Films." *Persuasions* 18 (1996): 171–181.

Katz, Ephraim. *The Film Encyclopedia.* Rev. by Fred Klein and Ronald Dean Nolen. Fourth ed. New York: Harper Collins, 2001.

Kelly, Rachel. "Business Sense and Sensibility Lift a Stately Star." *London Times* 22 Jan. 1996: 3, 17.

Kirkham, Margaret. *Jane Austen, Feminism and Fiction.* Totowa, NJ: Barnes and Noble, 1983.

Knight, Austen B., Col. Letter to the BBC. Feb. 1952. In the BBC Written Archives.

Kroll, Jack. "Jane Austen Does Lunch." *Newsweek* 18 December 1995: 66–68.

Lauritzen, Monica. *Jane Austen's Emma on Television: A Study of a BBC Classic Serial. Gothenburg Studies in English 48.* Gothenburg, Sweden, 1981.

Lellis, George, and Philip Bolton. "Pride but No Prejudice." *The English Novel and the Movies.* New York: Ungar, 1981.

Lethbridge, Nemone. *Pride and Prejudice.* Unpublished screenplay. BBC TV. August 1967. In the BBC Written Archives. Television Drama Scripts Microfilm 198/199.

Lew, Joseph. "That Abominable Traffic": *Mansfield Park* and the Dynamics of Slavery." *History, Gender and Eighteenth Century Literature.* Ed. Beth F. Tobin. Athens, GA: U of Georgia P, 1994. 271–300.

Libin, Kathryn. "'—A Very Elegant Looking Instrument—': Musical Symbols and Substance in Films of Jane Austen's Novels." *Persuasions* 19 (1997): 187–194.

Long, Edward. *The History of Jamaica or General Survey of the Antient* (sic) *and Modern State of that Island.* Ed. George Metcalf. 2 vols. Frank Cass, 1774.

Looser, Devoney. "Feminist Implications of the Silver Screen Austen." *Jane Austen in Hollywood.* Ed. Linda Troost and Sayre Greenfield. 2nd ed. UP Kentucky, 2001. 159–176.

_____. "Jane Austen Responds to the Men's Movement." *Persuasions* 18 (1996): 159–170.

Lyons, Donald. "Passionate Precision: *Sense and Sensibility.*" *Film Comment* Jan/Feb 1996: 36–41.

MacDonagh, Oliver. *Jane Austen: Real and Imagined Worlds.* New Haven: Yale UP, 1991.

Macdonald, Andrew and Gina. "Updating Emma: Balancing Satire and Sympathy in *Clueless.*" *Creative Screenwriting* 7.3 (May/June 2000): 22–30.

McFarlane, Brian. "It Wasn't Like That in the Book." *Literature/Film Quarterly.* 28:3 (2000): 163–169.

_____. *Novel to Film: An Introduction to the Theory of Adaptation.* Oxford: Clarendon Press, 1996.

McGrath, Douglas. "Raising Jane: A Diary of the Making of *Emma.*" *Premiere* Sept. 1996: 74–77+.

McNeil, Alex. *Total Television*. New York: Penguin, 1996.

Maeder, Edward, ed. *Hollywood and History: Costume Design in Film*. Los Angeles: Los Angeles Museum of Art, 1987.

Malins, Edward. *English Landscaping and Literature: 1660–1840*. London: Oxford UP, 1966.

Mansfield Park. Dir. David Giles. Screenplay by Ken Taylor. BBC TV. 1983. Videotape.

Mansfield Park. Dir., Screenplay by Patricia Rozema. BBC/Miramax. 2000. DVD. Commentary by Patricia Rozema.

Martin, John. "A Consuming Pride." 14 Jan. 1996. 4 Dec. 1996 <http://showbiz.starwave. tv/pride.html>. 1–2.

Mazmanian, Melissa. "Reviving *Emma* in a *Clueless* World: The Current Attraction to a Classic Structure." *Persuasions On-Line*, Occasional Papers, 3 (1999). 11 March 2001 <www.jasna.org/PolOPl/mazmanian.html>. 1–8.

Menand, Louis. "What Jane Austen Doesn't Tell Us." *New York Review of Books* 43:2 (1 Feb. 1996): B13–15.

Metro-Goldwyn-Mayer. Press Release. 1940.

Morgan, Susan. "Captain Wentworth, British Imperialism and Personal Romance." *Persuasions* 18 (1996): 88–97.

Morrison, Sarah. "*Emma* Minus Its Narrator: Decorum and Class Consciousness in Film Versions of the Novel." *Persuasions On-Line, Occasional Papers*, 3. (1999) 19 March 2001 <http://www.jasna.org/PolOPl/morrison.html>. 1–8.

Mudrick, Marvin. *Jane Austen: Irony as Defense and Discovery*. Princeton UP, 1952.

Myer, Valerie G. *Jane Austen: Obstinate Heart*. New York: Arcade, 1997.

Nachumi, Nora. "'As If!': Translating Austen's Ironic Narrator to Film." *Jane Austen in Hollywood*. Ed. Linda Troost and Sayre Greenfield. 2nd ed. Kentucky UP, 2001. 130–139.

Nixon, Cheryl L. "Balancing the Courtship Hero: Masculine Emotional Display in Film Adaptations of Austen's Novels." *Jane Austen in Hollywood*. Ed. Linda Troost and Sayre Greenfield. 2nd ed. Kentucky UP, 2001. 22–43.

Nokes, David. "Shepherd's Bush Gothic." *TLS* 20 Feb. 1987: 186.

North, Julian. "Conservative Austen, Radical Austen: *Sense and Sensibility* from Text to Screen." *Adaptations: From Text to Screen, Screen to Text*. Ed. Deborah Cartmell and Imelda Whelehan. London: Routledge, 1999. 38–50.

Northanger Abbey. Screenplay by Maggie Wadey. Dir. Giles Foster. BBC TV/A&E, 1987. Videotape.

O'Sullivan, Charlotte. "Fast Foreword: *Sense and Sensibility*." *Observer Preview* 24 Feb. 1996: 4.

Palmer, Sally. "Robbing the Roost: Reinventing Socialism in Diarmuid Lawrence's *Emma.*" *Persuasions On-Line: Occasional Papers* 3 (1999) 19 March 2001 <http:// www.jasna.org/PolOPl? palmer.html>. 1–6.

Pappas, Kali. "Costuming the Emmas." <http://www.pemberley.com/kip/emma/costume. html>.

_____. "*Emma* Two: A Defense of *Emma 2*" <http://www.pemberley.com/kip/emma/ kalem2def.html>.

Parrill, Sue. "The Cassandra of Highbury: Miss Bates on Film." *Persuasions On-Line, Occasional Papers*, 3 (1999) 19 March 2001. <http://www.jasna.org/PolOPl/ parrill.html>. 1–6.

_____. "Metaphors of Control: Physicality in *Emma* and *Clueless*." *Persuasions On-Line* 20: 1 (1998) 19 March 2001 <http://www.jasna.org/polOl/parrill.html>. 1–6.

_____. "Visions and Revisions: *Pride and Prejudice* on A&E." *Literature/Film Quarterly* 27.2 (1999): 142–148.

_____. "What Meets the Eye: Landscape in the Films *Pride and Prejudice* and *Sense and Sensibility*." *Persuasions* 21 (1999): 32–43.

Perkins, Moreland. *Reshaping the Sexes in Sense and Sensibility*. Virginia UP, 1998.

Persuasion. Dir. Roger Michell. Screenplay by Nick Dear. BBC/Sony Pictures Classics, 1995. Laserdisc.

Persuasion. Dir. Howard Baker. Screenplay by Julian Mitchell. ITV/Granada, 1971. Videotape.

Phillips, William, and Louise Heal. "Extensive Grounds and Classic Columns: *Emma* on Film." *Persuasions On-Line, Occasional Papers*, 3 (1999) 19 March 2001 <http://www.jasna.org/PolOPl/heal_phillips.html>. 1–8.

Pidduck, Julianne. "Of Windows and Country Walks: Frames of Space and Movement in 1990's Austen Adaptations." *Screen* 39 (1998): 381–400.

Pride and Prejudice. Dir. Robert Z. Leonard. Screenplay by Aldous Huxley and Jane Murfin. MGM, 1940. Videotape.

Pride and Prejudice. Dir. Cyril Coke. Screenplay by Fay Weldon. BBC, 1979. Videotape.

Pride and Prejudice. Dir. Simon Langton. Screenplay by Andrew Davies. Arts and Entertainment Television Networks, 1995. Laserdisc, DVD.

Punter, David. *The Literature of Terror: A History of Gothic Fictions from 1765 to the Present Day*. New York: Longman, 1980.

Purdum, Todd S. "From 'Saturday Night Live' to Jane Austen." *New York Times* 25 Aug. 1996: H 11, 16.

Radcliffe, Anne. *The Mysteries of Udolpho*. New York: Oxford UP, 1966.

Rafferty, Terrence. "Fidelity and Infidelity." *The New Yorker* 18 Dec. 1995: 124–126.

Rauch, Irmengard. "On the BBC/A&E Bicentennial *Pride and Prejudice*." *Interdisciplinary Journal for Germanic Linguistics and Semiotic Analysis*. 2.2 (Fall 1997): 327–346.

Rees, Jasper. "This Story Isn't Just Another Garden Party." Interview with Patricia Rozema. *Electronic Telegraph* 25 March 2000. <http://www.telegraph.co.uk.html>.

Renton, Alex. "A Break to Sweep You Off Your Feet." *Evening Standard* 23 March 1996: 23.

Reynolds, Lisa. "Now Emma on Screen in the Great Austen Revival." *Daily Express* 24 July 1996.

Richards, Irene. E-mails to author. 6 Jan. 2002, and 8 Jan. 2002.

Roberts, Janene. "Literature on PBS: Three Masterpiece Theatre Productions of Nineteenth Century Novels." *Text and Performance Quarterly* 9.4 (Oct. 1989): 311–321.

Roberts, Marilyn. "Adapting Jane Austen's *Northanger Abbey*: Catherine Morland as Gothic Heroine." *Nineteenth Century Women at the Movies: Adapting Classic Women's Fiction to Film*. Ed. Tepa Lupack. Bowling Green, OH: Bowling Green U Popular Press, 1999. 129–139.

"Roger Michell—Director." Press release, 1995. British Film Institute files.

Rozema, Patricia. "Mansfield Park." Unpublished screenplay, 3rd draft. 1998.

_____. *Mansfield Park: The Final Shooting Script*. Introduction by Claudia Johnson. New York: Talk Miramax Books, 2000.

_____. "A Place in the Sun." *Montage* (Spring 2000) 29 Mar.2001 <http://www.patriciarozema./a_place_in_the_sun.htm>.

Said, Edward. *Culture and Imperialism*. New York: Knopf, 1993.

Salber, Cecilia. "Bridget Jones and Mark Darcy: Art Imitating Art … Imitating Art."

Persuasions On-line 22. 1 (2000) 10/1/01 <http://www.jasna.org/pol04/salber. html>. 1–4.

Sales, Roger. "In Face of All the Servants: Spectators and Spies in Austen." *Janeites: Austen's Disciples and Devotees.* Ed. Deidre Lynch. Princeton, NJ: Princeton UP, 2000. 188–205.

_____. "It's That Man in Tight Trousers Again: Dishy Mr. Darcy Carries on Camping in a Raunchy Regency Romp also Called *Pride and Prejudice*." *Jane Austen and Cinema.* Ed. Judy Simons. London: Athlone Press (forthcoming).

_____. *Jane Austen and Representations of Regency England.* New York: Routledge, 1996.

Samuelian, Kristin Flieger. "Piracy Is Our Only Option": Postfeminist Intervention in *Sense and Sensibility. Jane Austen in Hollywood.* Ed. Linda Troost and Sayre Greenfield. 2nd ed. Kentucky UP, 2001. 148–158.

Sense and Sensibility. Dir. Ang Lee. Columbia/Mirage, 1995. Laserdisc.

Sense and Sensibility. Dir. Rodney Bennett. BBC, 1980. Videotape.

Sense and Sensibility. Original Motion Picture Soundtrack. (Notes on CD package) Sony, 1995.

Serpico, J. "*Mansfield Park*: Prosaic Magic." 1999. 29 Feb. 2000 <http://popmatters. com/film/-park>.

Sessums, Kevin. "Never Look Back." *Vanity Fair* Feb. 1996: 80–87, 142–144.

"Sex and Sensibility of a Classic Heroine." *London Times* 24 March 1996. Lexis/Nexis. Keyword: Emma.

Sheen, Erica. "'Where the Garment Gapes': Faithfulness and Promiscuity in the 1995 BBC *Pride and Prejudice*." *The Classic Novel: From Page to Screen.* Ed. Robert Giddings and Erica Sheen. Manchester: Manchester UP, 2000. 14–30.

Simons, Judy. "Classics and Trash: Reading Austen in the 1990's." *Women's Writing* 5.1 (1998): 27–39.

Sinyard, Neil. *Filming Literature: The Art of Screen Adaptation.* New York: St. Martin's Press, 1986.

Sokol, Ronnie Jo. "The Importance of Being Married: Adapting *Pride and Prejudice*." *Nineteenth Century Women at the Movies: Adapting Classic Women's Fiction to Film.* Ed. Tepa Lupack. Bowling Green, OH: Bowling Green U Popular Press, 1999. 78–105.

Solender, Elsa A. "Fidelity and Frustration: Janeites at the Movies" <www.jasna.org/ fidelity>. 1–2.

Sonnet, Esther. "From *Emma* to *Clueless*: Taste, Pleasure, and the Scene of History." *Adaptations: From Text to Screen, Screen to Text.* Ed. Deborah Cartmell and Imelda Whelehan. London: Routledge, 1999. 51–62.

Spencer, Mimi. "Hot Under the Collar for Men in Breeches." *Evening Standard* 21 February 1996: 19.

Stevenson, Lionel. *The English Novel: A Panorama.* Boston: Houghton Mifflin, 1960.

Stewart, Maaja A. *Domestic Realities and Imperial Fictions: Jane Austen's Novels in Eighteenth-Century Contexts.* Athens, GA: U of Georgia P, 1993.

Stovel, Bruce. "*Northanger Abbey* at the Movies." *Persuasions* 29 (1998): 236–247.

Tanner, Tony. *Jane Austen.* Cambridge: Harvard UP, 1986.

Taylor, Samuel. "*Pride and Prejudice*." NBC's *Philco Television Playhouse.* January 23, 1949. Library of Congress, NBC Television Collection. Microfilm.

Thomas, Evan. "Hooray for Hypocrisy." *Newsweek* 29 January 1996: 61.

Thomas, Gethyn S. "Plain Jane Puts On a Bold Face." *Western Mail* 21 Feb. 1987: 12.

Thompson, E. P. *The Making of the English Working Class.* New York: Vintage Books, 1966.

Thompson, Emma. *The Sense and Sensibility Screenplay and Diaries.* New York: New-market, 1995.

Thomson, David. "Riding with Ang Lee." *Film Comment* 35.6 (Nov/Dec. 1999): 4–9.

Thorpe, Vanessa. "Search for Sex in Austen's Abbey." *Sunday Independent* 12 July 1998:13.

Thynne, Jane. "Home News: 10m Viewers See Elizabeth Wed Mr. Darcy." *Electronic Telegraph* 31 Oct. 1995. 22 Nov. 1999 <http/www.telegraph.co.uk.html>.

Tilsley, Vincent. "*Emma.*" Unpublished screenplay. BBC TV. 1960. In the BBC Written Archives Centre. Television Drama Scripts Microfilm.

Tomalin, Claire. *Jane Austen: A Life.* New York: Knopf, 1997.

Trilling, Lionel. "*Mansfield Park.*" *Jane Austen: A Collection of Critical Essays.* Ed. Ian Watt. Prentice Hall, 1963. From *The Opposing Self.* New York: Viking, 1955.

Troost, Linda. "Jane Austen and Technology." *Topic: A Journal of the Liberal Arts* 48 (1997): iii–v.

Troost, Linda, and Sayre Greenfield. "Filming Highbury: Reducing the Community in *Emma* to the Screen." *Persuasions On-Line, Occasional Papers,* 3 (1999) 19 March 2001 <www.jasna.org/PolOP1/ troost_sayre>. 1–7.

_____. "The Mouse That Roared: Patricia Rozema's *Mansfield Park.*" Ed. Linda Troost and Sayre Greenfield. *Jane Austen in Hollywood.* 2nd Ed. Kentucky UP, 2000. 188–204.

Troyan, Michael. *A Rose for Mrs. Miniver: The Life of Greer Garson.* UP Kentucky, 1999.

Turan, Kenneth. "*Pride and Prejudice:* An Informal History of the Garson-Olivier Motion Picture." *Persuasions,* 1989:140–143.

Wagner, Geoffrey. *The Novel and Cinema.* London: Tantivy Press, 1975.

Wald, Gayle. "Clueless in the Neocolonial World Order." *Camera Obscura: A Journal of Feminism, Culture, and Media Studies* 42 (Sept. 1999): 51–69.

Watkins, Susan. *Jane Austen in Style.* London: Thames and Hudson, 1990.

Webster, Di. "Hindsite: In His Own Words," *WHO* Magazine (Australia), 11 March 1996. 23 Oct, 2000 <http://members.aol.com/dramaddict/ch/CHSPEAKS.Htm>.

Weldon, Fay. "Jane Austen and the Pride of Purists." New York *Times* 8 Oct. 1995, 2: 15.

_____. "*Pride and Prejudice.*" Unpublished screenplay. BBC TV. 1980. In the BBC Written Archives Centre. Television Drama Scripts Microfilm 446/447.

_____. "A Teenager in Love." *Radio Times* 14 February 1987: 98–101.

Whelehan, Imelda. "Adaptations, the Contemporary Dilemmas." *Adaptations: From Text to Screen, Screen to Text.* Ed. Deborah Cartmell and Imelda Whelehan. London: Routledge, 1999. 3–19.

Wilmington, Michael. "Adaptation of Austen's *Persuasion* Entertains Seamlessly." *Chicago Tribune* 27 Oct. 1995: H2.

Wilt, Judith. *Ghosts of the Gothic: Austen, Eliot, and Laurence.* Princeton UP, 1980.

Wiltshire, John. *Recreating Jane Austen.* Cambridge UP, 2001.

Winship, Frederick. "Jane Austen Revival Thrives." UPI 15 Jan. 1996. 20 March 2001 *Lexis-Nexis.* Keyword: Northanger Abbey.

Wright, Andrew. "Jane Austen Adapted." *Nineteenth Century Fiction.* 30 (1975): 421–453.

Young, R.V. "From Mansfield to Manhattan: The Abandoned Generation of Whit Stillman's Metropolitan." *The Intercollegiate Review* 35.2 (Spring 2000): 20–27.

Index